The Cooking of Italy

The Cooking of Italy

by

Waverley Root

and the Editors of

TIME-LIFE BOOKS

photographed by Fred Lyon

TIME-LIFE BOOKS, ALEXANDRIA, VIRGINIA

Time-Life Books Inc.
is a wholly owned subsidiary of
TIME INCORPORATED

FOUNDER: Henry R. Luce 1898-1967

Editor-in-Chief: Hedley Donovan
Chairman of the Board: Andrew Heiskell
President: James R. Shepley
Vice Chairmen: Roy E. Larsen, Arthur Temple
Corporate Editors: Ralph Graves,
Henry Anatole Grunwald

TIME-LIFE BOOKS INC.
MANAGING EDITOR: Jerry Korn
Executive Editor: David Maness
Assistant Managing Editors: Dale M. Brown,
Martin Mann, John Paul Porter
Art Director: Tom Suzuki
Chief of Research: David L. Harrison
Director of Photography: Robert G. Mason
Planning Director: Thomas Flaherty (acting)
Senior Text Editor: Diana Hirsh
Assistant Art Director: Arnold C. Holeywell
Assistant Chief of Research: Carolyn L. Sackett
Assistant Director of Photography: Dolores A. Littles

CHAIRMAN: Joan D. Manley
President: John D. McSweeney
Executive Vice Presidents: Carl G. Jaeger,
John Steven Maxwell, David J. Walsh
Vice Presidents: Peter G. Barnes (Comptroller),
Nicholas Benton (Public Relations), John L. Canova
(Sales), Herbert Sorkin (Production),
Paul R. Stewart (Promotion)
Personnel Director: Beatrice T. Dobie
Consumer Affairs Director: Carol Flaumenhaft

FOODS OF THE WORLD
SERIES EDITOR: Richard L. Williams
EDITORIAL STAFF FOR THE COOKING OF ITALY:
Associate Editors: Charles Osborne, Jay Brennan
Picture Editor: Donald Hinkle
Designer: Albert Sherman
Assistant Designer: Robert Pellegrini
Staff Writers: John Stanton, Geraldine Schremp
Chief Researcher: Helen Fennell
Researchers: Sarah Bennett, Elizabeth Gage, Penny Grist,
Penny Hinkle, Helen Isaacs, Julia Johnson,
Diana Sweeney
Test Kitchen Chef: John Clancy
Test Kitchen Staff: Fifi Bergman, Joel Levy,
Leola Spencer

EDITORIAL PRODUCTION
Production Editor: Douglas B. Graham
Operations Manager: Gennaro C. Esposito
Assistant Production Editor: Feliciano Madrid
Quality Control: Robert L. Young (director),
James J. Cox (assistant), Michael G. Wight
(associate)
Art Coordinator: Anne B. Landry
Copy Staff: Susan B. Galloway (chief),
Eleanore W. Karsten,
Grace Fitzgerald, Celia Beattie
Picture Department: Barbara S. Simon
Traffic: Jeanne Potter

CORRESPONDENTS: Elisabeth Kraemer (Bonn); Margot
Hapgood, Dorothy Bacon (London); Susan Jonas,
Lucy T. Voulgaris (New York); Maria Vincenza
Aloisi, Josephine du Brusle (Paris); Ann
Natanson (Rome).
Valuable assistance was also provided by: Carolyn
T. Chubet, Miriam Hsia (New York); Erik
Amfitheatrof (Rome).

THE AUTHOR: A veteran foreign correspondent, Waverley Root *(above, left)* has ceaselessly sought out good food on his travels, and from these researches came his book *The Food of France,* a classic on French provincial cooking, and another written with Richard de Rochemont, *Contemporary French Cooking.* Mr. Root first encountered Italian cooking in Rome in 1929. He has been exploring its delights at all opportunities ever since.

THE PHOTOGRAPHER: Fred Lyon *(above, right)* freelances in advertising and editorial photography from his home overlooking San Francisco Bay. He was a photographer-writer in World War II and later did New York fashion photography. For this book he traveled to all corners of Italy, eating two prodigious meals a day. He has produced two books of photographs, *Hawaii—The Other Islands,* and *Away from It All—Together.*

THE CONSULTING EDITOR: The late Michael Field *(above, left)* developed most of the recipes in this book from traditional Italian sources. One of America's first-rate cooks and teachers of cooking, he conducted a school in Manhattan and wrote many articles on the culinary arts for various magazines. His books include *Michael Field's Cooking School* and *Michael Field's Culinary Classics and Improvisations.*

THE CONSULTANT: Luigi Carnacina *(above, right),* the dean of Italian gastronomy, started as a waiter in his godfather's small hotel and rose to be manager of many famous hotels, among them the Hotel de la Ville in Rome, the Grand Hôtel Lido in Venice, the Plaza in Brussels and the Savoy in London. He also managed the Italian government's restaurants at the 1937 Paris Exposition, the 1939 New York World's Fair and the 1958 Brussels Fair. He has written 34 books on cooking, the most famous being *La Grande Cucina,* an encyclopedia of European cooking.

THE COVER: Shown are some of Italy's triumphs: a flask of Chianti, *provolone* cheese, olive oil and ripe tomatoes.

Contents

The Recipe Booklet that accompanies this volume has been designed for use in the kitchen. It contains all of the 83 recipes printed here plus 18 more. It also has a wipe-clean cover and a spiral binding so that it can either stand up or lie flat when open.

Introduction: A Robust Cuisine Based on a People's Character

All people are, in a sense, what they eat. Food therefore could be one of the more revealing indexes to personal and national proclivities, provided one could draw stable conclusions from an index so subject to individual and collective preference. The food of one's own country is too familiar to evoke anything but shadowy sensations; other peoples' cuisine may be too startlingly different to be anything but confusing. Perhaps the best way to make a judgment about the matter is to taste one's own cuisine after a long abstention, in order to rediscover its real nature, much as jaded husbands sometimes are advised to do to rediscover their wives' charms.

I tried the culinary experiment once. I was a correspondent for the Italian newspaper *Corriere della Sera* at the time, assigned to cover the marriage of a former King to an American lady in a château near Tours. Most of the visiting journalists stayed at the Hôtel de l'Univers, in Tours, whose cuisine was above the average. We had time on our hands. The Anglo-Saxons dedicated it to drinking a great number of identical drinks; others, myself included, to eating. Every day we chose a different *bistro* or restaurant to taste the local specialties and the wines that went with them, following the advice of well-qualified local inhabitants.

Later, when we could leave the château for a few hours at a time, we began favoring the little buffet of a nearby country railroad station. It belonged to a secondary line on which I never saw a train pass. The stationmaster's wife was the cook and waitress. The menu was so simple that I suspected that we were eating an extension of the family's normal luncheon. The local wine was excellent. The cheeses were unfamiliar and tasty.

On the scheduled date the wedding took place, the former King married his sweetheart, and the assignment was over. Herein lay my opportunity to essay the culinary experiment. I went to Paris to rest for a few days and to see the international exhibition that had been organized that summer. All the principal nations had built sumptuous pavilions on the banks of the Seine, filling them with all the products they presumed would provoke the admiration and envy of other people. The Italians had tried a daring innovation. They produced a *ristorante*. It was good, better than any in Italy at the time. It had the best Italian cook, taken from one of the transatlantic liners; the headwaiter was as handsome, pliant and courteous as an ambassador; the waiters, like members of an Olympic team, were hand-picked; the wines were poured by pretty girls in provincial costumes.

I tried the *ristorante* on my first night in Paris. This was, I knew, my chance to find out what my native food was really like, coming as I had from three weeks of steady French cuisine and wines, and possibly to deduce from my sensations a few revealing, definitive truths about my people and myself. I went with a friend who knew about food, a well traveled American. We ordered the usual things (novelties would have distorted the results of the experiment), drank good Chianti, and meditated.

This, in brief, is what we discovered: In contrast with the French food, which was always tenuously tinted in vague pastel or pearly shades, the Italian food was brightly colored, each thing unmistakably separate. The spinach was gaily green, the prosciutto delicately seashell pink, the peppers shiningly yellow, green or red like polished marble, the roast meat dark red, and so forth, each color as loud and clear as if made by children's crayons.

The distinct hues corresponded to distinct tastes. Each little ingredient harmonized with but was not confused with the others. It could be felt separately, if one paid attention, just as each voice in the sextet from *Lucia di Lammermoor* is meant to be heard separately. The sauces had little importance. There were no *fonds de cuisine*, velvety mousses, seductive gravies of the kind that permeate all tastes in French dishes and give them all a mysterious, vague, wonderful, all-pervading taste.

Italians obviously believe that the pleasure of eating (and living) is enhanced by preserving the characteristic tastes of separate ingredients (and the personalities of individuals), more than by blending them artistically. Their approach seems more direct, more straightforward. They are closer than the French to nature, less inclined to artifice. Are they?

To deal with the question, it should be said that the Italian nature is not real nature; it is a subtler and more deceptive form of artifice. The Italians' food and wines, like their music, literature and art, show that they have no inclination for the romantic, the ambiguous, the misty, the uncertain. Chianti is Rossini while Burgundy is Debussy.

My friend and I agreed that the apparently simple cooking of the Italians is, in fact, more difficult at times to achieve than the more elaborate and refined French cuisine. Things have to be good in themselves, without aid, to be exposed naked. In other words, a pleasant French dish can sometimes be made successfully even with very ordinary ingredients, while the excellence of many Italian dishes depends on the excellence of the things that go into them. The old saying that good cooking begins in the market is truer in Italy than in France.

A dish of pasta is only as good as the pasta itself, which must come from Gragnano, in the mountains behind Sorrento, or from Fara San Martino, in the Abruzzi. *Mozzarella di bufala* comes from a few square miles around Caserta. Fruit and vegetables must be picked at the right time, neither one day too early nor too late. They must not travel far, must not be preserved beyond their allotted season by chemicals or refrigeration.

In sum, if Italian cookbooks do not wish to deceive their readers, they should start out with these words: *Recipe* (this, as everybody knows, is not an English word but a Latin imperative meaning "procure") the best of ingredients, as fresh as they can be found, and within the bounds of skill, preserve their identity in the preparation. Thus forewarned, the reader could pursue the details given in the book and attain not only the true cooking of Italy—the *vera cucina Italiana*—but a deep understanding of Italy and Italians.   —*Luigi Barzini*, author of *The Italians*

I

The Mother Cuisine

A Renaissance salute to well-seasoned meals is the Italian sculptor Benvenuto Cellini's exquisite, symbolic golden saltcellar. The male Sea's miniature ship held the salt; the female Earth's Ionic temple contained the pepper.

Anyone who has ever seen, smelled and then eaten his way through a platter of the green noodles known as *fettuccine verdi* can readily accept Italian cooking as a symbol of Latin culture, and as a satisfying expression of a love of the good life as well. It would probably occur to very few people, however, to regard Italian cooking as the source of every other Western cuisine.

Nevertheless that is precisely what it is. The cooking of the Italian peninsula was the first fully developed cuisine in Europe. Its originators, the ancient Romans, found some of their culinary inspiration in Asia Minor and Greece, and they also drew on many resources and ingredients that were home grown. Combining all these, they made it possible for Italy to teach France—and all other Occidental cultures—the meaning of good cooking and eating. Indeed, *Larousse Gastronomique,* the bible of the French kitchen, goes so far as to make the concession that "Italian cooking can be considered, for all the countries of Latin Europe, as a veritable mother cuisine."

The Italian cuisine became a mother, most experts agree, in 1533, when Catherine de' Medici journeyed from Florence to France for her marriage to the future King Henri II. Both Catherine and her kinswoman Marie de' Medici, who followed in her footsteps to become the queen of King Henri IV in 1600, brought teams of expert cooks to France with them. These culinary aristocrats possessed, and delivered to France, the secrets of the most sophisticated cookery that had yet been developed. They knew the art of making modern pastry and desserts—cakes and cream puffs and ices.

Medici cooks also prepared, for the first time outside Italy, dishes including such now-familiar vegetables as artichokes, broccoli, and the tiny peas that the French took as their own and that the world now knows as *petits pois*. The French had never eaten so well.

Such culinary craftsmanship had taken a long time to develop—about 1,500 years. It began with the Romans—but not with the Romans that most people think of, a nation addicted to sumptuous banquets and unbridled orgies. This notion is made to order for wide-screen motion pictures in Flamboyant-Color, and the Hollywood and Italian movie-makers have not failed to exploit it. In Imperial times, we have been told, exotic eating was the rule. Like most gross exaggerations, this one contains an element of truth. From Petronius, Juvenal, Lucian, Martial and other Roman writers we learn that peacocks, flamingos and herons were in fact served with their full plumage carefully replaced after cooking; that wolves, hedgehogs and puppies were considered choice eating; that dormice—small rodents resembling squirrels—were confined in barrels to keep them from exercising and were force-fed to obesity for the table. According to Pliny, Maecenas was the first to serve ass's meat, in the First Century B.C. Most epicures seem to have preferred a wild variety of donkey, the onager. Elephant trunk is reputed to have been a great delicacy, and at least one emperor, Elagabalus, delighted in serving camel's foot. The food of the fabled Roman banquets, tradition has it, was not only exotic but was consumed in staggering amounts. The Emperor Maximinus (235-238 A.D.) is said to have eaten 40 pounds of meat daily, washed down with 40 quarts of wine. As a kind of command performance to amuse the Emperor Aurelian, the actor Farone on one occasion consumed a whole sheep, a suckling pig and a wild boar, along with 100 buns. He washed the repast down with 100 bottles of wine.

But although it is true that great feasts did occur in Rome, they were rare even during the spectacular death throes of the degenerating Empire. Most Romans simply did not have the means to offer extravagant meals to their guests. Aside from the court of the emperor himself, there were probably no more than 200 great houses that could afford a luxurious table. The most ostentatious banquets were staged not by patricians, but by the newly rich, who in all ages have been the most conspicuous spenders. Trimalchio, whose famous feast (one course involved a boar stuffed with live thrushes) is described in the *Satyricon* of Petronius, was a Levantine freedman, ostensibly a shipping magnate, but actually a profiteer in every shady traffic known to an age of license.

If Petronius and other writers described the lavish banquets of their times in meticulous detail, it was not because the events were typical of the ordinary life of Rome, but because they were not. These extravagant feasts aroused the attention of writers precisely because they were astonishing, extraordinary and excessive.

The more typical Roman cuisine, which is still making its influence felt in all the kitchens of the Western world, was several centuries in the making. Its beginnings were humble and austere. The first Romans were shepherds and small farmers, holding a strip of territory along the Tiber. Like sheep everywhere, those of the Romans needed salt, and their masters learned how to get it for them by evaporating sea water from the mouth of

The vines of the Valle d'Aosta, whose wines slaked the thirst of Caesar, grow on trellises supported by stone columns.

Rich Romans of the First Century A.D. reclined as they ate their evening meal. A few gourmands, who flaunted such specialties as dormice rolled in honey and poppy seeds, earned the whole period a reputation for extravagant gluttony. The old nobility scorned such ostentation.

the river. When they began to make more salt than they needed for themselves and their sheep, they started a profitable export trade with the Greek settlements to the south and the Etruscans to the north. The early expansion of Rome and the subsequent development of the Roman Empire and its cuisine were based partly on trade in salt, which was for many centuries a precious commodity on which fortunes were founded. One of the principal highways leading out of Rome is still called Via Salaria, the Salt Road.

The staple dish of these first Romans was *puls,* or *pulmentum.* It was a kind of mush made from grain—in those days usually millet or spelt, a primitive type of wheat, and sometimes chick-pea flour. *Pulmentum* could not have been a very inspiring food, but it served to nourish the conquerors of the ancient world. It was the field ration of the Roman soldier, who received daily about two pounds of the grain, which he roasted on a hot stone over his campfire, crushed, and put in his haversack. Whenever and wherever he might bivouac, the mixture was ready to be boiled into a more or less palatable gruel, which could be eaten as porridge or allowed to harden into a sort of unleavened scone, or cake. To this day the modern version of *pulmentum,* called *polenta,* can be eaten in either version—soft (and heated), with about the consistency of mashed potatoes, or hard (and usually cold), when it can be sliced like cake.

As time passed, the basic ingredients of *pulmentum* changed. Millet and spelt gave way to barley; and when the Romans found barley too bland they replaced it with *far,* a more palatable kind of wheat than spelt. (In Brittany, cakes of coarsely ground grain are still called *fars.*) Today, made

with corn meal, which was unknown to the Romans, *polenta (page 31)* remains a national dish of Italy. The soft variety is equivalent to American corn-meal mush, and the ancient Romans often ate it like mush, with milk. Honey was sometimes added for invalids and children.

Real bread, in the early days at least, was unknown; grain could not be ground fine enough to produce flour. When milling methods improved, the crushed grain of *pulmentum* was made into farina, genuine flour. Yeast was generally made with leftover dough (which will ferment by itself), but the most prized yeast was a cultivated type imported from Gaul, where it was used to make beer. Until about 170 B.C. the whole breadmaking process was carried out at home, from the grinding of the grain to the sprinkling of poppy seeds, fennel or parsley on the loaf. Then bakers appeared—Rome's first professional cooks. But the bread they baked remained a luxury until the Christian era, out of the reach of the poor— though wealthy Roman ladies could afford to use flour to powder their noses, and frequently did.

Though *pulmentum* was the early Romans' principal source of nourishment, they also ate quantities of cottage cheese, made from ewe's milk. They had wine as well, for they had learned the art of cultivating vines from the Etruscans. But since good wine was expensive, only the rich could afford it; poorer people drank leftovers, in the form of an unappetizing beverage derived from steeping the crushed residue of the grapes in water.

The early Romans raised sheep for wool and for food, and they usually roasted their mutton. But like the Greeks before them, the Romans had

The staple food of Caesar's legions, and of most other Roman citizens, was *polenta*, a type of porridge made of cereal grains. Still popular, it is cooked today much as it was in the First Century. One major innovation: corn, introduced from America, has replaced the wheat and millet of the Romans.

Continued on page 18

The Bustling Supermarket of Imperial Rome

From the early Second Century the dinner plates of Rome were filled from a bustling, superfragrant supermarket next to the Forum built by the Emperor Trajan. Also built on Trajan's orders, the market was a rambling multilevel structure on the slope of Quirinal Hill *(below)*. Its core was a semicircle containing arches that served as entrances to some of the shops, such as the *creopolion* (butcher shop), *taberna vinaria* (wine shop) and the *unguentarius* (cosmetic shop) shown in the drawing at left. Other shops offered fish from neighboring seas and streams, produce from the Italian countryside and many foods from afar: wheat from Egypt, olive oil from Spain, rare and costly spices from Asia. In this artist's conception of a section of the market as it looked in Trajan's time, buyers push through armies of jug- and basket-carrying porters. The towering dark wall to the right of the drawing masks the brawling scene and its noises from the sedate Forum.

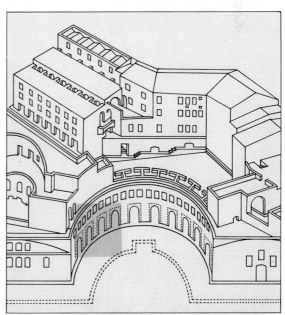

Stairs, ramps and roadways linked the various levels of Trajan's market. The section pictured in the scene at left is shaded in the drawing above. The dotted lines at the bottom show where the masking wall stood.

15

A Look inside the Shops

A vegetable dealer displays her wares on the trestle counter of her tiny stall.

Before the construction of Trajan's Market *(preceding pages)*, Roman butchers, grocers and dealers in fresh produce were scattered throughout the city. The market brought most of them together into one place. However, they still operated their own shops—most of them small, and probably much like those depicted in the reliefs shown on these pages. Shopkeepers in modern Rome still tend to cling to old ways, selling from small shops and stalls.

In a Roman poultry and produce shop, a counterwoman *(right, center)* sells a melon to one customer while at the far left another chooses a rabbit

butcher works at his block *(right)* under the eye of a female worker who is adding up the shop's accounts. Behind the butcher is a balance scale.

anging from the wall at left center are two unplucked fowl. The monkeys *(far right)* were kept to attract—and to entertain—customers.

kettles of bronze and iron, so they were also able to boil mutton. This put them more than 1,000 years ahead of the French, who until the 12th Century continued to cook their meat on spits, in consequence losing much of the juices into the fire.

As the ways of Rome became more sophisticated, vegetables were cultivated, prepared and served at table. By the Third Century B.C. the city had come to dominate all the Italian peninsula except the extreme north. As Roman legions conquered new territory, their leaders helped themselves to parcels of it. Eventually, their interest in exploiting their lands transformed them into squire-farmers. Cabbage, cultivated on their own acreage, was the most popular vegetable among the well-to-do, who believed it had some medicinal value. Less affluent citizens ate boiled greens, principally cultivated nettles and a variety of chard, as well as mallow, which today's farmers pull up as weeds. They ate these greens as modern Italians eat spinach, a plant Italy did not know until the Saracens introduced it in the Ninth Century A.D. from its native Persia. The *fava* bean was popular too, eaten raw when fresh, or boiled, or used to make soup.

Fruit was also a staple food among the ancient Romans. Among their favorites was the apple, which had long ceased to be a costly rarity, as it had once been for the Greeks. (In the Sixth Century B.C., Solon, attempting to control the extravagance of Athenian marriage feasts, had decreed that the bridal couple could eat only one apple between them.) Apricots were imported from Armenia and were expensive. So were peaches, which came from Persia. Lucullus is often credited with having introduced cherry trees into Italy, but a wild cherry seems to have been a native of the peninsula even before Roman times. Dates came from Africa, but figs were plentiful at home. Melons, in Roman times no bigger than oranges, were originally brought in from Persia. But their cultivation was soon established at Cantalupo, near Rome—hence the name of one of their larger descendants today.

By the Second Century B.C., Rome was well on its way to becoming a world power; the times were ripe for the enrichment and development of the Roman cuisine. In 185 B.C., Rome's Asiatic army returned from its war against the Emperor of Syria, Antiochus the Great, with appetite whetted for Oriental sybaritism and Oriental food. "The Army of Asia," Titus Livy wrote, "introduced foreign luxury to Rome. It was then that meals began to demand more preparation and more expense. . . . The cook, considered and employed until then as a slave at the lowest cost, became extremely expensive. What had been only a job became an art."

To meet the new demands made by changed tastes, Rome developed a sophisticated system of food production, importing and marketing. The heart of the system was the Central Market, a vast semicircular building of brick that still stands in the Forum of Trajan.

In Imperial times, the Central Market handled almost every kind of foodstuff. In it or in adjoining quarters butchers set up their small shops, even in the sacrosanct Forum Romanum. But the butchers rapidly acquired a reputation for selling spoiled goods, and the Imperial government eventually ordered them herded together outside the capital in the *macellum magnum*, a sort of professional ghetto in which it was easier for a special "meat squad" of the Roman police to enforce meat-handling regulations and to prevent the sale of any cuts that were unfit for human consumption.

The Romans of Imperial times were great eaters of meat. They had learned to prefer pork to mutton, as Romans do today, and they prepared it in many ingenious ways. One banquet recipe for "Trojan pork" called for whole pigs. They were first roasted on one side, which was slathered with a thick paste of barley meal, wine and oil. Then the other side, bare and uncooked, was suspended in water and boiled. The name "Trojan pork" was a reference to the wooden horse of Troy, which the Greeks had stuffed with soldiers; the Romans cleaned the pig and stuffed it with oysters and small birds.

Less of a banquet dish, but one still highly prized, was ham, both cured (dried or smoked) and fresh. A recipe attributed to Apicius—a gastronome of the First Century A.D. and one of the world's first famous cookbook writers—calls for fresh ham cooked in a crust of flour and oil and flavored with dried figs, bay leaves and honey pressed into small incisions in the flesh.

Birds of all kinds were highly popular in Imperial times. Chickens were sold in every market and were preferred in the form of capon. Guinea hens, known as Numidian or Carthaginian chickens, were imported from Africa, and domestic pigeons were crossed with wild ones to give them a gamier flavor. The Romans also ate wild duck, but disdained the drumsticks, eating only the breast meat and the brain. The goose was considered the most succulent bird, particularly the variety found in Picardy in northern Gaul. After the Roman legions conquered this region, tremendous flocks of geese often were driven on foot all the way from northern Gaul to Rome, living off the land; they were hardly more welcome to farmers along the route than the foraging legions had been.

Of the first creations of the professional cooks, many dishes are still in the Italian menu, somewhat modified. The Romans had an early version of *gnocchi,* or dumplings, and made a kind of double-boiler dish similar to the modern *sformato,* a cross between a soufflé and a pudding. Cato the Elder, the Roman statesman and writer, gives a recipe for this dish under the name of *torta scriblita.*

With the herbs and spices the Romans had at their disposal, they were able to produce a wide variety of flavors that they used with discrimination as long as their fare remained simple. But as the cooking of Rome became more ambitious and complex, they often tried to get all the available flavors into every dish, which of course made everything taste very much alike. They also favored an all-purpose sauce, *garum,* which they splashed on every food set before them. Historians disagree about what *garum* was made of, but there is little question that the sauce would be offensive to most modern palates. One description says that it was made from the entrails of mackerel.

Whatever the merits of *garum* may have been, one undisputable Roman success in the realm of sauces was the sweet-and-sour mixture. To Apicius is credited a version that combined pepper, mint, pine nuts, sultana grapes, carrots, honey, vinegar, oil, wine and musk. The family resemblance is still evident in the various *agrodolce* sauces applied in Italy today to duck and hare, to zucchini and cabbage, and to many other dishes.

Although the ancient Romans loved all sorts of condiments and spices, they had no cane or beet sugar. They had to make do with *defrutum* (grape syrup) and honey, which they ate with gusto throughout their meals. They also invented desserts that remain in use, one of which has given an important word to cooking: omelet, which comes from *ova mellita* (literally, "honeyed eggs").

Cheesecake is another Roman invention. An unsweetened variety was called *libum,* and the original recipe is the essence of simplicity: "Knead a pound of flour with two pounds of crushed fresh cheese and an egg. Bake in the oven under an earthenware cover." As *savillum* it becomes a dessert: "Mix half a pound of flour with two and a half pounds of cheese, one-quarter of a pound of honey, and an egg. Cook in a greased earthenware mold, tightly covered. After it is done, pour honey over it, and sprinkle it with poppy seeds."

The ancient Romans had at least 13 varieties of cheese, including one made from the milk of Gallic sheep; it may have been the ancestor of modern Roquefort. The cheese they used for cheesecake was similar to the *ricotta* of today, from which contemporary Italian cheesecakes and cheese puddings are made.

Most of the major contributions of Rome to the cuisine of the West were made before the end of the Second Century. Until about 180 A.D. the tempo of Roman life was sober and reasonable enough. But the pace was speeding up. The city had passed its crest with the first few of its emperors, the responsible ones such as Augustus, Trajan, Hadrian and Marcus Aurelius. Later, under the irresponsible ones—emperors like Commodus, Caracalla and Elagabalus—the state started coasting downhill, out of control. While the Roman Empire, top-heavy with power and luxury, softened and corrupt, was deteriorating, its cooking was in the wrong sense going to pot. Parvenus with fortunes made quickly from speculation, often in food, vied with each other in ostentatious spending.

Then, in the Third Century A.D., the Barbarians descended on Rome. For the next four or five centuries, the Italian cuisine did not progress. The Ostrogoths, a relatively civilized tribe of Barbarians, favored a wine called *vinum palmaticum,* which they sometimes drank mixed with egg, as Marsala is occasionally served today. The Barbarian occupations resulted, on the whole, in a salutary deflation of the overblown Roman cuisine. As the Empire disintegrated, the excesses in its cuisine disappeared—excesses in the use of spices, excesses in the ostentatious mixtures of all sorts of foods in the same dish (with even meat and fish cooked together). What was solid and worth preserving was retained. During the early Middle Ages the monasteries helped preserve the best of Roman gastronomy as well as other aspects of the old culture. Along with other manuscripts, the churchmen saved recipes. And because their food supplies were meager—as a consequence of both the uncertain times and the asceticism of early Christianity—the monks learned to cook even the meanest of vegetables (such as the turnip) so that they tasted good.

The status quo was not disturbed until the Ninth Century, when the East brought a new stimulus to the Italian cuisine, this time through the Islamic invasions of Southern Europe. The new conquerors' influence did not last as long in Italy as in most other parts of Europe, but the toehold they maintained for two centuries in Sicily and southern Italy eventually came to affect Italian cooking, and does to this day.

It was from the Arabs that the southern Italians learned how to concoct the desserts that are now so important in their cuisine. The art of making ice cream and sherbet was brought in by the Arabs, who had learned it, as the Persians and Indians had, from the Chinese. They also introduced various sweets based on honey, almond paste and marzipan, as well as cane sugar. The Arabs were the first to plant sugar cane in Europe, but the crop was difficult to cultivate. Until the late Middle Ages, the spread of sugar cane was limited by ignorance and poor communications.

Sugar did not gain a real foothold in Europe, either as a condiment or as a native crop, until the 11th Century, when the Crusades sent the soldiers of Christendom to invade the Saracen homelands. The Crusaders found sugar cane growing in the region of Tripoli, and brought both cane and refined sugar back with them. They called the refined product "Indian salt," because they believed it originally came from India (and they might very well have been right). Not realizing its possibilities, they considered sugar simply another kind of spice, to be used on fish or meat, and for a considerable period of time nobody thought of using it as a basis for sweet desserts.

From the land of the Saracens the Crusaders also brought back buckwheat (still called *sarrasin* in French, *sarraceno* in Spanish, *saraceno* in Italian). They rediscovered the lemon, which had been known to the ancient Romans, and lemon juice soon replaced the juice of green grapes and pressed herbs in meat sauces.

The culinary innovations brought back by the Crusaders did not achieve wide popularity until the 12th Century, long after the first of them had gone off to the Holy Land. A more immediate influence on Italian cooking was the increasing urbanization of the country—which produced new concentrations of wealth and new kinds of communities in which habits of living evolved toward greater luxury. Spices came back, including many of those known to the Romans. Other old Roman practices reappeared: the serving of meals in three or four courses, the artful building up of pyramids of food on serving platters and the custom of surprising guests with ingeniously disguised food—a whole "fish" that turned out to be made of vegetables, a roast of meat that turned out to be made of fish.

In the late Middle Ages in Italy, true bread appeared once more. The basic mixture of flour, water and yeast was elaborated into many varieties. One was sweetened with honey, flavored with spices and dotted with bits of dried fruit and figs—a direct ancestor of the modern *panforte* of Siena. The Genoese vegetable tarts *(torta pasqualina)* of today also had a late medieval forebear: similar vegetable tarts were listed in a cookbook by an anonymous author that was in use in the late 13th Century. In the same book, along with recipes for egg pies and milk tarts, appear the formulas for making *vermicelli*, *tortelli* and *tortelletti*——the first published reference to pasta. The latest date at which this book could have appeared is 1290, five years before Marco Polo returned from his historic journey across Asia to China, which should dispose of the fable that he brought back the art of making pasta from Cathay. The fact is that in the 13th Century Italians were already eating many forms of pasta, though it was by no means so important in their menu as it is today.

Marco Polo did perform one great gastronomic service for Italy, and for his hometown of Venice in particular: his writings led to the opening up

The table fork, unknown in Europe before the Renaissance, was first used in Italy. This one was part of an elaborate silver service made by a Roman artisan in the 16th Century.

of a direct route to the spices of the Far East, which until then had been bought from Arab middlemen. Venetian merchants quickly exploited spice importation as a near-monopoly and cornered the European market. During this period Venice bought spices cheap and sold them dear, and many of her glittering palaces were built on the profits. When the fall of Constantinople in 1453 finally closed this Far Eastern spice road, Venice turned again to the Muslims of the Near East. The cost was higher, but Venice was able to preserve its monopoly—and its high prices. This gave it another half century of wealth, until Portuguese captains succeeded in circumnavigating Africa and reaching the Spice Islands. Thereafter, Lisbon became the center of the spice trade, and at the same time replaced Venice as the most important refiner of sugar.

Marco Polo's return to Venice coincided with the dawn of the Renaissance. This rebirth of Classical civilization occurred in the culinary as well as other arts, a fact demonstrated by some of the books of the period. In 1305 Pietro de' Crescenzi, a native of Bologna, wrote his *Opus Ruralium Commodorum,* the first book on agriculture to appear in Europe since the Second Century. The most ambitious cookbook since Roman times was completed in 1475 by Bartolomeo Sacchi, librarian of the Vatican, who called himself Platina (a Latinization of Piadena, the name of his hometown). Printed in Venice under the title *De Honesta Voluptate ac Valetudine* ("Concerning Honest Pleasure and Well-being"), it was received so well that it appeared in six editions within 30 years.

The inspiration of Platina's cookbook was appropriately Classical. The book was based largely on the work of Apicius, but it also drew on Pliny the Elder, Varro, Columella and other ancient authors. Despite its Classical sources, it chided some of the excesses of Roman cooking—such as the lavish use of spices—which had been partly revived in the Middle Ages. Platina suggested that it was better to season food with lemon and orange juice, or wine. He also suggested starting a meal with the light, fresh taste of fruit. The advice was widely accepted (as one result, one of the most popular Italian hors d'oeuvre today is prosciutto, thin slices of dried ham served with melon or figs).

By the 16th Century the Italians' interest in gastronomy had become intense. One symbol of this culinary preoccupation was the founding in Florence of the first modern cooking academy, the Compagnia del Paiolo ("Company of the Cauldron"). It was limited to 12 members, all artists in the kitchen (and in some cases outside it: the most celebrated member was the painter Andrea del Sarto). Each member had to present a dish of his own invention at every meeting. One of Andrea's dishes was a temple built on a foundation of multicolored gelatin, with sausages for columns and wedges of Parmesan cheese for their capitals. Inside was a music stand that held a book with pages made of leaves of pasta, its lettering and musical notation picked out with grains of pepper. Near the stand, arranged like singers in a choir, were roasted thrushes.

It was all but inevitable that the Compagnia should have gathered in Florence, for it was in that shining city that Italian Renaissance cooking reached its greatest heights. Florentine skills did not go unchallenged; the Doges of Venice and great families in other parts of Italy also staged sumptuous feasts. But the most glittering menus of all were those of the Medicis in Florence, especially during the lifetime of Lorenzo the Magnificent.

Apart from the wealth of its first family, there was another reason for the culinary pre-eminence of Florence. There, more than anywhere else, the fine arts of the cuisine had worked their way down from the kitchens of the nobles into those of the humbler population.

Florentines generally ate two meals a day. The first was taken between 9 and 10 in the morning, the second just before nightfall. At the opening of the Renaissance, in the 14th Century, a meal was very light except in wealthy families: it might consist of bread (though bread was quite expensive), vegetables, and fresh or preserved fruit. Ordinarily, meat was eaten only on Sunday.

As the Renaissance progressed, the menu became more varied. Kid, and even boiled peacock, appeared on family tables. In middle-class families, the meal would begin with fruit (usually melon) or salad; it might continue with pigeon or *fegatelli*, a fine membrane rolled around a chopped liver stuffing, and conclude with goat cheese and grapes or figs. In addition there was pasta, which by the late 15th Century had become the mainstay of the Italian menu. (In Florence, pasta was always made at home. Its commercial production began during the Renaissance in Naples, still a center for the large-scale manufacture of macaroni and spaghetti.)

The wealthy Florentine merchants ate slightly more elaborately than the middle class, especially when they had guests. (The custom of the times was to have no more than nine persons at table; with more, as a contemporary writer pointed out, general conversation becomes impossible.) The meal began with something sweet: usually fruit or *berlingozzo*, a sort of cake. Next might come fattened capons, or veal with sausage, or a stew, or roast chicken, or a dish composed of thrushes, pigeon and pheasant, or trout. Finally, the meal would be concluded with cheese and a dessert of cookies or cakes.

Until the end of the 15th Century, this hearty but relatively simple kind of fare continued to be the style in Florence, the capital of Tuscany, where people still eat more simply than in any other part of Italy. Despite the example of conspicuous luxury provided by the later Medicis—in 1469 Lorenzo the Magnificent celebrated his wedding by giving five sumptuous banquets from Sunday to Tuesday—Florence followed the advice of Platina, who counseled moderation. The people used his recipes, which admittedly included the rich wine sauces and some of the heavily spiced dishes of the Middle Ages, but also offered many surprisingly humble ones: *fava* bean soup, for instance, or squash soup poured over slices of bread, and eaten as a meatless meal. Platina devoted a whole chapter to endive and romaine lettuce, with special notes on the preparation of asparagus. Grilled meat, spitted meat and veal steaks were eaten with the pasta that was now becoming universal, or sometimes with rice, though rice was usually sweetened and used to make puddings or cakes.

While Florence led Italy in the gastronomic arts, Italy as a whole had no competition whatever from the rest of Europe. Writing of 16th Century European cooking, the French culinary historian Georges Blond remarks: "Outside Italy, [the art] was in the Middle Ages." Not illogically it was Italy, led by Florence, that was to pass the torch to the rest of Europe—first of all to France. The tradition that credits Catherine de' Medici with introducing Italian cooking to France is factual enough, but perhaps some of the credit should go also to Francis I, her royal father-in-law, whose earlier fascination with Italy led him to popularize many Italian dishes in France.

The accounts of Catherine's arrival give considerable space to her pastry cooks, who introduced Italian pastries such as frangipane, macaroons and Milan cakes (which were only then being introduced in Italy itself). But Catherine also brought along other cooks, who gave her new court and country such delicacies as stuffed guinea hen, one version of which is still known in French cookbooks as *pintade à la Medicis*. The cooks imported truffles too, starting the French digging enthusiastically for these tasty underground fungoid growths.

Most Italians, certainly, were unaware that they had handed France the keys to greatness in cooking. They were too busy with their own culinary developments at home. For example, Italy gave the world the double boiler. According to one legend a lady alchemist who called herself Cleopatra the Wise invented it while composing a treatise on the relationships of magic, medicine and cooking. Since the lady's real name was Maria de Cleofa, her invention became known as "Mary's bath," *bagno maria*, and was later adopted in France as the *bain marie*.

Even more significantly, Renaissance Italy—which had a decided sweet tooth—introduced the rest of the Western world to its own predilections. As the use of the cane sugar provided by Venice became more common, sweet hors d'oeuvre began to take the place of salads as the opening dishes of banquets, so that meals now began as well as ended with sweets. Sugar went into everything, even macaroni—at least for the rich. But it was too expensive for the poor, who had to eat their macaroni unsweetened, as everyone does today. Even so, the poor seem to have fared reasonably well. One 15th Century Florentine preacher scolded his flock for the excessive embellishment of their food—even though sugar was not part of their diet. "It's not enough for you to eat your pasta fried," he protested. "No! You think you have to add garlic to it, and when you eat ravioli, it's not enough to boil it in a pot and eat it in its juice; you have to fry it in another pan and cover it with cheese!"

In the late Renaissance the Italian, and European, menu was to be enriched further by a major contribution from the East—coffee. The drink first entered Europe through the great trading port of Venice; that much seems well established. Its origin is less clear, though it probably came from Arabic-speaking territory (the Arabic word for "beverage" is *qahwah*—which to some scholars sounds enough like "coffee" to support that probability). The merits of coffee may have been discovered in Aden or Yemen, where it was supposedly used by Islamic hermits to keep them awake during their nightly prayers. Another story holds that an Arab goatherd discovered the beverage after observing that his charges, browsing on coffee beans, became particularly frisky. An early popularizer of the drink is reputed to have been a Muslim elder named Od-a-Makha, from the Red Sea port of Mocha; the names may be the origin of the word mocha, the fine variety of coffee first exported from the Arabian coast.

In any event, Gian Francesco Morosini, Venice's Ambassador to Turkey, reported to the Venetian Senate in 1585 on "the habit of the Turks of drinking a black water as hot as you can bear it, taken from seeds called *cavee*, and they say it has the power of keeping men awake." Not long afterward, coffee shops, called *botteghe*, appeared in Venice and from there coffee drinking soon spread to other parts of Europe. A Sicilian, Francesco Procopio dei Coltelli (Procope for short), is credited with popularizing the habit in France by opening the first coffeehouse, or café, in Paris in 1670; it still exists as Le Procope on the Rue de l'Ancienne Comédie. Procope also introduced a wealth of Italian pastries and sweetmeats, and two Italian specialties hitherto unknown in Paris—ice cream and sherbet. By the late 17th Century the habit of coffee drinking had become well established not only in France, but also in Italy, which many believe still offers the best coffee in Europe.

The "mother cuisine" of Italy also assimilated many products of the New World and helped introduce them to the Old. It is hard to imagine modern Italian cooking without the tomato, yet no European had ever set eyes on it before Cortés conquered Mexico. The first Italian description of a tomato, in 1554, called it *pomo d'oro* or "golden apple" (spelled *pomodoro* today). And in fact the first tomato seen in Europe was yellow in color, and about the size of a cherry. It took nearly two centuries for the Italians to develop new, bigger, red varieties and to use the tomato regularly in cooking; it was used at first as a salad vegetable.

The pimento, or red pepper, so important in Italian cooking today, was also one of the finds of the conquistadors. So was the potato, sent back to Europe around 1540 from Peru by Pedro de Cieza, one of Pizarro's men, who described it as being similar to a chestnut. A specimen potato was presented to Pope Clement VII, who asked the botanist Charles de l'Escluse to define it. De l'Escluse described it as "a small truffle," and the Germans still call potatoes and truffles by the same name, *kartoffel*. In Italy, too, potatoes were for centuries known as *tartufoli*, though they are called *patate* today. The potato was grown in Italian gardens as early as 1580 and in France somewhat later, but only as an ornamental plant. (The potato's acceptance as a food was not helped when it was first tried out in England at the court of Queen Elizabeth. No one thought to tell her cook what part of the plant was edible, so he served the leaves.) The Italians, supreme in raising vegetables such as spinach and squash, which are more subtle and delicate than the potato, have never depended on the latter for starch, as other countries do; they have traditionally preferred pasta and rice. The only characteristic dish into which the potato enters in Italy is a variety of *gnocchi* made with potato and flour.

Italy also was among the first to exploit corn, the grain used today in *polenta*. But the American grain was slow in supplanting other cereals. Columbus' sailors tried corn on their homeward voyage and did not like it. The Italians did not begin to eat it until about 1650. Another American vegetable became popular more quickly than corn: the haricot bean, one variety of which is the kidney bean. After their first presentation to Pope Clement VII in 1528, haricot beans quickly gained favor as substitutes for *fava* beans and peas. Turkey, also brought back from America and eventually raised in quantity in Italy, became popular, cooked according to existing recipes for peacock.

By the end of the 16th Century the Italian list of food resources was complete, and Italy's cooking techniques and eating habits had crystallized, approximately in the forms we know today. This did not prevent her citizens, particularly the upper classes, from making minor history in all manner of elaborate feasts. One such banquet, reputedly the most distinguished given in Rome during the entire 17th Century, was offered by Pope Alexander VII to Queen Christina of Sweden, who had become the Church's most illustrious convert. The guests seemed less impressed by the food than by the *trionfi di tavola,* the ornamental "triumphs of the table" that were a feature of great dinners of the day. Technically, some of these creations were edible, but most guests simply gaped at them in delight. Besides great statues of sugar, there were trees of marzipan, and other motifs in blancmange or aspic. The centerpiece for Christina's party was a model of the harbor of Messina; its buildings, piers and ships were reproduced in aspic and the water contained live fish.

By the 18th Century the days of such extravagancies were coming to an end. Rome saw its last great banquets for the reception of august visitors such as the Queen of Naples and the Emperor of Austria. At one lavish Holy Thursday dinner, the Pope gave his cardinals fresh cherries obtained before their season by forcing trees in the Naples region through heavy fertilization and watering them with warm water. The French Ambassador to Rome continued to give splendid banquets every December 13 to mark the anniversary of the conversion to Catholicism of Henri IV. But ostentation was meeting such general disapproval in Italy that the same Ambassador finally asked the permission of his superiors in Paris to replace the yearly banquet with a gift of dowries for poor girls. His superiors refused, but the banquets were toned down.

By now the prestige of French cooking, at least among the aristocracy, had begun to surpass that of the Italian cuisine; the country that had taught France how to cook was beginning to take lessons from its pupil. But a solid tradition had been built, and it has remained alive to the present, to the delectation of the country's citizens and the delight of her admirers.

A distinguished 18th Century visitor, the Elector of Cologne *(head of table, rear)* receives a traditional Venetian honor: a lavish banquet.

To make 1 nine-inch pie

PASTA FROLLA

2 cups unsifted all-purpose flour

12 tablespoons lard or butter, at room temperature but not soft

4 egg yolks

¼ cup sugar

3 tablespoons dry Marsala

1 teaspoon freshly grated lemon peel

½ teaspoon salt

RICOTTA FILLING

5 cups *ricotta* cheese (2½ pounds), or substitute whole-curd cottage cheese, rubbed through a sieve

½ cup sugar

1 tablespoon flour

½ teaspoon salt

1 teaspoon vanilla extract

1 teaspoon freshly grated orange peel

4 egg yolks

1 tablespoon white raisins, rinsed and drained

1 tablespoon diced candied orange peel

1 tablespoon diced candied citron

2 tablespoons slivered blanched almonds or pine nuts

1 egg white mixed with 1 tablespoon water

Crostata di Ricotta
CHEESE PIE

PASTA FROLLA (pastry crust): In a large mixing bowl, make a well in the center of 2 cups of flour. Drop into it the butter (or lard), egg yolks, sugar, Marsala, lemon peel and salt. With your fingertips, mix the ingredients together, incorporating as much flour as you can. With the heels of your hands, work in the rest of the flour until the dough is smooth and can be gathered into a ball. Do not, however, knead the dough or work it any more than necessary. (If you have an electric mixer with a paddle attachment, all of the ingredients can be placed in the bowl at once and mixed at low speed until they are just combined.) The dough can be rolled out at once, but if it seems at all oily, refrigerate it for about 1 hour, or until it is firm but not hard.

Break off about ¼ of the dough, dust lightly with flour and cover with wax paper or plastic wrap; set aside in the refrigerator. Reshape the rest of the dough into a ball and place on a lightly floured board or pastry cloth. With the heel of your hand, flatten the ball into a disk about 1 inch thick. Dust a little flour over both sides of the disk to prevent the dough from sticking, and begin rolling it out—starting from the center and rolling to within an inch of the far edge. Gently lift the dough, turn clockwise, and roll out again from the center to the far edge. Repeat lifting, turning and rolling until the disk is about ⅛ inch thick and at least 11 inches across. If the dough sticks to the board or cloth while you are rolling it out, lift it

gently with a wide metal spatula and sprinkle a little flour under it.

Lightly butter the bottom and sides of a 9-by-1½-inch spring-form or false-bottom cake pan. Then, starting at the nearest edge of the circle, lift the pastry and drape it over the rolling pin. Place the pin in the middle of the buttered pan, and unfold the pastry over it, leaving some slack in the center. Gently press the pastry into the bottom and around the sides of the pan, taking care not to stretch it. Roll the pin over the rim of the pan, pressing down hard to trim off the excess pastry around the top.

Unwrap the remaining pastry, place it on a lightly floured board or cloth, flatten it with your hand and roll it into a rectangle about 12 inches long. With a pastry wheel or knife, cut long strips about ½ inch wide.

RICOTTA FILLING: Preheat the oven to 350°. Combine the cheese with ½ cup of sugar, 1 tablespoon flour, ½ teaspoon salt, the vanilla, grated orange peel and egg yolks, and beat until they are thoroughly mixed. Stir in the raisins and the candied orange peel and citron. Spoon this filling into the pastry shell, spreading it evenly with a rubber spatula. Sprinkle the top with slivered almonds or pine nuts, then weave or crisscross the pastry strips across the pie to make a lattice design. Brush the strips lightly with the egg-white-and-water mixture. Bake in the middle of the oven for 1 to 1¼ hours, or until the crust is golden and the filling is firm.

Remove the pie from the oven and set it on a large jar or coffee can. Then slide off the outside rim of the pan. Cool the pie on a wire cake rack, leaving the bottom disk of the pan in place. If you prefer to remove the disk before serving, wait until the pie is cool, loosen the bottom crust with a wide metal spatula, and carefully slide the pie onto a round serving plate.

Fresh fruits like white grapes, served with *crostata di ricotta*, make a tangy, sweet contrast to the richness of the pie. *Crostata di ricotta* is one of the oldest of Roman dishes.

Prosciutto Fresco Brasato al Marsala
FRESH HAM BRAISED IN MARSALA

1 cup dry Marsala
¼ cup olive oil
2 teaspoons lemon juice
2 bay leaves, crumbled
A 4- to 6-pound half of fresh ham
½ cup coarsely chopped onions
¼ cup coarsely chopped carrots
¼ cup coarsely chopped celery
¼ cup olive oil
2 cups beef stock, fresh or canned
1 tablespoon arrowroot
2 tablespoons dry Marsala
Salt
Freshly ground black pepper

Combine 1 cup of Marsala, ¼ cup of olive oil, the lemon juice and bay leaves in a large glass or stainless-steel bowl. Turn the fresh ham in this marinade until it is thoroughly moistened. Marinate at room temperature for at least 6 hours or in the refrigerator for at least 12 hours—turning the ham 2 or 3 times.

Preheat the oven to 350°. Remove the ham from the marinade and pat it dry with paper towels. Strain the marinade into a small bowl. Combine the onions, carrots and celery and chop them together into very small pieces. (This mixture is called a *battuto*, which will be called a *soffritto* after it is cooked.) Heat 2 tablespoons of olive oil in a heavy 4- to 6-quart flameproof casserole just large enough to hold the ham comfortably. Add the *battuto* and cook over moderate heat, stirring frequently, for about 10 minutes, or until it is lightly colored. Heat the remaining 2 tablespoons of oil in a heavy 10- to 12-inch skillet until a light haze forms over the oil. Brown the ham in the skillet, starting it fat side down and turning it with 2 wooden spoons. When it is a golden-brown color all over, place the ham on top of the *soffritto* in the casserole and insert a meat thermometer deep into the thickest part of the meat.

Discard almost all of the fat from the skillet, leaving just a film on the bottom. Pour in the strained marinade and boil it briskly over high heat, stirring and scraping in any browned bits that cling to the pan. When the marinade has reduced to about half its original quantity, add it to the casserole along with the beef stock. If the liquid does not come ⅓ of the way up the side of the ham, add more stock. Bring the casserole to a boil on top of the stove, cover and place on the middle shelf of the oven. Braise the ham until the thermometer reaches 185°—which should take 3 to 3½ hours. Transfer the ham to a heated platter, and let it rest for about 15 minutes to make carving easier.

Strain the sauce from the casserole through a fine sieve into a 1½- to 2-quart saucepan, pressing down hard on the vegetables to extract all their juices before discarding them. Skim the surface of fat, then bring the sauce to a simmer over moderate heat. Mix the arrowroot with 2 additional tablespoons of Marsala and, when the arrowroot has dissolved, stir it into the simmering sauce. Continue cooking, stirring constantly, until the sauce thickens and clears. Do not let it boil. Taste the sauce for seasoning. Carve the ham into thin slices and arrange the slices in a row on a heated serving platter. Pour a few tablespoons of the sauce over the ham before serving it, and pass the rest separately.

Pesche Ripiene
FRESH PEACHES STUFFED WITH MACAROONS

6 firm but ripe peaches
5 stale macaroons, crushed in a blender
  or wrapped in a towel and crushed
  with a rolling pin (1 cup crumbs)
2 tablespoons sugar
4 tablespoons unsalted butter
2 egg yolks

Preheat the oven to 375°. Blanch the peaches, 2 at a time, in boiling water for about 20 seconds. Lift them out with a slotted spoon, plunge them into cold water and peel off the skins with a small sharp knife. Cut the peaches in half, and remove the pits. Scoop enough peach pulp out of each half to make a deep space in the center. Add this pulp to the crushed macaroons, then stir in the sugar, butter and egg yolks. Stuff the peach halves with the macaroon mixture. Arrange the peach halves side by side in a buttered 8-by-10-inch baking dish or on an ovenproof platter, and bake them for about 25 minutes, or until they are just tender. Baste with sugar syrup from the pan during baking. Serve hot or cold.

Polenta
CORN-MEAL PORRIDGE

In a heavy 3- to 4-quart saucepan, bring the water and salt to a bubbling boil over high heat. Pour the uncooked *polenta* or corn meal slowly into the boiling water, making sure that the boiling never stops, and stirring constantly to keep the mixture smooth. Reduce the heat and simmer the *polenta,* stirring frequently, for 20 to 30 minutes, or until it is so thick that the spoon will stand up unsupported in the middle of the pan.

The *polenta* can be served at once with gravy, butter and cheese, or tomato sauce *(page 47).* Or, if you prefer, it can be spooned out while it is still hot onto a large buttered baking dish or sheet and with a metal spatula or knife, spread into a thin layer about 8 by 16 inches in size. It should then be refrigerated for about 2 hours. Once cool it can be fried in oil, broiled or baked and served with sauce (Recipe Booklet).

To serve 6

1½ quarts water
2 teaspoons salt
1½ cups finely ground *polenta*
  or yellow corn meal

Ostriche all' Italiana
BAKED OYSTERS WITH BREAD CRUMBS AND GARLIC

Preheat the oven to 450°. Choose an ovenproof platter or a shallow baking-and-serving dish that is just large enough to hold the oysters in one layer (about 8 by 10 or 12 inches). Butter the dish generously.

In a heavy 6- to 8-inch skillet, melt 2 tablespoons of butter over moderate heat. When the foam subsides, add the fresh, white bread crumbs and the garlic, and toss them in the butter for 2 or 3 minutes, or until they are crisp and golden. Stir in the finely chopped parsley. Spread about ⅔ cup of the bread-crumb mixture in the bottom of the buttered baking dish, and arrange the oysters over it in one layer. Mix the rest of the bread-crumb mixture with the grated cheese and spread the combination on the oysters. Dot the top with the tiny bits of butter.

Bake the oysters in the top third of the oven for 12 to 15 minutes, or until the crumbs are golden and the juices in the dish are bubbling. Serve at once, either as a main course or as part of the *antipasto.*

To serve 4 to 6

2 tablespoons butter
1 cup fresh, white bread crumbs (made
  from about 3 slices of French or
  Italian bread)
1 teaspoon finely chopped garlic
2 tablespoons finely chopped fresh
  parsley, preferably the flat-leaf
  Italian type
2 dozen fresh oysters, shucked, or
  defrosted frozen oysters
3 tablespoons freshly grated imported
  Parmesan cheese
2 tablespoons butter, cut in tiny pieces

Cavoli in Agrodolce
CABBAGE IN SWEET AND SOUR SAUCE

Heat the olive oil in a heavy 10- to 12-inch skillet, add the onions and cook them over moderate heat, stirring constantly, for 2 or 3 minutes. When they are transparent but not brown, stir in the cabbage, tomatoes, vinegar, salt and a few grindings of pepper. Simmer uncovered, stirring frequently, for 20 minutes, or until the cabbage is tender. Then stir the sugar into the cabbage and cook a minute or 2 longer. Serve in a heated bowl, either as a vegetable accompanying a fish or meat course or as a separate dish preceding the main course.

To serve 4 to 6

3 tablespoons olive oil
½ cup thinly sliced onions
1½ pounds cabbage, cut into ¼-inch
  strips (about 8 cups)
3 large tomatoes, peeled, seeded and
  coarsely chopped
2 tablespoons wine vinegar
2 teaspoons salt
Freshly ground black pepper
1 tablespoon sugar

II

The Modern Cuisine

Olives, fish, ham, bread
sticks, sausages and
vegetables both raw and
cooked are combined for an
antipasto. What goes into
this dish depends on the
imagination of the cook and
on what foods are in season.
Only two of the *antipasto*
dishes shown at left,
caponata (double dish, top row)
and marinated mushrooms
(bottom, second from left),
need preparation.

To many a non-Italian, the cooking of Italy means pasta, served up as spaghetti, macaroni or noodles; outside of Italy, these starchy words have come to symbolize the nation's whole repertory of food. Actually, the Italian menu is lively and interesting: it ranges from rich, stomach-warming soups and dazzling *antipasti* (hors d'oeuvre), through subtle and sophisticated meat, fish and poultry dishes, to a profusion of delicious cheeses, cakes and ice creams.

Even within the category of pasta itself, there is astonishing variety. It is true that the sort of pasta one eats outside Italy—often from a can—may not seem very inspired; indeed, one may encounter unimaginative pasta in Italy too. Nevertheless, the basic food, like the rest of Italian cooking, is capable of taking on the most delicate nuances.

Far from being identical throughout Italy, styles of pasta cooking form a basis on which the whole country can be divided, north and south, into two quite separate culinary territories *(map, page 35)*. The north is the country of *pasta bolognese* (the noodles of Bologna), the flat ribbon type, often cooked fresh at home, usually made with eggs. The south is the territory of *pasta napoletana* (the macaroni of Naples), most often manufactured commercially in tubular form, frequently made without eggs and bought at the store in a dried form that makes it possible to keep it for long periods before cooking.

No doubt most non-Italians, if asked to name the different varieties of pasta, would mention macaroni, spaghetti, ravioli and—perhaps after a moment's hesitation—*vermicelli*. This is not many from a list that also embraces, among others, *agnolotti, amorini, anolini, bucatini, cannelloni, capellini, cappelletti, cavatelli, cavatoni rigati, conchiglie, ditali, ditalini, farfalle, farfallette, fedelini, fettucce, fettuccelle, fettuccine, frittelle, fusilli, lasagne, lasagne verdi, lingue di passero, linguine, lumache, maccheroncelli, mafalde, malfatti, manicotti, margherite, maruzzelle, mezzani, mostaccioli, mostaccioli rigati, nevi di Firenze, occhi di lupo, pappardelle, passatelli, pasta reale, pastine, penne, pennoni, perciatelli, ricciolini, rigati, rigatoni, spaghettini, spiedini, stelline, stivaletti, tagliarini, tagliatelle, taglio, tagliolini, tonnarelli, tonnellini, tortelli, tortellini, tortelloni, trenette, tripolini, tubettini, tufoli, tufoli rigati* and *ziti*.

This list reveals almost as much about the Italian language and spirit as it does about the varieties of pasta. Many of the labels are untranslatable nicknames (often in local dialect) describing the shapes, the origins or the fillings of different types of pasta. Among those that are translatable are *amorini* (little cupids), *agnolotti* ("little fat lambs"—rolls of pasta stuffed with meat), *cannelloni* ("big pipes"), *conchiglie* (conch shells), *farfalle* (butterflies), *fusilli* (spindles), *lingue di passero* (sparrows' tongues), *mostaccioli rigati* (little grooved moustaches), *ricciolini* (little curls), *stivaletti* (little boots), *vermicelli* (little worms).

This catalogue takes no account of the doughy varieties of *gnocchi,* or pastalike dumplings, which may be made of farina, semolina, potatoes and flour, or mixtures of these. Nor does it allow for the different effects that can be produced by different methods of cooking—simple boiling, boiling and frying, boiling and baking. Furthermore, it does not touch upon the endless varieties of sauces that can be combined with the varieties of pasta. Multifarious as pasta is, however, there is nothing mysterious about it. As the pictures on pages 39 through 45 show, all the variety and profusion proceed from very simple beginnings.

Just as pasta is anything but a simple dish, Italian cooking as a whole is anything but a simple cuisine. While it is not difficult to master, its diversity is inexhaustible. Part of this diversity results from the geographical fact that the Apennine Mountains, snaking across and down the peninsula, split the country into somewhat isolated compartments. Part comes from the political fact that the peninsula was divided until a century ago into many separate and often warring states, each with its own distinct cultural and culinary traditions. Economically as well as from the culinary standpoint,

Regional Styles: A Key to Italian Cooking

Each of the Italian regions has its own history and its own distinctive way of preparing food. These diverse styles give extraordinary variety to the national cuisine. Great as these regional differences are, however, there is an even more basic difference between the cooking of north and south. In the prosperous north, as shown on the map opposite, butter is the most common cooking fat. Flat noodles, usually made with eggs, are the favorite form of pasta. In the poorer south, dishes are cooked with cheaper ingredients—olive oil instead of butter, and dried tubular pastas like spaghetti and macaroni—and are more robust and highly seasoned than the foods of the north.

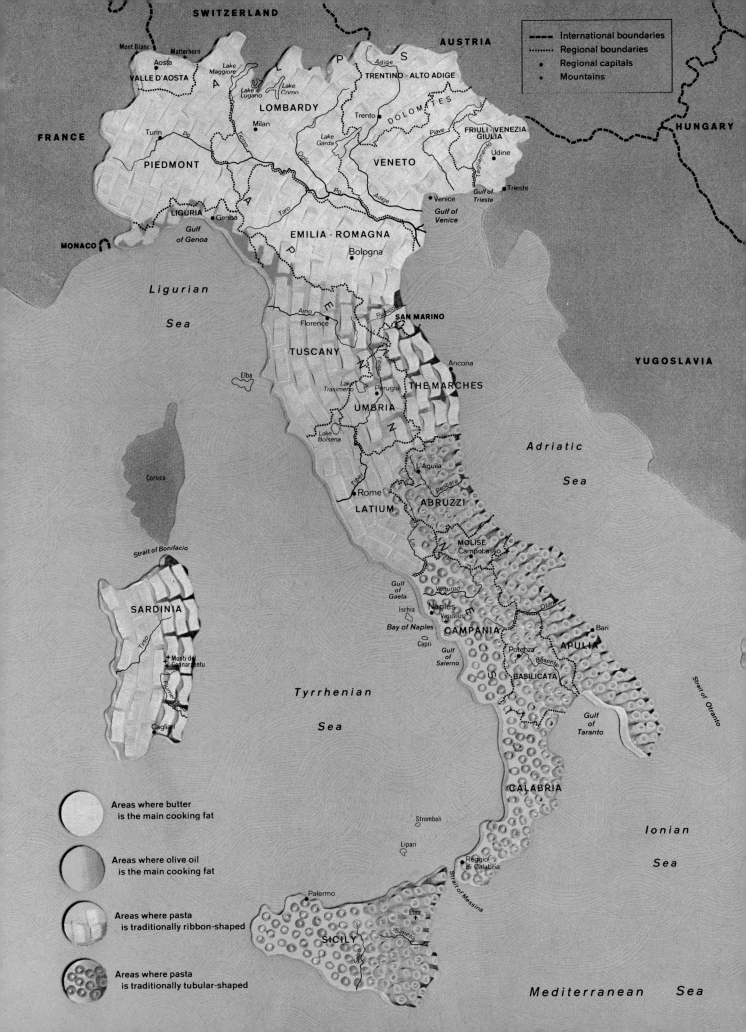

SWITZERLAND

AUSTRIA

International boundaries
Regional boundaries
• Regional capitals
+ Mountains

HUNGARY

FRANCE

Mont Blanc
Matterhorn
Aosta
VALLE D'AOSTA
Lake Maggiore
Lake Lugano
Lake Como
Lake Garda
A L P S
Adige
TRENTINO - ALTO ADIGE
Trento
DOLOMITES
Piave
FRIULI - VENEZIA GIULIA
Udine
Trieste
Gulf of Trieste

LOMBARDY
Milan
Turin
Po
Ticino
Oglio
PIEDMONT
VENETO
Adige
Venice
Gulf of Venice

A P E N N
LIGURIA
Genoa
Gulf of Genoa
Taro
Po
EMILIA - ROMAGNA
Bologna

MONACO

Ligurian Sea

Arno
Florence
Rubicon
SAN MARINO

TUSCANY
Elba
Lake Trasimeno
Perugia
UMBRIA
Tiber
THE MARCHES
Ancona

Adriatic Sea

YUGOSLAVIA

Corsica

Lake Bolsena
Tiber
L'Aquila
Pescara
Rome
LATIUM
ABRUZZI

Strait of Bonifacio

SARDINIA
Tirso
Monti del Gennargentu
Flumendosa
Cagliari

Liri
MOLISE
Campobasso

Gulf of Gaeta
Volturno
Ischia
Naples
Vesuvius
Bay of Naples
Capri
CAMPANIA
Gulf of Salerno
Potenza
Basento
BASILICATA

Ofanto
Bari
APULIA

Strait of Otranto

Tyrrhenian Sea

Gulf of Taranto

CALABRIA

Ionian Sea

Stromboli

Lipari

Reggio di Calabria

Palermo

Strait of Messina

Etna
Simeto
Salso
SICILY

Mediterranean Sea

Areas where butter is the main cooking fat

Areas where olive oil is the main cooking fat

Areas where pasta is traditionally ribbon-shaped

Areas where pasta is traditionally tubular-shaped

Italy is divided into the north (fertile, populous, industrialized and affluent) and the south (parched, sparsely settled and historically poor). As a consequence, while the north often cooks with butter, the south almost always cooks with olive oil; it costs less to maintain an olive tree than a cow, and the tree can live in poorer soil.

Overlying these north-south divisions are the differences between Italy's 20 regions, which in general are the same as the formerly independent states. The boundaries have been subject to many changes, but the regions tend to remain stubbornly individualistic. For example, although the north is known as "butter country," it contains a geographical triangle within which different types of fat shape the regional cooking of three adjacent provinces. Lombardy, to the northwest, prefers butter; Tuscany, to the south, uses olive oil; Emilia-Romagna, between the two, cooks with pork fat. Bologna, the capital of Emilia-Romagna, lies in the center and employs all three, though it favors the pork fat of its own region, especially for frying.

Even today, as a result of all these strong local differences, foods that are identified abroad as "Italian" may be associated in Italy only with a single city, and may be unobtainable elsewhere. For a visitor, this can lead to some unexpected misunderstandings. On my own trips through Italy, I have often asked tourist bureaus, members of the Italian Academy of Cooking, writers on food and other experts to direct me to the best restaurants of their own regions so that I could sample the local cooking. In place after place I have been advised not to go to certain well known and generally excellent restaurants. The explanation: "They attract too many tourists. They have become *internationalized.*"

At first I thought this meant that the restaurants had succumbed to the French-inspired cuisine, like so many successful restaurants outside France. But when, on occasion, I went ahead against all advice and did try an "international" restaurant, I discovered that though it might offer some of the dishes of the French haute cuisine, most of the menu was solidly Italian. What my advisers had meant by international was that the restaurant no longer confined itself to the Italian cooking of its own region. To a citizen of Bologna, a restaurant that serves Roman, Genoese or Sicilian dishes is international. On the other hand, a Bologna restaurant serving Milanese, Venetian or Florentine dishes is not regarded as international; those dishes from nearby cities have been assimilated into the Bolognese cuisine.

One reason many foreigners still have the impression that all Italian cooking is pretty much the same is that Italian restaurants abroad are almost all Neapolitan; it is from the relatively poor part of the country around Naples that emigration has been greatest.

In the broadest terms, the dominant city of northern Italian cooking is Bologna, as Naples is that of the south. Some regions, however, refuse to align themselves with either of these poles. One of them is the region of Latium, centered on Rome. As the historical headquarters of the Roman Catholic Church, Rome for centuries has attracted the cultural contributions of all Italy as well as those of other nations, becoming eclectic in cooking. Florence also enjoys a special status, which can be traced to its cultural leadership in the Renaissance. Sicily and Sardinia are special cases too, largely because they are especially dependent on the sea.

The sea, in fact, is the source of what, after pasta, is Italy's most important single category of food. Every Italian province with a seacoast has its own delicious variety of fish chowder—and most provinces have seacoasts. From the Tyrrhenian and Adriatic Seas, Italians net some 700 million pounds of fish a year, including red mullet, sole, sea bass, dentex, umbrine, anchovies, sardines, mackerel, tuna and eel. The sea also provides quantities of shellfish and crustaceans: oysters, clams, mussels, spiny lobster, shrimp, crayfish and the famous *scampi*, a close relative of the shrimp, which has no exact equivalent outside Italian waters. Finally, there is a class of seafood not very much fancied in Anglo-Saxon countries: squid, cuttle-fish and octopus.

While pasta and fish may be the nation's staples, the greater glories of Italy are its vegetables and fruit. Why these foods should taste so superior in Italy remains a mystery. Spinach, a rather lackluster vegetable in most countries, makes a royal dish in Italy. Asparagus melts in the mouth. The Italian variety of tomato, at its best in a simple salad, is so much tastier than its smaller, yellower American ancestor that the descendant has been transported back across the Atlantic into the New World.

The high quality of vegetables and fruit has been put down to a variety of causes: sea mists that carry salts and other minerals across the land and do for the taste of vegetables what they are said to do on the New England coast for the color and fragrance of flowers; the use of natural rather than artificial fertilizers; the vagaries of climate and soil; and, ultimately, know-how—the fine Italian hand.

Italy's genius for getting added taste into edible things has made it a country whose repertory of herbs is large and of high quality. No Italian kitchen is without fresh or dried bunches of parsley, sweet basil, wild marjoram, thyme, rosemary, sage, tarragon, bay leaves, oregano, mint, myrtle and borage. Fennel seeds and juniper berries are also favored seasonings. With spices—including cloves, coriander and especially saffron—and the use as seasoning of celery, onions, shallots, garlic, lemon juice, vinegar and olives, the Italian cook has a wide spectrum of flavorings to choose from.

In this list the olive deserves a special place. It may well be that the best olive oil in the world comes from Italy (along with some of poorer quality). According to connoisseurs, the finest comes from Lucca, in Tuscany, though a vote is sometimes cast for the region of Sassari, in Sardinia.

Rice is one other product of the Italian soil that deserves particular mention. This is an important food in Italian cooking, and an important item in Italian agriculture. Italy is Europe's biggest producer of rice, and the average production of rice per acre—530 bushels—is not matched anywhere in the world. Rice was known to a few privileged Italians by the 12th Century, but was not cultivated successfully until the 16th Century, when Italian farmers finally learned the techniques of growing it. But by the end of the 18th Century, the rice grown in the Piedmont region of the north was so superior to all other varieties, and so jealously guarded, that it was illegal to take seed grain out of the country. Some of the grain was smuggled out in 1787, by no less a person than Thomas Jefferson, who wanted to see how it would grow in American soil (it grew well). The Italian method of cooking rice leaves each grain separate and slightly resistant to the teeth: Italians think that most other countries overcook rice—and spaghetti and vegetables, as well.

Many foreigners, on the other hand, insist that Italians overcook meat. This may be because Italians are not ordinarily great meat eaters (though one who eats it every day is no longer accounted a rich man). It is even said that Italy *has* no good meat, but this is a canard: Italian pork and veal are superlative, and Italian beef is very good, too.

Like the ancient Romans, most modern Italians prefer veal to beef. On this subject, however—as on so many others—the country is divided. North of Florence, veal is *vitello*, or calf, and south of Florence, *vitella*, or heifer. In the north, especially in the plain of the Po Valley, the cows are reared solely for milk production, and only the steers are killed for meat. In the south, however, cattle are not great milk producers. They are raised chiefly for field work.

Besides veal, various other meats are available in Italy. Among the most popular are the processed forms of pork. Parma ham, cured in the mountain air, is world famous. Bologna is the center of the most prolific sausage-producing region; the English word "boloney" is evidence of this fact. What is called boloney (or more properly bologna) in the United States resembles the fragrant, subtly spiced Italian *mortadella*. The familiar salami comes in many forms from many parts of Italy.

In Italy the subject of sausage is invariably associated with that of cheese; a most satisfactory lunch, especially for workers in the fields, often consists of bread, sausage, cheese and a swig or two of wine. If Italy has not quite so many cheeses as France, it still has a respectable and highly varied selection, among the best known of which are Parmesan and Bel Paese. Even in a small Sicilian country market, I have seen more than 20 varieties of cheese on display, most of them local.

In no Italian market—whether the old-fashioned outdoor bazaars or the new indoor supermarkets—does the shopper have to search for a variety of poultry and game. Ducks and geese (in greater favor with Italians than with Americans); chicken (which Italians serve in a great variety of ways), and that immigrant from America, the turkey, are all on hand. Game is plentiful in season (and in Sardinia, the happy hunting ground of poachers, out of season too). Tiny field birds, including buntings, larks and warblers, are a favored dish in Italy for their delicacy and tenderness, especially roasted on a skewer. Rabbit, and sometimes the gamier hare, are widely served. There is bigger game in the wilder parts of the country—deer, wild boar and, in Sardinia, the *muflone*, or wild mountain sheep.

One of the many delights of an Italian market is the ice cream vendor, who usually sells his wares to be eaten on the spot. Italian ice cream is probably the best in the world. It comes in two basic varieties—*gelati*, resembling the milk-based chocolate or vanilla ices found in the U.S., and *granita*, an exquisitely light sherbet made with powdery ice and syrup strongly flavored with coffee, lemon or strawberry. The importance of the Italian contribution to ice cream is borne witness by the names under which many varieties are served throughout the world—Neapolitan, *biscuit tortoni, spumoni, cassata*—the latter not to be confused with the name of a famous Sicilian cake *(page 192)*.

Out of all this variety of food, the average Italian family, even the well-to-do family, customarily cooks a rather simple midday meal. Eaten at home, this lunch is the principal meal of the day. The usual beginning is

Light pressure with a rolling pin forces the dough through the wires.

The noodles are usually cooked and eaten immediately.

Italian cooks have devised many instruments for forming their basic dough into pastas of varying shapes and widths. One of the oldest, dating from the days before mass-production machines were invented, is the *chitarra*, a wooden frame strung with wires at close intervals. Its name is the Italian word for guitar. A strip of dough, forced through the thin wires, is thus transformed into long, narrow noodles called *maccheroni alla chitarra*.

pasta or soup. (An Italian might say simply pasta, since for him soup often *is* pasta—that is, it contains noodles. He calls it *pastina in brodo*, pasta in broth, as contrasted with *pasta asciutta*, dry pasta.)

Soups *(minestre)* are very important in the Italian cuisine, and every province has its own cherished varieties. Some Italians may tell you that *minestra* does not mean simply soup, that it is the name for the first course of the meal, whatever it may be; this is a colloquial use of the word, and not the proper one. Among *minestre, minestroni*—vegetable soups made with pasta—constitute a special class. They are rich, hearty and nourishing. A good *minestrone* can be a full meal *(page 48)*.

After soup in a typical Italian meal comes the main dish of fish or meat, usually accompanied or followed by a vegetable or greens. If this course is a salad, it includes tomatoes and other vegetables; it is not, as in France, simply lettuce with a dressing. In poorer homes, the main course is sometimes skipped and an abundant helping of pasta serves to blunt, if not to satisfy, the appetite. In this case the pasta may be accompanied by a sauce that affords a little taste of what a separate course might have included— bits of chopped meat, or tiny clams. Cheese or fruit, or both, come last. Elaborate desserts are likely to be indulged in only when there are honored guests, or at restaurants.

The range of Italian food, while broad, is a little narrower than that of French food: there are fewer high notes, but then there are fewer of the

At a factory in Fara San Martino, in central Italy, a worker checks a spaghetti-making machine *(below, left)*. The spaghetti dough, forced through small holes at the top of the machine, forms long curtains, which are draped on the racks at right to be carried to drying ovens.

abysmally low ones produced by bad French cooking. In the Italian school of cooking, it is hard to turn out inedible food. And if you take the trouble to look for them, as I have, you will find some truly towering and exquisite accomplishments in the Italian cuisine. They may be displayed more rarely, because the average is so comfortably satisfying. Most persons are content with that, so they do not go scouting about for miracles, nor do they get quite so excited about miracles when they occur.

Above all, Italian cooking at its best is in tune with the requirements of a changing modern world. It is undemanding, adaptable, inexpensive—characteristics that help it resist the pressures of rising costs, shortened schedules and the generally faster pace of living today.

But Italian cooking is also resistant to certain other kinds of change. One comment on a regrettable trend in modern agricultural practices was made by an Italian hotel owner who still manages to set a remarkable table. "Everything is losing its taste," he complained. "It's all but impossible to buy a tasty chicken anymore. That's the result of feeding them with antibiotics and stuffing them with hormones. The same thing is happening to meat. And even to vegetables—I suppose it's the chemical fertilizers."

I have noticed this decline in flavor myself, but more markedly in France than in Italy. In some important ways, Italy is still wedded to old-fashioned methods. Personally, I hope it will not be too quick to progress —if that is the right word.

Pasta in Plenty

It is no secret that Italians eat quantities of pasta; what is astounding is the variations they make out of the basically very simple dough. On the following pages are shown 42 different pastas keyed to the list below. Names sometimes vary; when purchasing, check visually to be sure you are getting the kind you want.

PASTA FOR SOUP
 1. Conchigliette
 2. Anellini
 3. Nocchette
 4. Acini di Pepe
 5. Semini di Melo

PASTA TO BE BOILED
 6. Fettuccine
 7. Fettuccine Verdi
 8. Fusilli
 9. Capellini
10. Fedelini
11. Spaghetti
12. Spaghettini
13. Ziti
14. Mezzani
15. Perciatelli
16. Perciatelloni
17. Lasagnette
18. Lingue di Passero
19. Mafaldine
20. Mafalde
21. Zitoni

PASTA FOR BAKING
22. Lasagne
23. Curly Lasagne
24. Lasagne Verdi
25. Occhi di Lupo
26. Conchiglie
27. Penne
28. Grosso Rigato
29. Pennini
30. Cappelletti
31. Spiedini
32. Elbow Macaroni
33. Ruote
34. Tortiglioni
35. Gramigna Rigata
36. Farfalle

PASTA TO BE STUFFED
37. Lumache
38. Agnolotti
39. Manicotti
40. Cannelloni
41. Ravioli
42. Tortellini

Pasta all'uovo

HOMEMADE EGG NOODLES

This recipe explains how to make—by hand or with the aid of a pasta machine—the basic dough for egg noodles. Using this recipe, you can prepare cannelloni, tortellini, ravioli, tagliarini, fettuccine, tagliatelle *and* lasagne.

To make about ¾ pound

1½ cups unsifted all-purpose flour
1 egg
1 egg white
1 tablespoon olive oil
1 teaspoon salt
A few drops of water

Pour the flour into a large mixing bowl or in a heap on a pastry board, make a well in the center of the flour and in it put the egg, egg white, oil and salt. Mix together with a fork or your fingers until the dough can be gathered into a rough ball. Moisten any remaining dry bits of flour with drops of water and press them into the ball.

TO MAKE PASTA BY HAND: Knead the dough on a floured board, working in a little extra flour if the dough seems sticky. After about 10 minutes, the dough should be smooth, shiny and elastic. Wrap it in wax paper and let the dough rest for at least 10 minutes before rolling it.

Divide the dough into 2 balls. Place 1 ball on a floured board or pastry cloth and flatten it with your hand into an oblong about 1 inch thick. Dust the top lightly with flour. Using a heavy rolling pin, start at one end of the oblong and roll it out lengthwise away from yourself to within an inch or so of the far edge. Turn the dough crosswise and roll across its width. Repeat, turning and rolling the dough, until it is paper thin. If the dough begins to stick, lift it carefully and sprinkle more flour under it.

To make *cannelloni*, *tortellini* and *ravioli*, follow the cutting directions in those recipes *(pages 62, 98 and 130)*. To make *tagliarini, fettuccine, tagliatelle* and *lasagne*, dust the rolled dough lightly with flour and let it rest for about 10 minutes. Then gently roll the dough into a jelly-roll shape. With a long sharp knife, slice the roll crosswise into even strips—⅛ inch wide for *tagliarini*, ¼ inch wide for *fettuccine* or *tagliatelle*, and 1½ to 2 inches wide for *lasagne*. Unroll the strips and set them aside on wax paper. In the same fashion, roll, shape and slice the second half of the dough.

A PASTA MACHINE will both knead and roll. Pull off about a third of the dough at a time, set the smooth rolls of the pasta machine as far apart as possible and feed the dough through them. Reroll this strip 4 or 5 more times, folding under the ragged edges and dusting the dough lightly with flour if it feels sticky. When the dough is smooth, shiny and elastic, it has been kneaded enough. Now roll it out, setting the machine to the second notch and feeding the dough through with the rolls closer together. Then set the machine at the third notch and roll the dough thinner. Repeat, changing the notch after each rolling, until the dough is about 1/16 inch thick.

To make *tagliarini*, feed the dough through the narrow cutting blades of the pasta machine; to make *fettuccine* or *tagliatelle*, feed it through the wide blades. For *lasagne*, roll the dough into a jelly-roll shape and cut it by hand into 1½- to 2-inch-wide strips.

Homemade egg noodles may be cooked at once or covered tightly with plastic wrap and kept in the refrigerator for as long as 24 hours. Cook them in 6 to 8 quarts of rapidly boiling salted water for 5 to 10 minutes, or until just tender *(al dente)*. To test, lift out a strand and taste it.

1 Start homemade pasta by breaking
an egg into the cuplike well you
have formed in a mound of flour.

2 Add egg white, oil and salt and
fill up the well with flour pushed in
from the edges of the mound.

3 Gather up the flour and begin
to knead, adding drops of water if
the crumbly mass proves too dry.

4 After 10 minutes of kneading, the
dough becomes smooth, shiny and
elastic. Divide it into two parts.

5 Complete the basic dough mixture
by dusting each part with flour and
rolling out into paper-thin sheets.

6 To make *fettuccine* from the dough,
roll each of the thin sheets into a long,
cylindrical jelly-roll shape.

7 Now cut the rolled-up pasta into ¼-inch slices and quickly unroll them into *fettuccine* strips before the layers of pasta stick together.

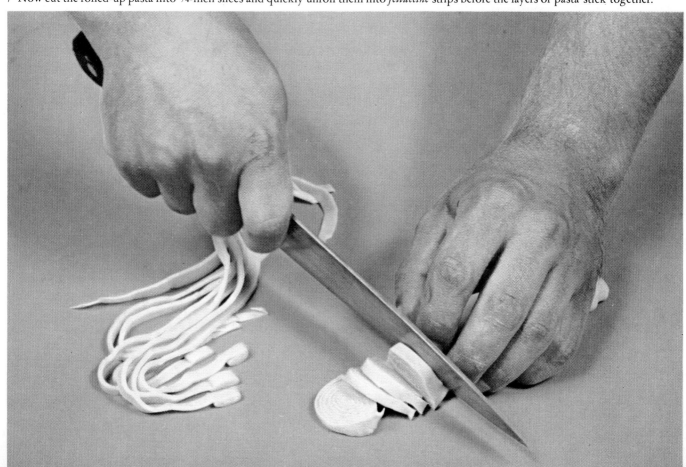

Fettuccine al burro is easy to prepare. Served with a butter, cream and cheese sauce, this rich pasta dish delights palate and eye.

Fettuccine al Burro
EGG NOODLES WITH BUTTER AND CHEESE

To serve 4

8 tablespoons (1 quarter-pound
    stick) butter, softened
¼ cup heavy cream
½ cup freshly grated imported
    Parmesan cheese
6 to 8 quarts water
1 tablespoon salt
1 pound *fettuccine*, homemade *(page 44)*
    or commercial
1 canned white truffle, sliced very thin
    or finely chopped (optional)
Freshly grated imported Parmesan
    cheese

Cream the ¼ pound of softened butter by beating it vigorously against the sides of a heavy bowl with a wooden spoon until it is light and fluffy. Beat in the cream a little at a time, and then, a few tablespoonfuls at a time, beat in ½ cup of grated cheese. Cover the bowl and set it aside—in the refrigerator, if the sauce is not to be used at once. If you do refrigerate the sauce, be sure to bring to room temperature before tossing it with the *fettuccine*.

Set a large serving bowl or casserole in a 250° oven to heat while you cook the *fettuccine*. Bring the water and salt to a bubbling boil in a large soup pot or kettle. Drop in the *fettuccine* and stir it gently with a wooden fork for a few moments to prevent the strands from sticking to one another or to the bottom of the pot. Boil over high heat, stirring occasionally, for 5 to 8 minutes, or until the pasta is tender. (Test it by tasting; it should be soft but *al dente*—that is, slightly resistant to the bite.) Immediately drain the *fettuccine* into a colander and lift the strands with 2 forks to make sure it is thoroughly drained. Transfer it at once to the hot serving bowl.

Add the creamed butter-and-cheese mixture and toss it with the *fettuccine* until every strand is well coated. Taste and season generously with salt and pepper. Stir in the optional truffle. Serve the *fettuccine* at once. Pass the extra grated cheese in a separate bowl.

46

Salsa di Pomodori
TOMATO SAUCE

Using a 2- to 3-quart enameled or stainless-steel saucepan, heat the olive oil until a light haze forms over it. Add the onions and cook them over moderate heat for 7 to 8 minutes, or until they are soft but not browned. Add the tomatoes, tomato paste, basil, sugar, salt and a few grindings of pepper. Reduce the heat to very low and simmer, with the pan partially covered, for about 40 minutes. Stir occasionally.

Press the sauce through a fine sieve (or a food mill) into a bowl or pan. Taste for seasoning and serve hot.

To make about 1½ cups

2 tablespoons olive oil
½ cup finely chopped onions
2 cups Italian plum or whole-pack tomatoes, coarsely chopped but not drained
3 tablespoons tomato paste
1 tablespoon finely cut fresh basil or 1 teaspoon dried basil
1 teaspoon sugar
½ teaspoon salt
Freshly ground black pepper

Scaloppine al Marsala
SAUTÉED VEAL SCALLOPS WITH MARSALA SAUCE

Season the veal scallops with salt and pepper, then dip them in flour and vigorously shake off the excess. In a heavy 10- to 12-inch skillet, melt 2 tablespoons of butter with the 3 tablespoons of oil over moderate heat. When the foam subsides, add the scallops, 3 or 4 at a time, and brown them for about 3 minutes on each side. After they have browned, transfer them from the skillet to a plate.

Pour off most of the fat from the skillet, leaving a thin film on the bottom. Add the Marsala and ¼ cup of chicken or beef stock and boil the liquid briskly over high heat for 1 or 2 minutes. Scrape in any browned fragments clinging to the bottom and sides of the pan. Return the veal to the skillet, cover the pan and simmer over low heat for 10 to 15 minutes, basting the veal now and then with the pan juices.

To serve, transfer the scallops to a heated platter. Add ¼ cup of stock to the sauce remaining in the skillet and boil briskly, scraping in the browned bits sticking to the bottom and sides of the pan. When the sauce has reduced considerably, and has the consistency of a syrupy glaze, taste it for seasoning. Remove the pan from the heat, stir in 2 tablespoons of soft butter, and pour the sauce over the scallops.

To serve 4

1½ pounds veal scallops, sliced ⅜ inch thick and pounded to ¼ inch
Salt
Freshly ground black pepper
Flour
2 tablespoons butter
3 tablespoons olive oil
½ cup dry Marsala
½ cup chicken or beef stock, fresh or canned
2 tablespoons soft butter

Funghi Marinati
MARINATED MUSHROOMS

Combine the ⅔ cup of olive oil, ½ cup of water, juice of 2 lemons, bay leaf, bruised garlic cloves, peppercorns and salt in a 10- to 12-inch enameled or stainless-steel skillet, and bring to a boil over moderate heat. Reduce the heat, cover and simmer for 15 minutes. Strain this marinade through a sieve and return it to the skillet; bring to a simmer over low heat. Drop the mushrooms into the marinade and simmer, turning them over from time to time, for 5 minutes.

Let the mushrooms cool in the marinade. Serve them at room temperature or, after they have cooled, refrigerate them and serve them cold. (The mushrooms will keep in the refrigerator at least 2 days.) Before serving, lift the mushrooms out of the marinade with a slotted spoon, draining them carefully, and arrange them on a platter or in a serving bowl. Serve as part of an *antipasto*.

To make about 2 cups

⅔ cup olive oil
½ cup water
Juice of 2 lemons
1 bay leaf
2 garlic cloves, bruised with the flat of a knife
6 peppercorns
½ teaspoon salt
1 pound small whole fresh mushrooms

To serve 4 to 6

2 slices French or Italian bread, torn into small pieces
½ cup milk
1 pound beef chuck, ground twice
¼ pound sweet Italian sausage, removed from casing
6 tablespoons freshly grated imported Parmesan cheese
2 tablespoons finely chopped fresh parsley, preferably the flat-leaf Italian type
1 tablespoon olive oil
2 teaspoons finely chopped garlic
1 teaspoon grated lemon peel
¼ teaspoon ground allspice
1 teaspoon salt
Freshly ground black pepper
1 egg, lightly beaten
Olive or vegetable oil

To serve 8

½ cup dry white beans
4 tablespoons butter
1 cup fresh green peas (about 1 pound unshelled)
1 cup diced unpeeled but scrubbed zucchini (about ½ pound)
1 cup diced carrots
1 cup diced potatoes
⅓ cup thinly sliced celery
2 ounces salt pork, diced
2 tablespoons finely chopped onions
½ cup finely chopped leeks
2 cups drained canned whole-pack tomatoes, coarsely chopped
2 quarts chicken stock, fresh or canned
1 bay leaf and 2 parsley sprigs, tied together
1 teaspoon salt
Freshly ground black pepper
½ cup plain white raw rice

GARNISH
1 tablespoon finely cut fresh basil or 1 teaspoon dried basil, crumbled
1 tablespoon finely chopped fresh parsley
½ teaspoon finely chopped garlic
½ cup freshly grated imported Parmesan cheese

Polpette alla Casalinga
MEATBALLS

Soak the pieces of bread in ½ cup milk for 5 minutes, then squeeze them dry and discard the milk. In a large mixing bowl, combine the soaked bread, the beaten egg, 1 pound of ground beef, ¼ pound of Italian sausage meat, grated Parmesan cheese, finely chopped parsley, 1 tablespoon of olive oil, garlic, lemon peel, allspice, salt and a few grindings of black pepper. Knead the mixture vigorously with both hands or beat with a wooden spoon until all of the ingredients are well blended and the mixture is smooth and fluffy.

Shape the mixture into small balls about 1½ inches in diameter. Lay the meatballs out in one layer on a flat tray or baking sheet, cover them with plastic wrap and chill for at least 1 hour.

Heat ¼ cup of olive or vegetable oil in a heavy 10- to 12-inch skillet until a light haze forms over it. Fry the meatballs 5 or 6 at a time over moderately high heat, shaking the pan constantly to roll the balls and help keep them round. In 8 to 10 minutes the meatballs should be brown outside and show no trace of pink inside. Add more olive or vegetable oil to the skillet as it is needed. Serve the meatballs hot with tomato sauce *(page 47)* or tomato and garlic sauce *(page 175)*.

Minestrone
VEGETABLE SOUP

Bring 1 quart of water to a bubbling boil in a heavy 3- to 4-quart saucepan. Add the ½ cup of beans (either marrow, Great Northern, white kidney or navy) and boil them briskly for 2 minutes. Remove the pan from the heat and let the beans soak undisturbed in the water for 1 hour. Then return the pan to the stove, and over low heat simmer the beans uncovered for 1 to 1½ hours, or until they are barely tender. Drain the beans thoroughly and set them aside in a bowl.

Melt the butter over moderate heat in a heavy 10- to 12-inch skillet. When the foam subsides, add the peas, zucchini, carrots, potatoes and celery. Tossing the vegetables constantly with a wooden spoon, cook for 2 or 3 minutes, or until they are all lightly coated with butter but not browned. Set aside.

Render the salt pork dice by frying them in a 6- to 8-quart soup pot or kettle over moderate heat, stirring frequently. When the pork dice are crisp and brown, lift them out with a slotted spoon and set them aside to drain on paper towels. Stir the onions and leeks (or if leeks are unavailable, substitute another ½ cup of onions) into the fat remaining in the pot and cook, stirring constantly, for 7 or 8 minutes, or until the vegetables are soft and lightly browned. Stir in the coarsely chopped tomatoes, the vegetables from the skillet, the chicken stock, the bay leaf and parsley sprigs, salt and a few grindings of pepper. Bring the soup to a boil over high heat, reduce the heat and simmer partially covered for 25 minutes.

Remove and discard the bay leaf and parsley sprigs, add the rice, white beans and salt pork dice and cook for about 15 to 20 minutes longer, or until the rice is tender. Taste the soup and season it with salt and pepper if needed. Serve, sprinkled with the herb and garlic garnish. Pass a bowl of the grated cheese separately.

Fritto Misto

DEEP-FRIED SWEETBREADS, CHICKEN AND VEGETABLES

Combine the flour, warm water, 3 tablespoons of oil and ½ teaspoon salt in a large mixing bowl, stirring gently but constantly until the ingredients form a fairly smooth cream. Do not beat or overstir. For best results, set the batter aside and let it rest at room temperature for about 2 hours, although it may be used at once if necessary. The 1 egg white should be beaten with a wire whisk or rotary beater until it is stiff enough to form unwavering peaks and folded into the batter just before using.

Soak the pair of sweetbreads in several changes of cold water for 1 hour; then place them in a 2- to 3-quart saucepan, add 1 quart of fresh cold water, 1 tablespoon of lemon juice or vinegar and 1 teaspoon of salt. Bring to a boil over moderate heat, reduce the heat and simmer the sweetbreads uncovered for 15 minutes. Remove them from the heat, drain and plunge them immediately into cold water for a few minutes to cool them. Drain them again and pat them dry with paper towels. Gently remove as much of the outside filament of the sweetbreads as possible without tearing them. Separate the two lobes from the tube between them and discard the tube. Cut the sweetbreads into 1-inch cubes.

Skin the chicken breast and cut the meat into strips about 2 inches long and ½ inch wide. Divide the cauliflower into small flowerets, place the flowerets in a saucepan with 2 or 3 quarts of boiling salted water and let them boil briskly for 3 minutes. Then plunge them into cold water and drain them. Peel the eggplant and zucchini and cut them into ½-inch strips; toss them with 2 tablespoons of salt to draw out their moisture and set them aside in a colander to drain. Dry and quarter the artichoke hearts.

Heat 3 to 4 inches of oil or shortening in a deep-fat fryer to 375°. Meanwhile, preheat the oven to 250° and line 2 large shallow baking dishes or baking sheets with paper towels. Dry the eggplant and zucchini strips with paper towels and place them with the sweetbread cubes, strips of chicken breast, cauliflower flowerets and quartered artichoke hearts where you can get at them easily.

Deep-fry the sweetbreads, chicken and vegetables separately: Drop 5 or 6 pieces at a time into the batter—into which you have just folded the beaten egg white. When they are well coated, lift the pieces out, one by one, with tongs or a slotted spoon. Hold them over the bowl for a second to let the excess batter drain off before placing them in the frying basket. Deep-fry, turning the pieces once or twice, for 5 or 6 minutes, or until the batter is golden brown. With tongs, transfer the browned pieces to a paper-towel-lined baking dish to drain, and place in the oven to keep warm. Then dip the next batch into the batter and deep-fry it. When the last piece is fried and drained, arrange the *fritto misto* as attractively as you can on a napkin-lined platter and serve it garnished with lemon quarters.

Insalata di Funghi Crudi

RAW MUSHROOM SALAD

In a serving bowl, toss the mushrooms with the lemon juice until the slices are lightly moistened. Then add the scallion greens, oil and salt and toss again. Chill the salad before serving it.

To serve 6

BATTER
1 cup all-purpose flour, sifted before
   measuring
¾ cup warm water
3 tablespoons vegetable oil
½ teaspoon salt
1 egg white

1 pair calf's sweetbreads
Water
1 tablespoon lemon juice or vinegar
Salt
1 whole chicken breast, boned
1 small cauliflower
1 pound eggplant
1 pound zucchini
1 nine-ounce box frozen artichoke
   hearts, thoroughly defrosted
Vegetable oil or shortening for
   deep-fat frying
Lemon quarters

To serve 4

½ pound fresh mushrooms, thinly sliced
2 teaspoons lemon juice
¼ cup thinly sliced scallion greens
3 tablespoons olive oil
½ teaspoon salt

To serve 6 to 8

A 3- to 3½-pound boneless veal roast,
 securely tied
3 flat anchovy fillets, cut into 1-inch
 lengths
1 to 2 garlic cloves, cut into thin
 slivers
1 quart chicken stock, fresh or canned
2 cups dry white wine
2 cups water
2 onions, quartered
2 carrots, cut up
3 celery stalks, cut up
2 bay leaves
6 parsley sprigs
10 whole peppercorns

TUNA SAUCE
¾ cup olive oil
1 egg yolk
1 three-ounce can tuna fish, preferably
 Italian tuna packed in olive oil
4 flat anchovy fillets, drained and
 soaked in water for 10 minutes, then
 cut into small pieces
2 tablespoons lemon juice
¼ cup heavy cream
¼ to ½ cup cooled, strained
 veal-braising stock (from above)
2 tablespoons capers, thoroughly
 washed and drained
Salt
White pepper

GARNISH
2 tablespoons finely chopped fresh
 parsley, preferably the flat-leaf
 Italian type
2 lemons, sliced
2 tablespoons capers
12 black olives, preferably
 Mediterranean style

Vitello Tonnato
COLD BRAISED VEAL WITH TUNA SAUCE

With a small sharp knife, make deep incisions along the length of the veal and insert a 1-inch piece of anchovy and a sliver of garlic in each one. Blanch the veal in a large pot by covering it with cold water and boiling it over high heat for 1 minute. Pour off the water and quickly rinse the meat of its scum in cold water.

Place the veal in a heavy saucepan or pot just large enough to hold it comfortably. Add the chicken stock, wine, water, onions, carrots, celery, bay leaves, parsley and peppercorns. If the liquid does not quite cover the meat completely, add more chicken stock or water. Bring to a boil, reduce the heat and simmer the veal slowly, partially covered, for about 1 hour and 40 minutes, or until the veal is tender when pierced with the tip of a sharp knife. Remove the pan from the heat and let the veal cool in the stock. Ladle out about ½ cup of the stock, strain it through a fine sieve, and set it aside in a cup or bowl to cool.

Meanwhile, prepare the tuna sauce. If you have a blender, all you need to do is to combine all of the olive oil, the egg yolk, tuna fish, 4 anchovy fillets and lemon juice in the jar of the blender and whirl the ingredients at high speed for no more than 10 seconds, or until the mixture is a purée. Transfer it to a small mixing bowl and stir in the cream gradually. Add the cooled, strained braising stock from the veal 2 tablespoons at a time until the sauce is thinned to the consistency of heavy cream. You probably will need about 4 tablespoons of the braising stock in all. Stir in the capers. Taste the sauce for seasoning.

If you do not use a blender, chop the tuna fish and anchovies by hand; then, using the back of a wooden spoon, force them through a fine sieve into a small bowl. With a wire whisk, rotary or electric beater, beat the egg yolk in another small bowl for 1 or 2 minutes. Stir the purée and lemon juice into the egg yolk, then dribble in the olive oil 1 teaspoonful at a time, beating constantly. After adding ¼ cup of the oil, the sauce should be very thick and smooth. Add the remaining ½ cup of olive oil, 1 table-spoon at a time, still beating. Then mix in the cream and enough of the cooled stock to thin the sauce to the consistency of heavy cream. Stir in the capers and taste for seasoning.

When the veal is cool, transfer it to a carving board. Strain the braising stock and refrigerate for use in soups or sauces. Trim the veal of any fat or gristle and cut the meat into thin, even slices. Spread a thin film of tuna sauce in the bottom of a large platter or baking dish and arrange the veal in the sauce, laying the slices side by side. Pour the rest of the sauce over the veal, smoothing it with a spatula to mask each slice. Cover the platter with plastic wrap and refrigerate the *vitello tonnato* for at least 2 or 3 hours—overnight, or longer, if possible.

About 1 hour before serving, remove the veal from the refrigerator and allow it to come to room temperature. Arrange the slices so that they overlap as neatly as possible in a circle on a large serving platter. Spoon all of the sauce over them. Sprinkle the veal and sauce with the chopped parsley, and garnish the platter with lemon slices, capers and black olives. Other possibilities for garnishing the *vitello tonnato* are sliced scallions, tomatoes or hard-cooked egg quarters.

This elegant dish of veal with tuna sauce known as *vitello tonnato*, garnished with capers, black olives and lemon slices, is often an appetizer but can be a main course.

Scaloppine al Limone
SAUTÉED VEAL SCALLOPS WITH LEMON

To serve 4

1½ pounds veal scallops, cut ⅜ inch thick and pounded until ¼ inch thick
Salt
Freshly ground black pepper
Flour
2 tablespoons butter
3 tablespoons olive oil
¾ cup beef stock, fresh or canned
6 paper-thin lemon slices
1 tablespoon lemon juice
2 tablespoons soft butter

Season the veal scallops with salt and pepper, then dip them in flour and shake off the excess. In a heavy 10- to 12-inch skillet, melt 2 tablespoons of butter with the 3 tablespoons of oil over moderate heat. When the foam subsides, add the veal, 4 or 5 scallops at a time, and sauté them for about 2 minutes on each side, or until they are golden brown. With tongs, transfer the veal scallops to a plate. Now pour off almost all the fat from the skillet, leaving a thin film on the bottom. Add ½ cup of beef stock and boil it briskly for 1 or 2 minutes, stirring constantly and scraping in any browned bits clinging to the bottom and sides of the pan. Return the veal to the skillet and arrange the lemon slices on top. Cover the skillet and simmer over low heat for 10 to 15 minutes, or until the veal is tender when pierced with the tip of a sharp knife.

To serve, transfer the scallops to a heated platter and surround with the lemon slices. Add the ¼ cup of remaining beef stock to the juices in the skillet and boil briskly until the stock is reduced to a syrupy glaze. Add the lemon juice and cook, stirring, for 1 minute. Remove the pan from the heat, swirl in 2 tablespoons of soft butter and pour the sauce over the scallops.

III

Regions of Rome

Sooner or later—and for most visitors it is sooner—all the gastronomic roads of Italy lead to Rome. And, as befits a capital, Rome manages to embrace the whole culinary character of its nation, north and south, as well as the refinements of the international cuisine.

The real pride of the Roman homeland, however, lies in its own native cooking—simple, hearty, vigorous, distinguished by the produce and specialties of its region, Latium, and the neighboring regions of Umbria and the Marches. If there is one characteristic shared by authentic *alla romana* dishes it is a robust directness, most delectably displayed in regional favorites like *porchetta:* suckling pig stuffed with herbs and roasted whole. In contrast, many dishes served outside Italy with the suffix *alla romana* seem merely fussy and contrived.

Rome approaches its eating with simplicity, but never austerity. Indeed, eating and enjoyment are synonymous in Rome: the word "gusto" stems from the ancient Romans' word for "to taste." The spirit is nowhere more evident than on holidays, both religious and seasonal, each of which has its own venerable traditions and specialties of the feast.

Among the most colorful of these are the city's Christmas festivities, which for many Romans begin in the big Via Ostiense wholesale market the night of December 23-24, when they can buy directly from the wholesale stands. (The proceedings become official when the mayor arrives at 2 a.m., and makes a few Christmas Eve remarks.) Known locally as the *Cottio* (from the Latin word for "quoting" a price), it is a genial, noisy, all-night buying spree, during which most good citizens purchase delica-

Rome is full of elegant restaurants catering to an international taste. But to savor the Romans' own hearty fare, one of the modest neighborhood restaurants, like the one at the left by the Portico di Ottavia, should be selected. Its specialty is flattened, fried artichokes.

cies for the Christmas table, especially live eels. On Christmas Day, the *piatto di resistenza* is likely to be roasted capon, stuffed with bread crumbs, sausages, giblets and grated *pecorino* cheese.

As the new year progresses, Romans celebrate other holidays and seasons with special foods. On St. Joseph's Day, March 19, a traditional delicacy is *bignè*, little deep-fried pastry puffs. *Maritozzi quaresimali*, light buns of flour, pine nuts, candied orange peel and sultana raisins, are eaten throughout Lent. At Easter, the family may drive out into the country after Mass to feast on suckling lamb roasted whole on an open spit. On St. John's Eve (Midsummer Night, June 24), Roman families traditionally eat snails that have simmered slowly with garlic, anchovy, tomato, fresh mint and pepper.

In July the open-air spits sizzle with succulent *porchetta*, especially at the rollicking week-long *festa di Noantri* ("festival of the rest of us"), which residents of the Roman quarter of Trastevere, across the Tiber, invented for themselves. In the clear, pleasant days of early autumn come the regional wine festivals, the first of which takes place on the last Sunday of September in Genzano, 18 miles out from Rome on the Appian Way and 1,500 feet up in the hills. *Porchetta*, once more, is the favored dish to be washed down with the wine. A week later, on the first Sunday in October, the festival scene shifts to Marino, 15 miles outside the city to the southeast. The stuffing in the *porchetta* served here comes from the nearby town of Ariccia, which has carefully kept its formula secret.

Between holidays and festivals, everyday eating in the Roman region may quiet down a little, but it continues to be hearty, both at home and in public. In the big, internationally minded *ristoranti*, the fare is less likely to be typically Roman. The places for real local food are the humbler *trattorie*, or taverns, where the fare and the service are closer to those of a private home. The Trastevere area, a world away from the glittering Via Veneto, is full of *trattorie*, many of them with gardens, where in fine weather the meals are served outdoors. *Osterie* (hostelries, or inns) are likely to be even more informal, with the kitchen visible from the dining room.

The proprietor of one Roman *osteria*, in fact, was so informal that he contributed the widespread expression *melafumo* to the Italian language. According to the story, the master of the *osteria*, on the Via Flaminia, was sitting out in the sun one day, smoking his pipe in a restful interval between meals. Suddenly the Pope's carriage drove up. Bystanders threw themselves to their knees and the Pope made the gesture of benediction. But the proprietor, absorbed in his pipe and his thoughts, failed to notice the commotion. One of the Pope's attendants, angry at this apparent disrespect, shouted, "Hey, you, there! What do you think you're doing?" "Me?" said the innkeeper; "I'm smoking—*me la fumo*." The name stuck to the inn, and today—the Italian word *melafumo* means "I couldn't care less."

Few Romans care much either about the gastronomic split between Italy's north and south: they know their own cuisine encompasses both tastes. One example of this eclecticism is *gnocchi*, a dish that is unclassifiable as either northern or southern. *Gnocchi* exists in many forms in many places, but it is especially esteemed in Rome, where it is made with flour and without the potatoes used elsewhere. The dish has a doughy, uninspired look that helps explain the dialect meaning of *gnocco* (the singular of *gnocchi*): "dullard," or "puddinghead." But its appearance belies its taste *(page 67)*.

54

In addition to *gnocchi,* Romans have also evolved their own local variations of both northern and southern pasta. The city is famous for its *cannelloni,* made in the northern style with thin, rectangular sheets of homemade dough that are rolled and stuffed with a meat filling. Another favorite is *fettuccine al burro (page 46),* also a ribbon-style pasta made with eggs, the same type known as *tagliatelle* in the north. In its nourishing simplicity, however, this *fettuccine* is peculiarly Roman: it can be served with no other sauce than a heavy lacing of butter *(al burro),* to which the diner may add as much grated Parmesan cheese as he wants.

As for southern pasta, Rome has many dishes involving macaroni and spaghetti. *Maccheroni alla ciociara* ("peasant style") is served with a sauce containing fat bacon, ham and sausage; *spaghetti a cacio e pepe* is served with the local cheese *(cacio)* and pepper *(pepe).* Any pasta dish *alla carrettiera* ("in teamster's style") involves tuna and mushrooms; *alla prestinara* ("baker's style") means cooked with garlic and oil; *all'arrabbiata* is "rabid" with hot red peppers. A pasta dish familiar to few Americans, cooked simply with salt pork belly and egg, is *spaghetti alla carbonara (Recipe Booklet).*

The rest of the Roman menu following pasta is vast and varied, but a few items demand mention. Among meat dishes, probably the most important after *porchetta* is *abbacchio:* suckling lamb that has never tasted grass, roasted whole in an oven or outdoors on a spit. There are various ways of seasoning it, but an essential herb is rosemary. A favorite way of cooking *abbacchio* in the oven is *alla cacciatora* with an anchovy sauce containing olive oil, vinegar and garlic, along with rosemary *(Recipe Booklet).*

Other baby lamb dishes favored by Romans include *costolette a scottadito,* called "burn-your-finger chops," because they are cooked on a grill or a flat skillet, and then—traditionally, anyway—turned over very quickly with the fingers. *Abbacchio brodettato (page 65)* consists of small chunks of lamb cooked in a sauce of egg yolks flavored with lemon juice.

Among other meat dishes considered particularly Roman is *saltimbocca,* slices of ham laid upon slices of veal, seasoned with sage, sautéed in butter, and braised in white wine. The name means "jump into the mouth"; and when superbly cooked it does all but that.

Among the most ancient and authentic of Roman vegetable dishes— originating in what was once the Jewish ghetto—is *carciofi alla giudìa* (artichokes Jewish style). Still considered best when eaten in the restaurants of the old ghetto, they are made with tender young artichokes deep fried in olive oil, and flattened out in the cooking so that they are shaped like roses on the plate. Another outstanding artichoke dish is the city's own *carciofi al tegame alla romana:* the boiled artichokes are stuffed with bread crumbs flavored with garlic, vinegar and mint and baked *(Recipe Booklet).*

Selected from among other Roman favorites are the following, arranged in the sequence of a Roman menu, with page numbers of recipes indicated for some of the most representative:

SOUP: *Stracciatella* ("little rags"), a liquid batter of eggs, flour and grated Parmesan cheese, poured into boiling broth. The egg breaks up into little flakes in the soup (the recipe for one variation is in the Recipe Booklet).

FISH: *Filetti di baccalà,* thin strips of salt cod, dipped in a batter and fried in olive oil.

ENTRÉES: *Crostini alla provatura,* slices of bread topped with *provatura*

Rome and its environs are well supplied with the makings of excellent dining and wining. Nearby hillsides produce the famous Frascati wine. From Latina and the Gaeta coast come lobster and shrimp; the Sabine hills supply sharp cheeses and fine sauces. Umbria has hams, sausages, truffles, excellent vegetables and quantities of rich chocolates. The Marches provide savory fish soups of all kinds.

cheese, which melts in the oven and envelops the bread. Or *supplì al telefono*, deep-fried rice croquettes with *mozzarella* cheese inside; it gets its name ("croquettes on the telephone") because the melted cheese draws out into long "wires" as it is forked from the plate *(page 64)*.

MEAT: *Pajata di vitello*, Roman dialect for veal innards, sliced with *pecorino* cheese and *rigatoni* (thick, ribbed macaroni). Few foreigners might be attracted to lamb's head, but *testicciuola di abbacchio*—seasoned with a mixture of bread crumbs, garlic and parsley, and well basted with olive oil and baked in the oven—is highly appreciated in Rome. So is *coda alla vaccinara*, or braised oxtail *(page 67)*.

VEGETABLES: Broccoli, among the best of the fresh produce that abounds around Rome, is likely to appear on dinner tables as *broccoli alla romana*, simmered in white wine and olive oil, with garlic *(Recipe Booklet)*. Other notable vegetable dishes include *pomodori con riso*, tomatoes stuffed with rice; *cipolline in agrodolce*, tiny onions in a sweet-and-sour sauce; *fagioli con le cotiche*,

The flanks of the Via Appia, oldest and most illustrious of the great highways to ancient Rome, are a favorite picnic site for modern Romans. This family has spread its lunch under a roadside tree near a tower dating from the Middle Ages.

white haricot beans cooked slowly with thick slices of pork rind; and *fave al guanciale*, broad beans steamed with onions and fat bacon or pig's cheek (*guanciale*). Little new peas may be steamed the same way, as *piselli al guanciale*, or converted into *piselli al prosciutto* by being cooked with morsels of prosciutto ham (*Recipe Booklet*). *Finocchio* (fennel) is often served as a salad with *pinzimonio*, a dressing concocted of the purest obtainable olive oil (from the Sabine hills or Tivoli), with salt and pepper. *Funghi arrostiti* are grilled mushrooms with olive oil, garlic and parsley.

DESSERTS: Besides such seasonal and holiday dishes as *bignè* and *maritozzi quaresimali*, Roman specialties in this category include *biscottini con le mandorle* (dry cookies made of flour, eggs and toasted almonds) and *zuppa inglese*. Despite its name ("English soup") it is very Italian, and it is a cake. It is also layered with custard, which gives it a resemblance to an English trifle —which may explain its name—and is drenched in rum.

As might be expected, Rome tends to overshadow other parts of its home

At the Noantri festival, held every summer in the workers' quarter of Trastevere, a young Roman demonstrates one method of eating spaghetti, draping it over the fork and maneuvering it rapidly toward the mouth. Rolling the spaghetti up around the fork, with or without the aid of a spoon, is also permissible.

province, but the Latina district of Latium boasts at least two specialties worthy of note. *Aragosta con maionese* combines mayonnaise with fresh, cold spiny lobsters from the Pontine Islands of Latina, where the lobsters are kept alive in underwater traps until they are ready for the market. Equally delicious are *mazzancuogni*, somewhat larger cousins of the Venetian *scampi*. Both crustaceans live in Latina's Gulf of Gaeta and in waters near Venice, and nowhere else.

The northern part of Latium, near Rieti, is Sabine country, home of the legendary women "raped" by the early Romans. Actually the Romans badly needed wives and therefore probably avoided any real violence. There is even a story that the Sabine women exacted a promise of freedom from kitchen work as compensation for their kidnaping, but today's Sabine cuisine—locally described as "home cooking, healthy, tasty and sincere"—makes it difficult to believe that Sabine women, unwilling wives though they may have been, ever stayed long out of a kitchen.

The Sabine district is dairy country, and the local cheese is excellent. The towns of Accumoli and Vallecupola are especially known for their *pecorino*, a firm, sharp cheese that is not only grated but also eaten as a table cheese. *Pecorino* is a very old cheese, produced since early Roman times not from cow's milk but from whole sheep's milk, treated with rennet, a curdling agent made from the stomach lining of unweaned lambs.

The Sabine town of Amatrice has given its name to a spaghetti sauce (*amatriciana*), now also known as a specialty of Rome. In Amatrice the original sauce is served with *bucatini*, a form of spaghetti. The sauce is composed of tomatoes, onion and bacon cooked in pork fat, and is served with sharp grated *pecorino* cheese.

Another Sabine town with a local specialty is Antrodoco, known for its *stracci*, little disks of paper-thin pastry. The disks are built up in layers and stuffed with a filling of meat, ground vegetables and grated cheese; they are served very hot, moistened with gravy and sprinkled with more cheese.

An inscription on the wall of a villa in the town of Fara in Sabina makes reference to *crustulum*, the oil-soaked cake that was given by the authorities to the people of ancient Roman times on important civil or religious feast days in December and January. Today, during those months, when the olive oil of the region is extremely light and fresh, the direct descendant of *crustulum*, a sort of coarse, flat bun called *bruschetta*, is served. The bun is impregnated with the young oil, which still has the somewhat sharp taste of the newly pressed fruit, occasionally set off with the flavor of garlic. Other seasonal Sabine dishes include *nociata*, a Christmas sweet of honey and ground walnuts in lozenge shape, and the rustic *pizza pasquale*, a little Easter cake made with eggs, *ricotta* cheese and honey. (Pizza is originally and basically a word signifying any pie or cake, not simply the familiar Neapolitan pie with cheese and tomato.)

Latium is rich in wines to wash all these local delicacies down. Best known are the Castelli Romani wines, named for the castle-dominated villages near Rome that cling to the crests and slopes of the Alban hills—former volcanoes whose soil is well suited to the culture of wine grapes. The wines are mostly whites, quite dry. The most famous is Frascati, the dry wine that comes in distinctive funnel-shaped bottles and has a sharp, clean taste.

Two wines of the province of Latina, famous since ancient Roman times, were praised by Horace: Falerno, bottled as a dry white and also as a red; and the red *cecubo* (*caecubum* in Latin), the wine of Tiberius and Nero.

The pride of the Viterbo district is a wine called Est! Est! Est! which comes from Montefiascone and is described by some as the finest wine of Italy. I suspect that its reputation is overblown because of the 800-year-old story that accounts for its name (tastes have largely changed since then from sweet to dry wines, and Est! Est! Est! is decidedly sweet). The story goes that in the 12th Century the German prelate Johann Fugger, a famous wine lover, made a journey to Rome from Augsburg. He sent his steward ahead to sample the wine along the way, ordering him to chalk the word *Est!* ("It is!") on the doors of the taverns and wineshops where the wine was good. When the Cardinal reached Montefiascone, he found the door of an inn marked, *Est! Est!! Est!!!* He entered and found his steward still there, in a state of blissful unconsciousness. The Cardinal outdid him: he drank so much of the wine of Montefiascone that he died on the spot and was buried in the town; the inn, and the wine, are still called Est! Est! Est!

One last, fond word for the beverages of Latium: don't overlook Sambuca, the clear, sweet, anise-flavored liqueur much favored in Rome as an after-dinner drink. The approved way to drink it is *con la mosca*, "with a fly." The "fly" is a coffee bean (or several) floating in the glass, a piquant solid to be crunched as you sip. It is a most pleasant combination; the bitter coffee bean makes a delightful complement to the sweetness of the liqueur.

When it comes to sweet tastes, Perugia, the capital of the region of Umbria, north of Rome, produces the best chocolates in Italy—perhaps the best in the world. But Perugia has other specialties that are equally famous locally: *torcolo,* a sort of bun coated in olive oil that traditionally marks Christmas, New Year's and St. Constant's Day (January 29), and *porchetta perugina,* the local, highly spiced version of roast suckling pig.

Umbria, in fact, excels in pigs. The acorn-fattened hogs of Norcia deserve first mention, chiefly because of the variety and excellence of their hams, sausages and smoked meat. Norcia is so famous for its processed pork that when a Roman talks of a *norcino,* he is not referring to a citizen of Norcia—he is talking about a salami seller. Among Norcia's other products are a variety of fresh and dried sausages, and *mazzafegati,* pig's liver sausage seasoned with garlic, pepper and pine nuts. The finished product is perfumed with fennel, and the result has a nutty, spicy flavor.

Umbria is also rich in vegetables, particularly in the Tiber Valley. The town of Trevi is noted for its celery, which is stewed in tomato sauce. The specialty of Cannara is onions. Umbrian mushrooms—flap mushrooms, honey mushrooms, orange-milk agaric—appear under the shade of the trees in the beech and chestnut groves. Among the more humble of Umbria's dishes is *cardi alla perugina,* an edible thistle that is marinated in olive oil, lemon juice and chopped parsley, then dipped in batter and fried in oil.

More exotic are the magnificent black truffles of Umbria, richer in taste than the French variety. Made with these truffles, *spaghetti ai tartufi* is a remarkable dish. As I ate it in Perugia, the truffles had been chopped fine, and marinated a day in advance in a mixture of olive oil, garlic and anchovy paste. The truffles came out tasting like particularly delicious chicken livers.

Norcia is such a center for eating that it gets credit for the best truffles in Umbria. But the fact is that Spoleto is just as distinguished a truffles center and even claims to have known the truffle before Norcia did. In any case, the ancient Romans considered Spoleto truffles especially delicious. Even the French, who have their own truffles, import Spoleto's in large quantities.

Among the other food resources of Umbria are the fresh-water fish from the lakes of Piediluco and Trasimeno. A specialty of Trasimeno is *lasca,* or European roach—sent by the citizens to the bishop of Perugia since the 16th Century in memory of Pope Pius V. There are trout and perch in the lake, too, as well as fresh-water gray mullet and eels.

Umbrian wines are pleasant, honest table vintages, without any great distinction. So little fuss is made about them that some of the wines do not even have a name. I was once served an anonymous red wine in a carafe in the spectacular, triple-walled medieval town of Todi. The wine was warm, with a slight, piquant natural sparkle. When I asked its name, I was told it had none. "It's just what we grow outside the walls," the waiter said. Very similar to this nameless vintage was a red wine I had tasted earlier at Perugia; it was semi-dry, with a velvety texture. It did have a name (Montefiascone), but I find it listed nowhere. With these wines I was served a dish I also find listed nowhere—a local combination of veal steak with liver.

One Umbrian wine that does have a name—and a famous one—is Orvieto. Best known as a white wine, Orvieto was originally sweet; in the Middle Ages, when the sweet taste was more prized than it is today, the wine was a favorite of popes. A sweet Orvieto is still made, but the favorite now is dry, bottled in bulbous straw-covered flasks. It is pale yellow, with a delicate taste that becomes pleasantly sharp after the wine has been swallowed.

Medieval popes, sipping their Orvieto in Rome, were protected—part of the time, anyway—from jealous rivals to the northeast by outposts in the Marches ("frontiers" or "borderlands"). This is the region that was, for nearly a thousand years, the boundary of the Papal States. In the Ninth Century the Marches consisted of three districts—the March of Ancona, the March of Fermo, and the March of Camerino; but they were amalgamated by Pope Innocent III in the 13th Century. Today, the Marches comprise four districts: Ancona, Ascoli Piceno, Macerata and Pesaro-Urbino..

A typical dish of the Marches is *brodetto marchigiano*, fish soup, a favorite in Ancona. The people of Ancona also have a special way of dressing up dried cod: *stoccafisso in potacchio*, cod stewed with onions, tomatoes, olive oil, pepper, parsley, rosemary, ground anchovies and—added at the last moment—a little butter and white wine.

Ascoli Piceno has such a special fondness for the suckling pig that the municipal statutes of some of its cities—for instance, Fermo—at one time enjoined the city fathers to distribute free *porchetta* to the citizens when distinguished visitors came to town. The vegetables of Ascoli Piceno are extremely good and the inhabitants of the area claim that nowhere else can *olive ripiene* (stuffed olives breaded and fried) be so delicious. Olives, the Piceni argue, are naturally available everywhere, but the peculiarly fat and fleshy olives of Piceno are not. The snails of Piceno are also specially prized because they are flavored with the region's own fennel.

The towns in the province of Ascoli Piceno have their particular prides: Offida's are *funghetti*, cakes shaped like mushrooms; Montegiorgio's are *caciunitti*, sweets that are actually little ravioli stuffed with chocolate. Fermo also preens itself on its sweets, which include *casarecal*, a sort of bun, and *ciambelle col mostocotto*—small, sugared, doughnut-shaped cakes.

In the district of Pesaro-Urbino, the most notable culinary achievement is the Duke of Urbino's legendary sauce. The town of Urbino rose to relative importance in the 15th Century through the power of its ruling family, the Montefeltro. Power is often unpopular, and Federigo da Montefeltro, a 15th Century Duke of Urbino, was afraid of poison: he ordered all his dishes to be cooked without seasoning because it was harder to insinuate poison into an unseasoned dish. But the Duke, as fond of seasoning as the next aristocrat, had his own private sauce—prepared for him at the table by a trusted servant from secret ingredients, and ladled onto the dishes when they had been judged safe to eat. A few years ago a playwright named Paolo Serano, doing research for a historical play, came upon the recipe for this forgotten sauce, tried it, and found it so good on meat that he decided to make it commercially. The ingredients are still a secret, though it is known that one of them is honey. The sauce is sold in bottles with a label bearing the Duke's portrait—a profile view that is the more striking and memorable because the Duke's nose ends abruptly in a depression just below his eyes. This disfigurement, though self-inflicted, resulted from another of the Duke's fears. Having lost his right eye to the claws of a falcon, he feared being stabbed from the blind side—so he had the bridge of his nose removed to give his left eye a broader field of vision.

CHAPTER III RECIPES

To serve 6 to 8

PASTA

Pasta dough *(page 44)*
6 to 8 quarts water
1 tablespoon salt

FILLING

2 tablespoons olive oil
¼ cup finely chopped onions
1 teaspoon finely chopped garlic
1 ten-ounce package frozen chopped
 spinach, defrosted, squeezed completely dry and chopped again
 (about ¾ cup) or ¾ pound
 fresh spinach, cooked, drained,
 squeezed and finely chopped
2 tablespoons butter
1 pound beef round steak, ground
 twice, or 1 cup finely chopped
 leftover beef
2 chicken livers
5 tablespoons freshly grated imported
 Parmesan cheese
2 tablespoons heavy cream
2 eggs, lightly beaten
½ teaspoon dried oregano, crumbled
Salt
Freshly ground black pepper

BESCIAMELLA

4 tablespoons butter
4 tablespoons flour
1 cup milk
1 cup heavy cream
1 teaspoon salt
⅛ teaspoon white pepper

TOPPING

3 cups tomato sauce (double the
 recipe on page 47)
4 tablespoons freshly grated imported
 Parmesan cheese
2 tablespoons butter, cut in tiny pieces

Cannelloni

PASTA TUBES FILLED WITH MEAT AND BAKED IN TOMATO AND CREAM SAUCE

PASTA: On a floured board or cloth, roll out the pasta dough until it is paper thin, then cut it into about 36 rectangles of 2 by 3 inches. Bring the water and salt to a bubbling boil over high heat in a large soup pot or kettle. Drop in the pieces of pasta and stir gently with a wooden fork or spoon for a few moments to be sure they don't stick to one another or to the pot. Return the water to a boil and cook the pasta over high heat, stirring occasionally, for 5 minutes, or until the pasta is tender but not soft. Drain, cool slightly, then spread the pasta pieces side by side on paper towels to dry.

FILLING: Heat the olive oil in an 8- to 10-inch enameled or stainless-steel skillet. Add the onions and garlic, and cook over moderate heat, stirring often, for 7 or 8 minutes until they are soft but not brown. Stir in the spinach and cook, stirring constantly, for 3 or 4 minutes. When all moisture has boiled away and the spinach sticks lightly to the pan, transfer to a large bowl. Melt 1 tablespoon of butter in the same skillet and lightly brown the beef, stirring constantly to break up any lumps. Add it to the onion-spinach mixture. Melt 1 more tablespoon of butter in the skillet and cook the livers, turning them often, for 3 or 4 minutes, until they are somewhat firm, lightly browned but still pink inside. Chop them coarsely, and add to the mixture in the bowl along with the Parmesan, cream, eggs and oregano. Mix the ingredients gently but thoroughly. Taste and season with salt and pepper.

BESCIAMELLA FOR CANNELLONI: In a heavy 2- to 3-quart saucepan, melt the butter over moderate heat. Remove the pan from the heat and stir in the flour. Pour in the milk and cream all at once, whisking constantly until the flour is partially dissolved. Then return the pan to high heat and cook, stirring constantly with the whisk. When the sauce comes to a boil and is smooth, reduce the heat. Simmer, still stirring, for 2 or 3 minutes longer, or until the sauce is thick enough to coat the wires of the whisk heavily. Remove the sauce from the heat, and season with salt and white pepper.

ASSEMBLING AND BAKING THE CANNELLONI: Preheat the oven to 375°. Place a tablespoon or so of the filling on the bottom third of each of the pasta rectangles and roll them up. Pour just a film of the tomato sauce into two 10-by-14-inch shallow baking-and-serving dishes. Lay the *cannelloni* side by side in one layer on the tomato sauce. Pour the *besciamella* over it and spoon the rest of the tomato sauce on top. Scatter in 4 tablespoons of grated cheese and dot with 2 tablespoons of butter. Bake the *cannelloni* uncovered in the middle of the oven for 20 minutes, or until the cheese is melted and the sauce bubbling. Slide the baking dishes under a hot broiler for 30 seconds to brown the top. Serve the *cannelloni* from the baking dish.

NOTE: The pasta can be cooked, spread between 2 layers of wax paper, and refrigerated for a day or 2. The *cannelloni*, filled and combined with its sauce, also can be refrigerated—tightly wrapped in plastic or foil—up to 2 days. The *cannelloni* may be sauced differently by reversing the above order: after laying the *cannelloni* in the thin layer of tomato sauce, cover them with the rest of the tomato sauce and pour the *besciamella* over the dish. Sprinkle with cheese, dot with butter, and bake.

Tubes of *cannelloni*, stuffed with chopped chicken livers and beef, spinach and cheese, are placed in a long casserole, then topped with *besciamella* and tomato sauce. So prepared *(above)*, and sprinkled with Parmesan cheese, the pasta is ready for baking; finished *(below)*, it is one of Italy's heartiest concoctions.

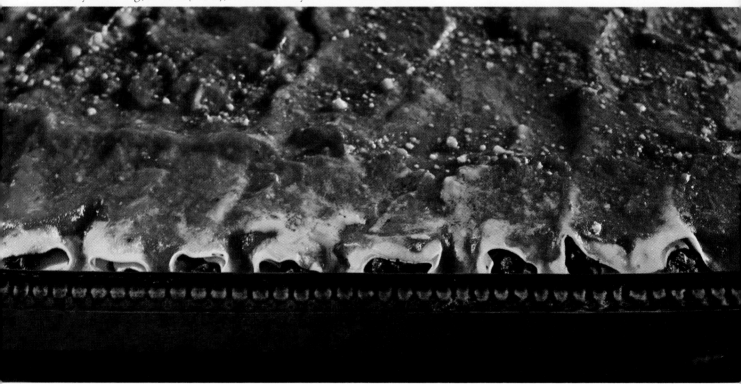

To serve 4 to 6

2 eggs
2 cups freshly made or leftover *risotto*
  (*page 144*)
4 ounces *mozzarella* cheese, cut in
  ½-inch cubes (about 1 cup)
¾ cup fine dry bread crumbs
Vegetable oil or shortening for deep
  frying

Supplì al Telefono
DEEP-FRIED RICE-AND-CHEESE BALLS

Beat the eggs lightly with a fork until they are just combined. Then add the *risotto* and stir gently but thoroughly, taking care not to mash the rice. Scoop up 1 tablespoon of the mixture in a spoon, place a cube of *mozzarella* in the middle, and top with another spoonful of *risotto*. Press the two spoons together or use your hands to shape a ball. Roll the ball in bread crumbs and place on wax paper. Similarly, shape other balls. The balls may be fried at once, but they are easier to handle if refrigerated for 30 minutes.

Heat the oil in a deep-fat fryer to 375°. Preheat the oven to 250°, line a large baking dish with paper towels and put the dish in the oven. Fry the balls, 4 or 5 at a time, for about 5 minutes until they are golden brown and the cheese has melted. Transfer to the baking dish to drain. They may be kept warm in the oven for 10 minutes or so if they must wait.

Place a tablespoon of rice in one hand, add cheese, then cover with rice.

Pat the mixture into a ball; the cheese must be completely surrounded.

Roll the ball in bread crumbs and fry it. The cheese should then resemble the "telephone wires" extending from the rice ball at right.

64

Abbacchio Brodettatto
BRAISED LAMB WITH EGG AND LEMON SAUCE

Preheat the oven to 500°. Fry the diced pork fat in a heavy 10- to 12-inch skillet over high heat, stirring frequently, until the dice are crisp and brown. Remove them with a slotted spoon and discard them. In the fat remaining in the skillet, brown the lamb, 4 or 5 chunks at a time. As the chunks become golden brown on all sides, transfer them to a heavy 2½- to 3-quart flameproof casserole. Then pour off all but a thin film of fat from the skillet and set the pan aside; it will be used again.

Sprinkle the lamb with salt and a few grindings of pepper, and add the flour, tossing the meat with a wooden spoon to coat the chunks as evenly as possible with the seasoning and flour. Place the casserole in the upper third of the oven and brown the lamb uncovered, turning it 2 or 3 times, for about 10 minutes, or until no trace of gummy flour remains and the chunks are lightly crusted. Remove the casserole from the oven, and reduce the oven heat to 350°.

In the fat remaining in the skillet, cook the garlic over moderate heat, stirring constantly for 1 minute. Pour in the wine and boil briskly until it is reduced to ¼ cup. Scrape in any browned bits clinging to the bottom and sides of the skillet. Stir in the stock and bring to a boil, then pour the entire contents of the skillet over the chunks of lamb in the casserole. Bring the casserole to a boil on top of the stove. Add the bay leaf, cover the casserole and cook in the middle of the oven for 1½ hours, or until the lamb is tender when pierced with the tip of a sharp knife. With a slotted spoon, transfer the lamb to a deep, heated platter, and cover it lightly with aluminum foil to keep it warm. Strain the braising stock from the casserole through a fine sieve into a small saucepan. Let the stock settle for a minute or so, then skim the fat from the surface. In a small bowl, beat the egg yolks and lemon juice together with a whisk, and stir in 2 tablespoons of the hot stock. Add 2 more tablespoons of stock, stirring constantly, then whisk the now warmed egg-yolk-and-lemon mixture into the stock remaining in the pan. Over moderate heat, bring this sauce to a boil, stirring constantly, and cook it for 30 seconds, or until it is thick enough to coat the wires of the whisk lightly. Taste for seasoning. Pour the sauce over the lamb, sprinkle with parsley and serve.

To serve 6

2 ounces fresh pork fat, diced (about ½ cup)
2 pounds boneless lamb shoulder, cut in 1½-inch chunks
½ teaspoon salt
Freshly ground black pepper
3 tablespoons flour
½ teaspoon finely chopped garlic
½ cup dry white wine
3 cups beef stock, fresh or canned
1 bay leaf
2 egg yolks
1 tablespoon lemon juice
2 tablespoons finely chopped fresh parsley

Piselli al Prosciutto
BRAISED PEAS WITH PROSCIUTTO

In a heavy 1- to 2-quart saucepan, melt the 2 tablespoons of butter over moderate heat and cook the finely chopped onions for 7 or 8 minutes, stirring frequently until they are soft but not brown. Stir in the green peas and chicken stock, cover, and cook for 15 to 20 minutes. When the peas are tender, add the strips of prosciutto and cook, uncovered, stirring frequently, for 2 minutes more, or until all the liquid is absorbed. Taste for seasoning. Serve the peas in a heated bowl.

NOTE: One 10-ounce package of frozen peas may be substituted for the fresh peas. Defrost the peas thoroughly before using them, and add them to the onions without any stock. Cook the peas uncovered, stirring frequently, for about 5 minutes, then add the prosciutto, heat through and serve.

To serve 4

2 tablespoons butter
¼ cup finely chopped onions
2 cups fresh green peas (about 2 pounds unshelled)
¼ cup chicken stock, fresh or canned
2 ounces prosciutto, cut in 1-by-¼-inch julienne strips (about ¼ cup)
Salt
Freshly ground black pepper

When a spoon can stand
unsupported in semolina,
the mixture is thick enough.

Spread the *gnocchi* batter into a sheet ¼ inch thick,
cool it in the refrigerator and then, with a round
cookie cutter, cut it into 1½-inch circles.

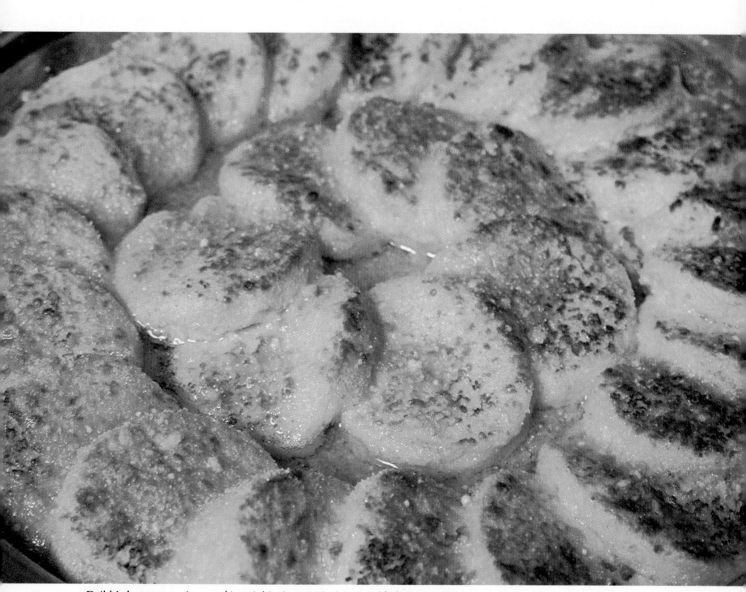

Dribble butter over the *gnocchi,* sprinkle them with cheese and bake them crisp
and golden at 400°. They should be served at once while the entire dish is alive—
still popping and bubbling from the heat of the oven.

Gnocchi alla Romana
SEMOLINA CAKES BAKED WITH BUTTER AND CHEESE

Butter a large baking sheet and set it aside. In a heavy 2- to 3-quart saucepan, bring the milk, salt, nutmeg and a few grindings of pepper to a boil over moderate heat. Add the semolina or farina gradually, so the milk never stops boiling, stirring it constantly with a wooden spoon. Continue cooking and stirring until the semolina or farina is so thick that the spoon will stand up unsupported in the middle of the pan. Remove the pan from the heat.

Beat the eggs lightly with a fork, add ¾ cup of freshly grated Parmesan cheese and stir the mixture into the semolina. When the ingredients are well blended, spoon the mixture onto the buttered baking sheet. Using a metal spatula or knife, which should be dipped in hot water from time to time to make the semolina easier to handle, smooth and spread the semolina into a sheet about ¼ inch thick. Refrigerate for at least an hour, or until the semolina is firm.

Preheat the oven to 400° and butter an 8- or 9-inch shallow baking-and-serving dish. With a 1½-inch biscuit cutter, cut the semolina into small circles. (Or use a sharp knife to cut it into triangles.) Transfer them to the baking dish, dribble in the melted butter, and sprinkle the top with the remaining ¼ cup of cheese. Bake the *gnocchi* on the middle shelf of the oven for 15 minutes, or until they are crisp and golden; if you want them browned, put them under a hot broiler for 30 seconds. Serve the *gnocchi* at once, while they are hot.

To serve 4 to 6

3 cups milk
1½ teaspoons salt
Pinch of ground nutmeg
Freshly ground black pepper
¾ cup semolina or farina
2 eggs
1 cup freshly grated imported
   Parmesan cheese
4 tablespoons butter, melted

Coda alla Vaccinara
BRAISED OXTAIL WITH CELERY HEARTS

Preheat the oven to 325°. Season the pieces of oxtail with salt and freshly ground black pepper, then roll the pieces in flour and shake or brush off all of the excess. In a heavy 10- to 12-inch skillet, heat the 3 tablespoons of olive oil until a light haze forms over it. Brown the pieces of oxtail over high heat, 5 or 6 pieces at a time, turning them with tongs until they are richly colored on all sides.

Transfer the oxtail to a heavy 3- to 4-quart flameproof casserole. Now discard most of the fat from the skillet, leaving only a thin film on the bottom. Add the finely chopped onions and garlic and cook them over moderate heat, stirring frequently, for 8 to 10 minutes, or until they are soft and lightly colored. Pour in the red wine and boil it briskly over high heat, stirring constantly. When the wine has cooked almost completely away, stir in the beef stock, cook for a minute or 2, then pour the entire contents of the skillet over the oxtail. Add the drained tomatoes, tomato paste and cloves. Bring the casserole to a boil over high heat, cover it and place it on the middle shelf of the oven, regulating the heat if necessary to keep the casserole at a slow simmer.

Meanwhile, cook the celery strips in the 2 cups of boiling water for 5 minutes. Drain and set aside. When the oxtail has cooked for 3½ hours, gently stir in the blanched celery. Cover the casserole again and cook for another 30 minutes. Skim off as much fat as possible from the sauce and serve the oxtail directly from the casserole.

To serve 6

3 pounds oxtail, cut into 1½-inch
   pieces
Salt
Freshly ground black pepper
Flour
3 tablespoons olive oil
1 cup finely chopped onions
1 teaspoon finely chopped garlic
½ cup dry red wine
1 cup beef stock, fresh or canned
1½ cups Italian plum or whole-pack
   tomatoes, drained and coarsely
   chopped
1 tablespoon tomato paste
4 whole cloves
2 cups water
1 celery heart cut into 2-by-¼-inch
   julienne strips (about 1 cup)

IV

Florence
and Tuscany

Framed by a window in the
Belvedere Fort, Florence's
ancient bastion, Giotto's
belltower and the dome of
Santa Maria del Fiore
dominate the Tuscan skyline.
On the table sit equally
familiar Florentine sights—
beans in a flask, olive oil and
garlic, basic ingredients in the
city's popular dish, *fagioli
nel fiasco*.

Tuscany, the region that caps the knee of the Italian boot between Genoa
and Rome, is considered the heartland of the nation, the place where the
language is the purest, the traditions the strongest and the culture the live-
liest. It is also the region where the cooking is thought to be the least
"corrupted" by outside influences. Indeed, the one characteristic shared by
the best of Tuscan dishes is a single-minded avoidance of unnecessary complications. Great attention is paid to raw materials of the highest quality,
cooked with a minimum of sauces and seasonings. It is spare home cooking, healthy and with no pretense to sophistication. Perhaps that is the
highest sophistication of all.

The heart of this heartland is Florence; Tuscany as a whole is overshad-
owed by its brilliant capital. Even outside Italy, the designation *alla fiorentina* (Florentine) is famous—but it is likely also to mean that, in one way
or another, spinach dominates the recipe. In France, one has only to incor-
porate spinach into a dish to make it automatically "Florentine"—at least
to a Frenchman. Out of 29 recipes listed as Florentine in that encyclopedia
of cookery, *Larousse Gastronomique*, 27 involve spinach. But in three Italian
cookbooks chosen at random, I found only one recipe identified as Florentine that contains spinach. To an Italian, therefore, *alla fiorentina* merely
connotes the way Florentine cooks prepare a particular kind of food and
whether it contains spinach has nothing to do with the case.

This becomes clear when a few Florentine dishes are compared. One of
the simplest, and best, is *trippa alla fiorentina*, tripe stewed in chicken or
beef stock with herbs and vegetables, and served with grated Parmesan

cheese *(Recipe Booklet).* Another is *arista alla fiorentina,* saddle of pork seasoned with garlic, cloves and rosemary, and roasted slowly. Others are *pollo alla diavola,* tender chicken, quartered, basted with a spicy butter sauce and broiled *(page 80),* and the Florentine omeletlike dish, *tortino di carciofi,* which calls for tiny, tender artichoke hearts to be quartered and mixed with the eggs *(page 81).*

The authentic local cuisine of Tuscany is best sampled not in its big-city restaurants, but in smaller eating places similar to the *trattorie* of Rome. These *taverne caratteristiche* are well worth seeking out, particularly those whose names start with the word *buca* (meaning, literally, "hole"). A *buca* is usually very small, sometimes below street level, like the Buca di San Francesco in Arezzo, but the word is also a punning reference to *bocca,* the Italian word for mouth; what is served there is certain to be what pleases the mouth of the proprietor, who has his own positive and often unique ideas of how to cook certain dishes. A *buca* offers a *table d'hôte,* a table of the host, in its most literal sense; there is no written menu, and the customer is invited to accept what the host, in his own way, chooses to put before him.

Whether they are observed in a *buca,* in a *ristorante* or at home, Tuscany is best known for three gastronomic traditions: beef, beans and Chianti. Probably the oldest as well as the tallest and heaviest breed of beef cattle in the world is the Chianina of Tuscany. The breed goes back centuries; it supplied some of the animals sacrificed to the gods by the priests of ancient Rome. "It is no wonder that our cattle give the best beef," a cattle judge once declared irreverently at a Chianina show. "In all ages, priests have always been gluttons." In the pre-Christian days when priests officiated at the sacrifice, gluttony must have been almost an occupational disease: the gods were given the sacrificed animals' entrails, which were burned, and the poor priests were left to consume the lowly leftovers in the form of large quantities of freshly killed beef.

The best Italian beef comes from animals like this Tuscan Chiana Valley bull. Known since ancient times for their tenderness, these cattle were prized by the Romans.

The Chianina cattle are remarkable for their speedy growth, as well as for their great weight. A year-old bull weighs more than 1,000 pounds; a two-year-old may easily go over a ton. On the 500-acre farm of the Contessa Marietta di Frassineto, in the Chiana Valley, south of Arezzo, I saw a prize four-year-old that weighed nearly 4,000 pounds. Chianina steers are ordinarily killed at what would seem an unusually early age in some countries—15 to 17 months. In most cattle the result of such early slaughter is what is known as "baby beef," which has the merits neither of beef nor of veal. However, because the Chianina cattle grow rapidly, their flesh is not baby beef. It is called *vitellone,* which might be translated as "large veal," and is definitely red meat, virtually without fat and with an exceptionally high percentage concentrated in the choicer cuts. When it reaches the table, Chianina beefsteak is the most famous dish of Florence—although more than a few Florentines, characteristically dissenting from the general opinion, prefer their beef from outside Tuscany. Wherever the meat originates, beef is listed on the menu either as *bistecca alla fiorentina (page 80)* or *costata* (rib steak) *alla fiorentina.* Many consider *costata,* grilled over coal and softwood embers and then seasoned with olive oil, salt and pepper, the best of the best that can be had in Florence.

Besides being beef fanciers, Tuscans are called *mangiafagioli* (bean eaters) by non-Tuscan Italians, and not always with an intent to be complimentary;

beans are widely regarded as peasant fare. But the addiction to beans, common to all classes of Tuscans, goes far back into history: Alessandro de' Medici, Duke of Florence, started the fashion among his subjects of eating *fagioli* in the 16th Century, when haricot beans were first introduced to Europe from the New World.

Beans appear in the Tuscan menu at almost every stage of the meal except dessert, and they are used in combination with practically every other kind of food. There is bean soup, or *zuppa di fagioli; minestrone di fagioli,* in which tomatoes and celery are added to the beans; there is *riso e fagioli,* rice and beans; and a pasta soup, *zuppa di fagioli con la pasta (page 83),* in which spaghetti is added to bean soup. For the fish course, a favorite is beans with tuna fish, *fagioli toscanelli con tonno (page 80).* Florentine beefsteak is often served with beans or *piselli* (small peas) as a side dish. *Ribollita,* any leftover dish from Sunday dinner, is "reboiled" (actually just heated up) on Monday—and served with beans.

Other bean dishes may turn up as *antipasti,* entrées or separate vegetable dishes. *Fagioli nel fiasco,* to mention one of the more picturesque, does not mean "disastrous beans"; the beans are boiled in an empty fiasco, or Chianti wine flask, to preserve as much of their aroma and flavor as possible— including a lot of it that normally escapes as steam when the cooking is done in an open vessel. They are served cold, with an uncooked seasoning of oil, salt, pepper and a little lemon juice.

Chianti, with its distinctive flask full and ready for the pouring, is the one Italian wine that almost every non-Italian can recognize and name. But not all the wine sold as Chianti is the real thing. The Chianti country proper straddles the districts of Florence and Siena; its boundaries are defined by law, and only wine produced within them has a right to the name of *Chianti classico.* The growers try to protect themselves from imitators by placing on the neck of every bottle a trademarked seal, bearing a serial number and displaying the insignia of the medieval Chianti League: a black rooster framed in light red on a golden background.

Not to be left behind, exporters of Chianti from areas near the legally defined region have devised a seal that looks almost identical. This imitation mark does not necessarily denote a bad or spurious wine. The Arezzo Chianti, for example, is very good. Such related wines are called *tipo Chianti,* or Chianti-type wines. When you find a "Chianti" coming from outside of Tuscany, however, you are entitled to regard it with some suspicion until it proves its worth in the drinking.

One of the best of the true classical Chiantis is Chianti Brolio, an ancient name in Tuscany. The Brolio Castle and vineyards where the grapes are grown—shown in the pictures on the following pages—lie in the mountains between Florence and Siena.

In addition to Chianti there are many other fine wines to be found in Tuscany. In fact, Siena is generally considered to be the wine capital of Italy. The Italian Academy of Wines and Grapes is located there, and there is a permanent exposition of Italian wines in the cellars of the Medici castle. The region offers robust wines to be served with the roast and delicate wines to accompany the fish. A *moscato* from the island of Elba, rich in iron and phosphates, is both nourishment and a tonic. A *moscatello* from Montalcino, low in alcoholic content, is not only healthful but considered by

Tuscany and its treasure-house city of Florence eat simply, and drink largely of Chianti, the hearty wine grown in the mountains between Florence and Siena. From the Chiana Valley come world-renowned beefsteaks plus giant melons and small game. Arezzo offers hams and Casentino river trout. Lucca has the finest olive oil in all Italy.

Continued on page 78

The author *(at right, below)* lunches with the Ricasolis in the dining room of Brolio Castle, where the family has lived since 1141.

The Chiantis of Brolio

The vineyards of Brolio Castle, the baronial estate of the Ricasoli family, yield some of the finest and most illustrious of the classical Chianti wines. Wine has been made at Brolio since the year 1000 but, during the Renaissance, the Ricasoli barons were more occupied with the wars between neighboring Florence and Siena than with the improvement of their vintages. The wars ended in the 16th Century, and the Brolio Chiantis have enjoyed a high reputation ever since. Among the outstanding wines produced at Brolio are Castello di Meleto, a light, ruby-colored red; Brolio Bianco, a pale dry white; Brolio Vin Santo, a sweet white made from dried grapes and aged in oak; and Castello di Brolio, a dark red that, in the best years, is bottled as Brolio Riserva. Brolio wines are among the few estate-bottled wines in Italy.

At the Brolio winery, Baron Bettino Ricasoli *(left)* and his technical director sample one of the leading Brolio reds to adjudge its bouquet and flavor.

Piled in a storeroom, Brolio flasks are straw-covered, but many have a lyre shape rather than the common pear shape.

Overleaf: Workers load grapes on a cart for transport to the winery.

A Sampling of Wines

Italy produces hundreds of different wines, and exports many of the best to the United States, where they can be purchased at reasonable prices. The bottles shown here, varying from dry to sweet and coming from vineyards in the far north, the center and the south, suggest the extraordinary range of these wines. The numbered descriptions below correspond to numbers in the photograph opposite.

1 BARDOLINO, a light red with a dry, spicy, pleasantly bitter flavor, is grown on the shores of Lake Garda, near Verona.

2 RAVELLO ROSATO is a delicately sweet rosé grown near Salerno. Its light, fruity taste makes it most refreshing with the rich desserts of southern Italy.

3 VERDICCHIO DEI CASTELLI DI JESI, grown in the Marches of central Italy, is a dry white wine with a slightly bitter taste. It is a superior table wine, particularly good with fish.

4 FREISA, a red from Piedmont, has a slight flintiness (a winetaster's word connoting a taste that is slightly abrasive but not sour or tart) that makes its fruity flavor all the more refreshing.

5 FRASCATI, the table wine of Rome, is unpredictable. It can be very good or very bad, but it should never be expensive. It can be dry or semisweet, is straw-colored and, when it is good, has a mellow and refreshing taste.

6 ORVIETO, a white from Umbria, is a pleasantly fruity wine. Usually served as a dessert wine, it comes in both dry and semisweet varieties.

7 GRIGNOLINO, grown in the Piedmont, is one of the more delicate of Italian reds. Its pleasant, nutty flavor goes well with beef and other meat dishes.

8 VALPOLICELLA, a dark, mellow red from Verona, can be served at the most formal meals. It will not overpower delicate flavors, but it has enough body to hold its own with highly seasoned dishes.

9 BARBARESCO, a red from the region of Turin, is full bodied and very flinty. It is a fitting accompaniment for the finest roasts.

10 BAROLO, greatest of the Piedmontese reds, is smooth and full bodied, with a high alcoholic content. It should be aged for at least three years, and the finer vintages should mature for eight.

11 BROLIO, a fine *Chianti classico*, hides a rich and subtle flavor behind the familiar tang. It is produced in Tuscan areas known as the *zona classica*.

12 SOAVE, grown near Verona, is considered by some the finest of Italian whites. It is mild and delicate, but its flavor and bouquet are so distinctive that no one who has drunk it ever forgets it.

13 EST! EST! EST! ("It is! It is! It is!"), whatever the authenticity of the 800-year-old story *(page 59)* that explains its cheerful name, is still made at Montefiascone, near Rome. It is a pleasant wine, one variety of which is slightly tart, the other semisweet.

14 CHIANTI bears the name usually associated with the classic Tuscan product, but this fresh, fruity wine comes from a neighboring region and is therefore not a *Chianti classico*.

Italians to be suitable for children. And of course there is the simple *vino santo toscano,* pressed by every farmer in the province from the grapes nearest at hand. The farmers jealously guard their best wine-making efforts and serve glasses of their finest only on important occasions or as a sign of great honor to a favored guest.

Florence dominates its own district so completely as to obscure nearly every neighboring town. Yet a brave culinary challenge to Florence comes from Arezzo, an ancient town with an independent history that goes back to Etruscan times. "Does a well-fed race produce more geniuses than others?" asks a local gastronomy writer. "The list of great men from Arezzo seems to confirm it." Indeed, during the Middle Ages and the Renaissance, the roster of distinguished Aretini was impressive, including Guido d'Arezzo, inventor of the musical scale, the poet Petrarch and the satirist Aretino. The painter Piero della Francesca, famed for his 15th Century frescoes, was born in nearby Sansepolcro, and Michelangelo, greatest of the sculptors and painters of Italy, came from the little town of Caprese, 14 miles from Arezzo.

Seamed with valleys and crowned with wooded hills, the region produces the raw materials of a solid cuisine. The Casentino River, running in a long, narrow cleft between two ranges of forested mountains, is especially favored with small, juicy Arezzo hams, delicately flavored trout and particularly tasty chestnuts and walnuts. From the Arno Valley come excellent chickens; giant melons are grown in the Chiana Valley. This is also good country for small game; a hare that has hung for at least two days furnishes the sauce for a kind of special Arezzo-region *lasagne* called *pappardelle con la lepre.*

Such a sauce—or any sauce—would be the better for the inclusion of the olive oil of Lucca, the finest oil in Italy. It is not surprising that the best season for eating in Lucca is late summer and early autumn, when the olives are pressed, and fresh, new oil is on hand. It is also the time when pigs are slaughtered; many pork dishes are on the menu, and housewives make *biroldo,* blood pudding flavored with herbs. It is game season too and a time for picking chestnuts to be served as a purée with the game, or ground into flour for desserts.

Lucca was an independent state from 1160 to 1847, and has preserved state archives reaching as far back as 790. For many centuries its inhabitants seem to have been endowed with a sweet tooth. One of the specialties of the region is *buccellato,* a ring-shaped cake made of flour, sugar, vanilla, raisins and anise seed served with strawberries that have been marinated in sugared wine. Another favorite dessert—one which Lucca shares with other Tuscan regions (including Massa-Carrara), is *cenci*—literally, "tatters." *Cenci alla fiorentina (page 83),* strips of pastry dough, tied in knots or bows and deep fried, are excellent ingredients for a children's party, as festive and delicious as their distant cousins, New England cinnamon sticks, made with leftover pie crust.

Over toward the coast, the influence of the sea enters Tuscan cooking. But it is only a partial influence. In Grosseto, south of Florence, fishing shares precedence with hunting, a fact evident in a list of 58 specialties drawn up by local gastronomes. Twenty come under the heading of fish and fish soups, 15 under game. One of Grosseto's finer foodstuffs is an especially tasty fat eel known as *capitone;* at the holiday season most of the eel catch goes to market in Rome and Naples, to be sold for the traditional Christmas Eve meal. The district of Grosseto runs well inland, and as a result its specialties include a great deal of game, not only birds and rabbits but deer and even wild boar.

Pisa, six miles inland, is not often thought of in connection with the ocean. Nevertheless, it was one of the world's greatest maritime powers in medieval times when the Arno was navigable from the coast upstream as far as the city. Still standing on the banks of the Arno in the city is the lovely Church of Santa Maria della Spina, built by the devout citizens of Pisa in 1230 as a chapel for seamen. The river, which is now silted up at the mouth, is the source of Pisa's most distinguished specialty: *le cee*. This strange word, which seems more French than Italian, is local dialect; in classical Italian it is written *cieche*. Either way it refers to the young, still-blind eels of the Arno, cooked in oil and seasoned with sage and pepper.

One of the great fish soups of the Mediterranean region takes its name from Livorno (Leghorn), another Tuscan city that is still one of Italy's busiest ports. The stew, called *cacciucco alla livornese (page 81)*, contains various kinds of fish, white wine and a tingling assortment of spices. It is worthy to stand beside the *bouillabaisse* of Marseilles, to which it bears a Mediterranean family resemblance. The kinds of fish cooked for *cacciucco* can include halibut, cod and mackerel, but purists insist that at least some shellfish be included.

Part of the Livorno district is the island of Elba, Napoleon's first place of exile, where he spent 10 months before his return to France and eventual defeat at Waterloo. Elba is good hunting country, and game in season offers a variation on the year-round seafood menu, which includes spiny lobster; the sharp-toothed, white-fleshed dentex, a fish resembling the striped bass of American waters; and octopus, called *polpi*. The menu may change, but on Elba one certainty is freshness: no islander would think of buying fish not actually still alive.

Livorno, like other parts of Italy, has always attracted the English. The Scottish novelist Tobias Smollett lived, and died, there, and in 1819 Percy Bysshe Shelley wrote a tragic epic, the *Cenci* (about the murder of the wicked count Francesco Cenci of Rome by his wife and daughter) in his villa near Livorno. Shelley cared little about food, and in any case was a vegetarian who probably would not have countenanced, let alone enjoyed, the local seafood.

Much more enthusiastic—and particular—about his eating was the terrible-tempered English writer Walter Savage Landor, who lived in Florence for almost 30 years as a member of the English-speaking colony that also included Robert and Elizabeth Barrett Browning and the American sculptor William Wetmore Story. Landor studied and perfected ways of making his own wine, and was a keen gardener who raised all his own vegetables. He also loved flowers—so much that he refused to have them picked. One day his passion for flowers and his concern about good food met head-on in a collision that was not softened by his legendary temper. Presented by his cook with what he regarded as a badly prepared dish, he seized the poor man in a furious rage and threw him out the window. Then, as the body hit the ground, Landor cried in horror: "My God, I forgot—our best tulip bed is under that window!"

Pollo alla Diavola
BROILED DEVILED CHICKEN

To serve 4

8 tablespoons (1 quarter-pound stick)
   butter, melted
2 tablespoons olive oil
¼ teaspoon crushed dried red pepper
¼ cup finely chopped onions
2 tablespoons finely chopped fresh
   parsley, preferably the flat-leaf
   Italian type
½ teaspoon finely chopped garlic
A 2½- to 3-pound chicken, quartered
1 teaspoon salt
Lemon quarters

Preheat the broiler. Combine the melted butter, oil and red pepper in a small bowl, and in another bowl mix together the chopped onions, parsley and garlic. Add 4 teaspoons of the butter-oil mixture to the onion-parsley mixture, stir it into a paste and set it aside.

Wash the chicken quickly under cold running water and dry with paper towels. Brush both sides of the chicken with half the remaining butter-oil mixture and salt it lightly. Put the quarters skin side down on the broiler pan rack and broil 4 inches from the heat. After 5 minutes, baste the chicken with the remaining butter-oil mixture and broil for 5 more minutes. Baste again and turn skin side up. Then broil, basting every 5 minutes with pan drippings, for another 10 to 15 minutes, or until the juice runs clear when a thigh is pierced with the tip of a sharp knife. With a metal spatula spread the top of each quarter with the onion-parsley paste (patting it firmly in place) and broil another 3 or 4 minutes, or until the coating is lightly browned. Arrange the chicken on a heated serving platter and pour the drippings over it. Garnish with lemon quarters.

Bistecca alla Fiorentina
BROILED MARINATED STEAK

To serve 4

¾ cup olive oil
¼ cup wine vinegar
2 tablespoons finely chopped fresh
   parsley, preferably flat-leaf
½ teaspoon finely chopped garlic
½ teaspoon dried oregano
A 2½- to 3-pound T-bone,
   porterhouse or sirloin steak, cut
   1 inch thick
Salt

Choose a shallow baking dish large enough to hold the steak comfortably, and in it combine the olive oil, vinegar, parsley, garlic and oregano. Lay the steak in the marinade and turn it about until the meat is well coated. Let the steak marinate at room temperature for at least 4 hours or in the refrigerator for 6 hours, turning it over from time to time.

Preheat the broiler to its highest temperature and remove the steak from the baking dish. Discard the marinade. Pat the steak dry with paper towels and broil it 3 inches from the heat for about 4 minutes on each side, or until it is done to your taste. (Test it by pressing it with a finger: when it is slightly resilient, neither soft nor firm, the steak is medium rare.) Transfer the steak to a heated serving platter and season with salt before slicing.

Fagioli Toscanelli con Tonno
WHITE BEAN AND TUNA SALAD

To serve 4 to 6

4 cups canned *cannellini* or other
   white beans (2 one-pound cans) or
   2 cups dry white kidney, marrow,
   Great Northern or navy beans and
   2 quarts water
¼ cup olive oil
1 tablespoon lemon juice
½ teaspoon salt
Freshly ground black pepper
¼ cup finely chopped scallions
2 tablespoons finely chopped fresh
   parsley, preferably the flat-leaf
   Italian type
1 seven-ounce can tuna fish, preferably
   Italian tuna packed in olive oil

If you are using canned beans, drain them in a colander, wash them in cold water, then drain them again and spread on paper towels to dry before transferring them to a serving bowl. If you are using dry beans, combine them with water in a 3- to 4-quart saucepan and bring to a boil. Boil briskly for 2 minutes, remove from the heat and let the beans soak for 1 hour. Then cook them in the soaking water over low heat for 1 to 1½ hours, or until they are tender. Drain, transfer them to a serving bowl and cool.

Combine the olive oil, lemon juice, salt and pepper and pour them over the beans. Add the scallions and parsley and mix them all together. Transfer the beans to a platter, break the tuna into chunks and arrange on top. This salad may be served alone as a first course or as part of an *antipasto*.

Cacciucco alla Livornese

LEGHORN SEAFOOD STEW

Place the lobsters one at a time on their backs on a chopping board and slice off the whole tail section. Cut the tail in half lengthwise down the center. Then cut the large claws from the body and separate the joints from the claws. Gash the flat underside of each claw with a sharp blow of a knife to make it easy to extract the meat later. Cut off the antennae and then split the body section in half lengthwise. Remove and discard the gelatinous sac (or stomach) near the head and the long intestine attached to it. Then remove and set aside the greenish-brown tomalley (or liver) and the black caviarlike eggs (or coral), if any.

Heat the olive oil in a heavy 4- to 6-quart saucepan or flameproof casserole. Add the onions and cook them over moderate heat, stirring frequently, for 8 to 10 minutes, or until they are lightly colored. Add the garlic and sage and cook, stirring, for 1 minute longer. Pour in the wine and boil briskly over high heat, stirring constantly, until it has reduced to about ¼ cup, then add the tomato paste and water, clam broth, bay leaves and salt. Reduce the heat and simmer the sauce, partially covered, for 10 minutes.

Drop the squid into the simmering sauce, cover and cook for 10 minutes. Add the lobster, cover and cook for another 5 minutes. Then place the firm white fish in the sauce, cover the pan and cook for 5 minutes. Finally, add the scallops and cook, covered again, for 5 minutes longer. With a large slotted spoon, carefully transfer the cooked fish and seafood to a heated serving platter, arranging them as attractively on the plate as you can. Force the tomalley and coral through a fine sieve and stir them into the hot sauce. Simmer for a moment, taste for seasoning, then spoon the sauce over the fish and seafood and sprinkle chopped parsley and grated lemon peel on top. Arrange the slices of garlic toast around the platter.

GARLIC TOAST: Preheat the oven to 325°. Spread the slices of bread on a lightly oiled baking sheet and bake them on the middle shelf of the oven for 15 minutes. Combine the oil and garlic and brush both sides of each slice lightly with the mixture. Then turn the slices over and bake for another 15 minutes, or until they are lightly browned.

To serve 6

2 live 1-pound lobsters
¼ cup olive oil
½ cup finely chopped onions
1 teaspoon finely chopped garlic
½ teaspoon crumbled dried sage leaves
½ cup dry white wine
2 tablespoons tomato paste dissolved in 1 cup water
½ cup fresh or bottled clam broth
2 bay leaves
1 teaspoon salt
½ pound squid (optional), cut into ½-inch rings
½ pound each of 2 kinds of firm white fish—such as halibut, cod, flounder, mackerel, haddock, pollack, snapper, bass or rockfish—cut into 2-inch serving pieces
½ pound whole bay scallops or sliced sea scallops
2 tablespoons finely chopped fresh parsley, preferably the flat-leaf Italian type
1 tablespoon freshly grated lemon peel

GARLIC TOAST
6 to 12 one-inch-thick slices Italian bread
2 to 4 tablespoons olive oil
1 to 2 teaspoons finely chopped garlic

Tortino di Carciofi

BAKED ARTICHOKE HEART OMELET

Preheat the oven to 400°. In a small bowl, beat the eggs and salt with a whisk or rotary beater until they are frothy and well combined. Set them aside. Heat the olive oil in an 8- to 10-inch enameled or stainless-steel skillet. Drop in the artichoke hearts and cook them over moderate heat, stirring frequently, for 5 minutes, or until they are golden brown. Spread the artichoke hearts over the bottom of a buttered 1-quart baking-and-serving dish and pour the beaten eggs over them. Bake in the upper third of the oven for 15 minutes, or until the omelet is firm and a knife inserted in its center comes out clean. Serve the *tortino* at once.

NOTE: In Italy this *tortino* is traditionally made with tiny artichokes. The whole artichokes are cleaned, trimmed and cooked in boiling water for about 15 minutes, or until tender, before they are sautéed.

To serve 4

4 eggs
½ teaspoon salt
2 tablespoons olive oil
1 cup frozen artichoke hearts (about half of a 9-ounce package), defrosted and cut lengthwise in quarters

Zuppa di Fagioli con la Pasta
BEAN SOUP WITH PASTA

In a 3- to 4-quart saucepan, bring the beans and 2 quarts of water to a boil over high heat and boil them for 2 minutes. Remove from the heat and let the beans soak for 1 hour. Drain the beans, saving the water. Add enough fresh cold water to make 2 quarts. Chop together the ham, onions, celery and garlic into very small pieces. This mixture is called a *batutto*. Heat the olive oil in a large pot or kettle, stir in the *batutto* and cook, stirring frequently, for 10 minutes, or until it is lightly colored. Add the beans, water and salt pork, and season with salt and a few grindings of pepper. Bring to a boil, reduce the heat and simmer partially covered for 1 to 1½ hours, or until the beans are tender. Discard the salt pork and skim the fat off the soup. With a slotted spoon, remove about half the beans from the soup and purée them through a sieve or food mill, then return them to the soup. Simmer over low heat, stirring constantly, for a minute or 2. Add the spaghetti and simmer 10 to 15 minutes, or until it is tender. Taste for seasoning, ladle into a large tureen or soup bowls and sprinkle with grated cheese.

To serve 4 to 6

1 cup dry white beans (marrow, Great Northern, navy or white kidney)
2 to 2½ quarts water
½ pound cooked smoked ham, cut in ¼-inch cubes (about 2 cups)
½ cup finely chopped onions
¼ cup finely chopped celery
½ teaspoon finely chopped garlic
2 tablespoons olive oil
¼ pound lean salt pork in 1 piece
1½ teaspoons salt
Freshly ground black pepper
½ cup of 1-inch pieces of spaghetti
Freshly grated imported Parmesan cheese

Cenci alla Fiorentina
DEEP-FRIED SWEET PASTRY

Place 1¾ cups of the flour in a large bowl, make a well in the center and add the eggs, egg yolks, rum, 1 tablespoon confectioners' sugar and salt. Using your hands or a fork, mix until all the flour has been incorporated and you can gather the dough into a rough ball. Sprinkle the remaining ¼ cup of flour on a board or pastry cloth and knead for 10 minutes until the extra flour is worked in and the dough is smooth. Cover with a damp towel and let rest for 30 minutes. Heat 3 to 4 inches of oil or shortening to 350° in a deep-fat fryer or large heavy saucepan. On a floured board or pastry cloth, roll out one fourth of the dough at a time. When paper-thin, cut the dough with a pastry wheel or sharp knife into strips 6 or 7 inches long and ½ inch wide. Tie the strips into loose knots and deep-fry them, 4 or 5 at a time, for 1 or 2 minutes, or until they are golden brown. With tongs or a slotted spoon, transfer the *cenci* to paper towels to drain. Repeat with the rest of the dough. Just before serving, sprinkle the *cenci* with confectioners' sugar.

To make about 4 dozen

2 cups all-purpose flour
2 whole eggs
2 egg yolks
3 tablespoons rum
Confectioners' sugar
⅛ teaspoon salt
Vegetable oil or shortening for deep frying

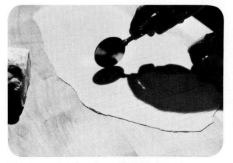

The process of making finished *cenci* (*opposite page*) begins when the paper-thin dough is cut into half-inch strips, 6 to 7 inches long.

Hold each strip of dough gently. Fold into a loop and thread one end through to form a loose knot. Do not try to pull the knot tight.

The twists are dropped into a deep-fat fryer, a few at a time. During the frying process, they puff up to form their characteristic shape.

V

Bologna: Northern Center

Ⅰf Tuscany and Florence offer the purest of Italian cooking, *Bologna la grassa*—"Bologna the fat"—offers by all odds the richest, and must be considered the gastronomic center of the north. The Italians refer to the Bolognese (and by implication, the people of the surrounding region of Emilia-Romagna) as gluttons. But it might be fairer to call them the trenchermen of Italy, as the Burgundians are the trenchermen of France. "Emilia has the richest style of cooking in Italy," says a contemporary writer. "When you hear mention made of Bolognese cooking, drop a little curtsy, for it deserves it," says an older author, the 19th Century expert Pellegrino Artusi, in his *La scienza in cucina e l'arte di mangiar bene (Science in the Kitchen and The Art of Good Eating)*. "It is a rather heavy cuisine . . . but how succulent it is, and what good taste it displays! It is wholesome, too . . . in fact octogenarians and nonagenarians abound [in Bologna] as nowhere else."

The well-fed region of Emilia-Romagna owes the first part of its double-barreled name to Marcus Aemilius Lepidus, a Roman consul of the Second Century B.C., who built the Emilian Way across the plain from Rimini to Piacenza. The road, now an automobile highway, is still there. The northern part of the region has taken the name of Emilia. The southern part was named Romania by Byzantine colonists who occupied it in the Middle Ages, and later generations Italianized the name to Romagna.

The region is one of the flattest parts of mountainous Italy (though it has lovely mountains, too) and one of the most fertile. Wheat and to a lesser extent maize are intensively cultivated; sugar beets are grown to feed the refineries of Ferrara. The tomatoes of the region are as juicy as any in

Checking her purchases, a woman leaves a Bolognese butcher shop that specializes in game. Near the shopper's feet lies a wild boar holding in its mouth a sprig of the laurel often used to garnish the roasted dish; at right hangs a whole deer. The rich yet refined cuisine of Bologna sets a standard in northern Italy.

Italy. Since ancient Roman times one of its cities, Ravenna, has had the reputation of producing the best asparagus in Italy. Vignola is credited with growing the country's best cherries, a dark-colored variety.

The cattle of Emilia-Romagna are famous even in Tuscany, and the Bolognese are fond of veal. They particularly like to embellish it with ham, cheese, herbs and spices, as in *involtini alla cacciatora*, veal rolls stuffed with prosciutto and chicken livers, scallions, and flavored with sage *(page 100)*; or *cuscinetti di vitello*, veal scallops stuffed with cheese and ham, moistened with wine and cooked in a skillet (a variation is on page 100).

Famous as they are for these delicacies, Bologna and Emilia-Romagna are even better known, in Italy and throughout the world, for the delicacy of their pasta, their processed pork (ham and sausages), and the great drums of cheese that come from the district of Parma.

The pasta of Emilia-Romagna, say the local inhabitants, is unbeatable. In its various forms, Bolognese pasta is almost always served with a *ragù* (the word is a corruption of the French *ragoût*, or stew). This is a thick sauce made from such ingredients as onions, carrots, finely chopped pork and beef, celery, butter and tomatoes *(page 98)*

One of the best known of Bolognese pasta is *tagliatelle*. According to a Bolognese legend, *tagliatelle* was first served on the table of a nobleman whose cook was inspired by the flaxen hair of the principal guest—Lucrezia Borgia. Lucrezia is not so well known for her hair as for the gastronomically unsound habit of poisoning her own guests, but the story makes a kind of sense: uncooked *tagliatelle* should have the lightness that fine blond hair suggests. This quality is one of the reasons Emilia-Romagna claims that its *tagliatelle* and other pasta dishes cannot be equaled elsewhere.

The other reasons are superlative raw materials and painstaking preparation. Starting from the local wheat, which is ground into a type of pure wheat flour, strained in a silk sieve, and then kneaded, the pasta dough is finally rolled to a thinness approaching translucence.

Other pasta specialties start from this same dough. In Bologna, Christmas dinner traditionally begins with *tortellini (page 99)*—little rings of dough, stuffed with such things as chopped pork, turkey, prosciutto and sausage, cheese, egg yolks and nutmeg, boiled and then served in consommé, or with butter, or *ragù* and grated cheese, or (best of all) with butter, cream and grated cheese. "*Tortellini* is more essential than sun for a Saturday and love for a woman," said an anonymous article in the *Gazzetta di Bologna* of December 27, 1874. "The origin of *tortellini* is lost in the mists of time," the article continues. But there are local legends. In 1925, a Bolognese named Ostilio Lucarini wrote a play called *The Inventor of Tortellini*. The play is the story of a cook who claimed to see his employer's wife sleeping in the nude and fell in love with her; as a token of his hopeless passion, he cooked and served pasta made in the shape of her navel.

Lasagne, the pasta that comes in wide ribbons, is found in many forms in different parts of Italy, but the citizens of Emilia-Romagna lay claim to it as their own. The preferred recipe is *lasagne pasticciate* (baked in the oven). After boiling, the lasagne is placed in a baking dish in layers alternating with *ragù* and cream sauce, topped with grated cheese *(page 98)*.

Besides *tortellini*, *tagliatelle* and *lasagne*, another popular form of pasta in Emilia-Romagna is *cappelletti*—("little hats," so called because of the

shape of their doughy envelopes stuffed with ricotta cheese, minced chicken, Parmesan cheese, egg and spice. These may be served dry, with *ragù*, melted butter and grated cheese, or in chicken soup.

Sausage is made throughout Italy, but Emilia-Romagna leads all other parts of the country in the processing of pork. Boloney, as made in the United States, is an excellent sausage but lacks the subtlety of its forebear, the famous *mortadella*. A specialty of the city of Bologna, *mortadella* is a large, tasty sausage. It releases a mouth-watering smell when it is cut in paper-thin slices, and is distinguished by the even smoothness of its meat and the delicacy of its flavor. Already well established when the guild of sausage makers was formed in 1376, *mortadella* is quite ancient. It probably originated in the monasteries, where the process of making it began by crushing the pork with a pestle in a special mortar called *un mortaio della carne di maiale* ("mortar for the meat of a pig"), later shortened to *mortadella*.

Mortadella has been called the noblest of pork products, but the famous Parma ham, *prosciutto di Parma*, may be the most delicate. When it has been properly matured, it is a pale red shade. The simon-pure ham is made from the boned rear legs. Sweet and tender, it is sliced extremely thin; occasionally, it becomes an ingredient in a dish that involves a different flavor: chicken, for example—as in *petti di pollo alla bolognese (page 101)*.

The early part of the curing of Parma ham includes a salting process, but the excellence of the finished product lies in half a year of drying in the air, said to be particularly favorable in the Parma region for the aging of ham. Local tradition decrees that the most propitious curing place is in the hills, at moderate altitudes—never too high, never too low.

The center of Parma ham curing is the hill town of Langhirano, which has a reputation for the best air for ham-curing: hams from all parts of Italy are sent there to be aged. In the drying season of a particularly prosperous year, Langhirano homes have been known to be virtually invaded by hams, hung to dry all through the house.

The foreleg of the pig—particularly its foot—is the raw material of *zampone*, a specialty of Modena. The bone is taken out of the foot and replaced by minced spiced pork. It is ordinarily bought already prepared, but until recently it still had to be cooked, which was a long, slow process. The sausage was first soaked in water for 10 to 12 hours, and then boiled over a low flame for three or four more, according to its weight: the heavier the sausage, the longer it was boiled. Since 1964, however, *zampone* has been packaged in precooked form. Sold in aluminum foil bags, the sausages need be boiled for only 20 minutes before serving. *Zampone* is then served sliced, usually with other boiled meats, such as beef or calf's head, accompanied by vegetables or mashed potatoes. Modena also produces *cotechino*, made with the same stuffing used for *zampone*, but sold in ordinary sausage casing instead of the actual pig's forefoot. In addition to their skill with

The Emilia-Romagna region, whose chief city, Bologna, gave its name to American boloney, is rich in fare that gives pleasure to many serious eaters. Besides sausage, the Romagna makes fine stuffed pasta; its pork rivals the best anywhere. Parma produces fine hams and Parmesan cheese; Ravenna, delicate asparagus; Vignola, sweet cherries. From the lagoon of Comacchio come quantities of eels.

Salt-cured Langhirano hams are aged in an open attic overlooking the hillsides of Emilia-Romagna. Local farmers maintain that the hams of the region derive their special flavor from prolonged aging in the mountain air.

sausages, the Modenese have given the world a special way of cooking pork chops—*costolette di maiale*—which they braise in white wine *(page 101)*.

Between Modena and Parma is the country of Parmesan cheese (*Parmigiano* in Italian). The most famous of Italian cheeses, it is superb for sprinkling thickly over pasta, rice, soup and many other dishes. Perhaps because Parmesan cheese marries so well with so many foods, one manufacturer advertises it as "the husband of Italian cooking." Actually the appellation could be applied to almost all the Italian cheeses—some of which, along with Parmesan, are shown on the following pages.

It is easy to think of cheese in terms of robustness, and the same is true of ham and sausage. But Emilia-Romagna also has one quite delicate product—indeed, a rather rare culinary flower—in *aceto balsamico* (vinegar perfumed with herbs). "The history of our aromatic vinegar is more or less the domestic history of the dukes of Modena," a local gastronomy writer affirms. And, in fact, this product is often marketed as *aceto del duca*. The dukes were those of the glamorous house of Este; driven out of Ferrara, the Estes transferred their capital to Modena in 1598. In those days, the vinegar was so highly esteemed that wills sometimes began: "I, the undersigned, being of sound mind and body, leave my vinegar to . . ." Less treasured goods were disposed of in later paragraphs. Today this herb-perfumed vinegar serves—on special occasions—to give sparkle to salads and to marinate or pickle meat. A less valuable vinegar goes into the pickling and packing of the eels of Comacchio in the Ferrara district. Comacchio, a sort of fisherman's Venice, is built on sand and water, threaded with canals crossed by bridges that look as if they had been designed for an opera. Its great lagoon, the Valli di Comacchio, is a huge fish-breeding tank—part salt water, part fresh. Ten thousand fishermen make their living from the lagoons of Comacchio, taking many varieties of fish, but concentrating on eels. The men are busiest in autumn; during this period some eels are allowed to leave the lagoon to spawn. Work piles up again in the spring when the young eels, moved by some mysterious sense, return to grow to maturity in waters that they have never known.

Comacchio and the other towns and cities of the Ferrara district are surrounded by enormously fertile land, reclaimed by the draining of coastal marshes. The rich soil gives special savor to fruit and vegetables. There are nearly 100,000 acres of orchards in the district, and they produce 10 million tons of fruit yearly. Between 60 and 65 per cent of this acreage is devoted to apples, including some with outlandish names like Rome Beauty, Stark Delicious and Golden Delicious. Also important in the region is the Passacrassana pear, which grows best in the Ferrara area, especially around Tresigallo.

A typical Ferrarese dessert is *pan pepato di cioccolato,* a sort of brioche or light, yeasty roll. Traditionally, *pan pepato* was eaten from the week before Christmas through Twelfth Night, though today it is considered a New Year's Eve delicacy. The ingredients are flour, cocoa, milk, sugar (or preferably honey), spices, almonds and bits of lemon peel. It has chocolate frosting and is dusted with sugar and tiny candies. The Duke Borso d'Este, at a banquet he gave in 1465 to mark the feast of St. Martin, served *pan pepato* that was made even more attractive by the insertion of a piece of gold in each cake. The bakers of Ferrara used to send *pan pepato* as presents to their rulers and to the Pope. Continuing the tradition, the Ferrarese sent an 11-pound *pan pepato* to General Dwight D. Eisenhower during World War II.

The bread of the Ferrara district is especially good in the seaside town of Porto Garibaldi, named because it was here that Giuseppe Garibaldi, fleeing from the Austrians, landed in 1849. The bread comes in the form of a ball, with the crust drawn up into four points at the top, forming a sort of crown.

Just southeast of Ferrara is Ravenna, the city where Dante Alighieri died. Faenza, in the province of Ravenna, is the town whose name is the origin of *faïence,* the brightly colored earthenware with an opaque glaze that originated there in the 12th Century. Faenza was one of the first cities in Europe to manufacture tableware—as it still does.

The best dishes of Ravenna are those of the sea—particularly *brodetto* (fish chowder). *Brodetto* appears in various guises and often under other names (such as *zuppa di pesce,* page 114) all along the Italian coast. Just south of Ravenna at Rimini, in 50 B.C., Julius Caesar is reputed to have fortified himself with a copious helping of the local *brodetto* before crossing a small stream that runs into the sea near the town—the Rubicon. Caesar's last taste of *brodetto* before becoming the most powerful man in the Roman Empire was probably very similar to the dish consumed in this region some 2,000 years later by another famous field general—Bernard Law Montgomery—during the Italian campaign of 1943. The Bolognese are pleased when such specialties please any visitor, regardless of rank.

Cheeses in Profusion

Save for a few faddists, Italians never have displayed much enthusiasm for a simple glass of fresh milk. Yet the national milk bucket is kept filled by more than 3.4 million cows and more than 7 million sheep, goats and water buffalo. Roughly half of all their milk goes into cheese, and Italy takes just pride in producing some of the most glorious and luxurious varieties on earth. They range from the rock-hard Parmesan *(below)* and the malleable *provolone (right),* both originated at least 1,000 years ago, to the soft and subtle Bel Paese, first made scarcely 50 years ago. And there are perhaps a hundred others, old and new, with local, national or international reputations for excellence. The great cheeses have the qualities of great wines. Noble in themselves, they enhance the savor of all other foods and so they appear everywhere in the Italian menu, sprinkled on soups and salads, cooked with the pasta, meat and vegetables, proud companion of fruits and true friend of the wine. The Italian kitchen could not exist without them.

A workman taps a wheel of Parmesan cheese with a hammer to make sure it is aging properly. When ready, the wheel gives off a distinctive thump recognizable to the trained ear.

Pig-shaped *provolone* cheeses honor the animal source of the hams and sausages that flavor many Bolognese dishes.

A Sampling of Cheeses

Displayed on the opposite page are 11 of the finest Italian cheeses available in the United States. Grouped below as grating, table (eating) or cooking cheeses, they are keyed by number to the picture.

Grating Cheeses

1 PARMIGIANO REGGIANO, the original Italian Parmesan, is salty and sharp, the world's only true seasoning cheese. It is produced in certain officially designated places in a small section of northern Italy, and is made, under carefully controlled conditions, only between April 15 and November 11. To be at its best, Parmesan should be grated just before use. When freshly cut and moist, it makes an excellent table cheese.

2 PECORINO ROMANO is a sharp cheese made of fresh sheep's milk curdled with lamb's rennet (the lining from the stomach of an unweaned lamb). Americans who like Italian cooking should know it well: it flavors the pasta in most Italian restaurants in the United States.

Table Cheeses

3 TALEGGIO, originally from the Bergamo area but now produced elsewhere, is made from dry, salted curds and has a slightly aromatic flavor.

4 FONTINA, among the greatest of cheeses, is a sweet and delicate semisoft product of the Valle d'Aosta at the foot of the Great St. Bernard pass. It blends magnificently with truffles in a hot, melted cheese *fonduta (page 156)*.

5 PROVOLONE, a variety of CACIOCAVALLO (6), is delicate and creamy for two or three months, spicy and sharp thereafter. Provolone is fashioned into many amusing shapes—pears, melons, little pigs, little people, sausages, saints, sinners and cylinders.

7 ASIAGO, sharp but palatable, is hard and granular and is made from two cow milkings. One milking is skimmed, the other partly skimmed.

8 GORGONZOLA, lightly spiced and sharp, ranks with the greatest veined cheeses. It is a *stracchino,* meaning that it is made from the milk of "tired" cows that had been grazing on Alpine slopes. At one time, many "tired" cows wintered at Gorgonzola near Milan, and there the bacteria-mottled masterpiece evolved. It is now produced mainly in the Po River flatlands.

9 BEL PAESE, a luxury cheese, soft, smooth and daintily flavored, was developed in the 1920s by the cheese-maker Egidio Galbani. The company he founded now makes it in Brazil and Wisconsin as well as in Italy.

Cooking Cheeses

10 RICOTTA, a fresh, moist, unsalted variety of cottage cheese, goes well in sandwiches, salads, *lasagne* and blintzes. Mixed with Marsala wine, *ricotta* makes an excellent and highly flavorful dessert.

11 MOZZARELLA, a pleasant, slightly sour cheese made from the milk of cows or water buffalo, is used often on pizza or, mixed with *ricotta,* in *lasagne.*

In the first step the curds, produced by adding a natural coagulant to the buffalo milk, are carefully broken up by hand into small pieces.

Cheese as the Italians Make It

The Italians devote a great deal of attention to the art of cheese making, for cheese is a basic ingredient in the cooking of all of its regions. In the north, the most important cooking cheese is *grana,* of which Parmesan is the most widely known variety; in the south, it is *mozzarella.* True *mozzarella* is made from buffalo milk. But, since cows vastly outnumber buffalo in Italy, cow's milk cheeses are more frequently produced. True *mozzarella* has a mellow flavor and can be eaten by itself at the end of a meal. The cow's milk varieties have a rather faint flavor and are suitable mainly for cooking (the *mozzarella* sold at Italian stores in the United States is made from cow's milk). Pictured on these pages is a small factory near Mondragone, about 25 miles from Naples, owned by the Puoti brothers. Here, in the traditional manner, only buffalo milk is used; and each step, from the initial forming of the curds to the molding of the finished cheeses, is meticulously carried out by hand.

Boiling water is poured over the curds by Renato Puoti to start another step in the cheese-making process. The hot water melts the curds, then blends with them to form a rubbery mixture.

Stirred with a paddle and a bowl, the rubbery mixture gradually approaches the proper consistency. As in virtually every other step in cheese making, the worker relies on his experience to tell him exactly when the mixture is ready.

Standing by a caldron of boiling water, Renato Puoti (*opposite*) checks the consistency of a nearly finished batch of *mozzarella:* it should be stringy and rubbery but not tough. Above, workers are molding the partly cooled mixture into individual balls of *mozzarella*. After further cooling in salted water, the completed cheeses will be wrapped in wax paper for shipment to market.

Lasagne Pasticciate
BAKED LASAGNE WITH MEAT AND CREAM SAUCES

To serve 6 to 8

LASAGNE
6 to 8 quarts water
1 tablespoon salt
½ pound *lasagne*

BESCIAMELLA FOR LASAGNE
6 tablespoons butter
6 tablespoons flour
2 cups milk
1 cup heavy cream
Pinch of ground nutmeg
1 teaspoon salt
3½ cups *ragù bolognese (below)*
½ cup freshly grated imported
   Parmesan cheese

LASAGNE: Generously butter the bottom and sides of a 9-by-12-by-3-inch serving casserole or baking dish. In a large soup pot or kettle, bring the water and salt to a bubbling boil over high heat. Add the *lasagne*, stirring gently for a few moments to prevent the strips from sticking together. Boil over high heat, stirring occasionally, until the *lasagne* is tender, but *al dente*, or somewhat resistant to the bite—the time may vary between 10 and 25 minutes, depending on whether you use homemade or commercial *lasagne*. Set the pot under cold running water for a few moments to cool the pasta. Then lay the strips side by side on paper towels to drain.

BESCIAMELLA FOR LASAGNE: In a heavy 2- to 3-quart saucepan, melt the butter over moderate heat and stir in the flour. Remove the pan from the heat and pour in the milk and cream all at once, beating with a wire whisk until the flour is partially dissolved. Return the pan to high heat and cook, stirring constantly with the whisk. When the sauce comes to a boil and thickens into a smooth cream, reduce the heat and simmer, still stirring, for 2 or 3 minutes. Remove from the heat and season with nutmeg and salt.

Preheat the oven to 350°. Spread a layer of *ragù bolognese* (made without the cream) about ¼ inch deep over the bottom of the casserole. Spread over it about 1 cup of *besciamella*. Lay one third of the *lasagne* on the *besciamella*, overlapping the strips slightly. Repeat the layers of *ragù, besciamella* and *lasagne* twice more; top with the rest of the *ragù* and *besciamella*. Sprinkle with grated cheese. Bake 30 minutes, or until the sauce is bubbling hot.

Ragù Bolognese
NORTH ITALIAN MEAT SAUCE

To make about 3½ cups

¼ pound smoked ham, coarsely chopped
   (about 1 cup)
1 cup coarsely chopped onions
¼ cup coarsely chopped carrots
½ cup coarsely chopped celery
4 tablespoons butter
2 tablespoons olive oil
¾ pound beef round, ground twice
¼ pound lean pork, ground twice
½ cup dry white wine
2 cups beef stock, fresh or canned
2 tablespoons tomato paste
½ pound chicken livers
1 cup heavy cream
Pinch of ground nutmeg
Salt
Freshly ground black pepper

Combine the chopped ham, onions, carrots and celery on a cutting board, and chop into very small pieces. (This mixture is called a *battuto*; when cooked it is a *soffritto*.) Melt 2 tablespoons of the butter over moderate heat in a heavy, 10- to 12-inch skillet. When the foam subsides, add the *battuto* and cook, stirring often, for 10 minutes, or until it is lightly browned. With a rubber spatula, put the *soffritto* in a heavy 3- to 4-quart saucepan. Heat 2 tablespoons of olive oil in the same skillet, and lightly brown the beef and pork over moderate heat, stirring constantly to break up any lumps. Pour in the wine, increase the heat, and boil briskly, still stirring constantly, until almost all liquid has cooked away. Add the meat to the *soffritto* in the saucepan, and stir in the stock and tomato paste. Bring to a boil over high heat, then reduce the heat and simmer, partially covered, for 45 minutes, stirring occasionally. Meanwhile, over high heat melt 2 more tablespoons of butter in the original skillet, and when the foam subsides, add the chicken livers. Cook for 3 or 4 minutes, or until firm and lightly browned. Chop the chicken livers into small dice, set aside, and add to the sauce 10 minutes before it is done. A few minutes before serving, stir in the cream and let it heat through. Taste the *ragù* and season with nutmeg, salt and pepper. Serve on pasta or—without the cream—use it in *lasagne pasticciate (above)*.

Tortellini

PASTA RINGS STUFFED WITH CHICKEN AND CHEESE

Mix the chicken, cheese, egg yolks, lemon peel and nutmeg in a large bowl until they are thoroughly combined. Season with salt and pepper. Break off ¼ of the pasta dough, and keep the rest moist by covering with foil or a damp cloth. Roll out the dough on a floured board until it is paper thin, then cut into 2-inch rounds with a biscuit cutter or a small glass. Place ¼ teaspoon of the chicken mixture in the center of each round. Moisten the edges of each round. Fold the circles in half and press the edges firmly together. Shape into little rings by stretching the tips of each half circle slightly and wrapping the ring around your index finger. Gently press the tips together. The *tortellini* are best if they are cooked at once, but they may be covered with plastic wrap and refrigerated for a day or so.

Bring the water and salt to a boil in a heavy pot or kettle. Drop in the *tortellini* and stir gently with a wooden spoon for a moment to make sure they do not stick to one another. Boil, stirring occasionally, for about 8 minutes, or until they are tender. Drain them into a large sieve or colander. Serve with *ragù bolognese (opposite)* or in hot beef or chicken stock.

To make about 80
(Serving 8 to 10)

FILLING

2¼ cups finely chopped cooked chicken (3 single chicken breasts, boned and skinned, and poached in stock for 15 minutes)
½ cup freshly grated imported Parmesan cheese
2 egg yolks, lightly beaten
⅛ teaspoon grated lemon peel
⅛ teaspoon ground nutmeg
Salt
Freshly ground black pepper

1 double recipe of pasta dough (*page 44*)
6 to 8 quarts water
Salt

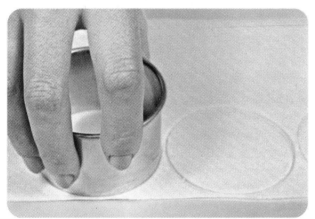

1 On a floured board, cut evenly rolled pasta dough into two-inch circles with a biscuit cutter or drinking glass.

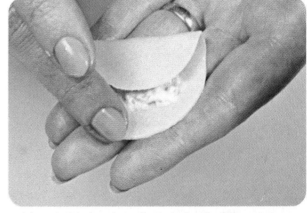

2 After wetting the edges of a circle, lay the filling on the top. Fold over. Wetted edges will adhere.

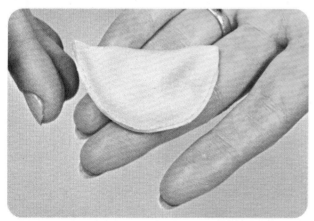

3 Gently press wetted edges together with fingertips to make certain that filling will not emerge during cooking.

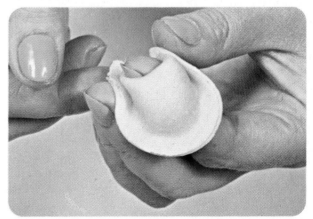

4 Now wrap the piece of dough around your finger and press ends together, forming a ring of the *tortellini*.

Cuscinetti di Vitello
BRAISED VEAL SCALLOPS WITH PROSCIUTTO- AND CHEESE-STUFFING

To serve 4

16 thin 4-inch-square veal scallops
8 thin 3½-inch-square slices Fontina or Gruyère cheese
8 thin 3-inch-square slices prosciutto
Salt
Freshly ground black pepper
Flour
2 tablespoons butter
3 tablespoons olive oil
½ cup dry white wine
¾ cup chicken or beef stock, fresh or canned

Place a square slice of cheese and a square of prosciutto on each one of eight veal scallops and top with the remaining scallops. The veal should cover the cheese and ham completely. Press the edges of the veal together and seal them by pounding with the flat of a cleaver or the bottom of a heavy bottle. Season with salt and pepper; dip them in flour and shake off the excess. In a heavy 10- to 12-inch skillet, melt the butter with the oil over moderate heat. When the foam subsides, add the *cuscinetti* 3 or 4 at a time and cook in the hot fat, turning gently with a slotted spoon or spatula until they are golden brown on both sides. As the *cuscinetti* are browned, transfer them to a platter.

Discard most of the fat from the skillet, leaving a thin film on the bottom. Pour in the wine and boil it briskly, stirring and scraping in any browned bits that cling to the skillet. Continue to boil until the wine has been reduced to about ¼ cup. Add ½ cup of stock and bring it to a simmer. Then return the veal to the skillet, cover, and simmer 20 minutes over low heat, turning the *cuscinetti* over after 10 minutes. Transfer the *cuscinetti* to a heated serving platter, and add the remaining ¼ cup of stock to the skillet. Bring the stock and the pan juices to a boil, and let them cook briskly for a minute or so. Taste and season the sauce with salt and pepper, then pour the sauce over the *cuscinetti* and serve.

Involtini alla Cacciatora
ROLLED VEAL SCALLOPS WITH CHICKEN LIVER STUFFING

To serve 4 to 6

2 tablespoons butter
¼ pound chicken livers
1 ounce prosciutto, cut in tiny pieces
1 green scallion stem, finely chopped
2 teaspoons finely chopped fresh parsley
⅛ teaspoon sage leaves, crumbled
⅛ teaspoon salt
Freshly ground black pepper
1 pound veal scallops, sliced ⅜ inch thick and pounded ¼ inch thick, then cut into 4-by-4-inch squares (about 12 squares)
Flour
2 tablespoons butter
3 tablespoons olive oil
½ cup dry Marsala
1 cup chicken stock, fresh or canned

Over moderate heat melt 2 tablespoons of butter in a heavy 8- to 10-inch skillet. When the foam subsides, add the livers and cook them, turning frequently, for 4 or 5 minutes, or until they stiffen and are lightly browned. Cut them into ¼-inch cubes and place them in a large bowl. Sauté the prosciutto and scallions in the same skillet for about 2 minutes, adding more butter if necessary. Then, with a rubber spatula, scrape them into the bowl of livers, and add the parsley, sage, salt and a few grindings of pepper. Stir together gently and taste for seasoning.

Place about 2 tablespoons of the chicken-liver mixture on the bottom third of each veal scallop. Roll up the scallops and tie both ends with soft string. Dip the rolls in flour, then shake off the excess. Melt 2 tablespoons of butter with the oil in a heavy 10- to 12-inch skillet. When the foam subsides, add the veal rolls, 4 or 5 at a time, and cook over moderate heat, turning them frequently, until they are golden brown on all sides, transferring them to a plate when done. Now discard almost all of the fat from the skillet, leaving a thin film on the bottom. Pour in the wine and ¾ cup of chicken stock, and boil briskly for 1 or 2 minutes, scraping in any browned fragments clinging to the pan.

Return the veal to the skillet, reduce the heat, cover and simmer, basting once or twice with pan juices, for 15 minutes, or until the veal is tender when pierced with the tip of a sharp knife. With tongs, transfer the veal to a heated serving platter. Pour the remaining stock into the skillet and boil briskly, until the liquid has reduced to ½ cup and thickened slightly. Pour it over the veal rolls and serve.

Costolette di Maiale alla Modenese
PORK CHOPS BRAISED IN WHITE WINE

Combine the sage, rosemary, garlic, salt and a few grindings of pepper and press a little of this mixture firmly into both sides of each pork chop. In a heavy 10- to 12-inch skillet, melt the butter with the olive oil over moderate heat. When the foam subsides, place the chops in the hot fat and brown them for 2 or 3 minutes on each side, turning them carefully with tongs. When the chops are golden brown, remove them from the pan to a platter. Pour off all but a thin film of fat from the pan, add ½ cup of the wine and bring it to a boil. Return the chops to the pan, cover and reduce the heat to the barest simmer. Basting with the pan juices occasionally, cook the chops for 25 to 30 minutes, or until they are tender when pierced with the tip of a sharp knife. Transfer the chops to a heated platter, skim off all the fat from the braising liquid, and pour the remaining ¼ cup of wine into the skillet. Boil briskly over high heat, scraping in any browned bits that cling to the bottom and sides of the pan, until it has reduced to a few tablespoons of syrupy glaze. Remove the skillet from the heat. Taste for seasoning and stir in the parsley. Pour the sauce over the pork chops and serve.

To serve 4

1 teaspoon dried sage leaves, crumbled
1 teaspoon dried rosemary leaves, crumbled
1 teaspoon finely chopped garlic
1 teaspoon salt
Freshly ground black pepper
4 center-cut loin pork chops, about 1 inch thick
2 tablespoons butter
1 tablespoon olive oil
¾ cup dry white wine
1 tablespoon finely chopped fresh parsley, preferably the flat-leaf Italian type

Petti di Pollo alla Bolognese
BONED CHICKEN BREASTS WITH PROSCIUTTO AND CHEESE

Preheat the oven to 350°. With a very sharp knife, carefully slice each chicken breast horizontally to make 8 thin slices. Lay them an inch or so apart on a long strip of wax paper and cover them with another strip of wax paper. Pound the chicken slices lightly with the flat of a cleaver or the bottom of a heavy bottle to flatten them somewhat. Strip off the paper. Season the slices with salt and a few grindings of pepper, then dip them in flour and shake off the excess. In a heavy 10- to 12-inch skillet, melt the butter with the oil over moderate heat. Brown the chicken to a light golden color in the hot fat, 3 or 4 slices at a time. Do not overcook them.

Transfer the chicken breasts to a shallow buttered baking-and-serving dish large enough to hold them comfortably. Place a slice of prosciutto and then a slice of cheese on each one. Sprinkle them with grated cheese and dribble the chicken stock over them. Bake uncovered in the middle of the oven for about 10 minutes, or until the cheese is melted and lightly browned. Serve at once.

To serve 4

4 individual chicken breasts, ½ pound each, skinned and boned
Salt
Freshly ground black pepper
Flour
3 tablespoons butter
2 tablespoons oil
8 thin 2-by-4-inch slices prosciutto
8 thin 2-by-4-inch slices imported Fontina or Bel Paese cheese
4 teaspoons freshly grated imported Parmesan cheese
2 tablespoons chicken stock, fresh or canned

Slice the filleted breasts as indicated in the picture above.

Cover fillets with wax paper; pound them thin with the flat of a cleaver.

After the fillets have been browned, cover them with prosciutto and cheese.

VI

Venice and the Northeast

For a pleasant surprise, the traveler journeying to Venice for the first time should take the train. On the last leg of the trip, between Mestre on the mainland and Venice out in the lagoon, all that can be glimpsed through the window are a few masts and a crane or two—skyline features like those of every port in the world. The train arrives in a station that is like every big-city station—trains pulling in and out, loudspeakers bawling, a hubbub of hurrying travelers, long caterpillars of freight-laden carts, porters with loads of baggage. The mind automatically sets the scene for what must be outside the railroad station—what is always outside such a station in Italy: a square with buses and cars wheeling in eccentric patterns and streams of pedestrians overflowing the sidewalks and recklessly pitting their lives against motor scooters and taxis.

Not in Venice. There, the traveler steps through the station portals and lo—instead of a teeming, landlocked square, there are half a dozen wide steps stretching the whole length of the building and leading down into water. Along the bottom of the steps, the tall bows of gondolas bob up and down in the choppy wakes of motor boats. Before the eye lies the incredible spectacle of the Grand Canal, which Goethe called "the most beautiful street in the world." It leads to the culinary center of the city, the Piazza San Marco, which Napoleon, another traveler given to superlatives, characterized as the most elegant ballroom in Europe. On the canal, in the piazza itself and in the narrow streets behind the bell tower of St. Mark's basilica are some of the finest restaurants in Europe.

Almost all the buildings on the Grand Canal, except the churches and

Coffee and ice cream are served in Florian's, one of the famous and elegant cafés within the arcades that line the Piazza San Marco in Venice. The Venetians, who introduced coffee to Western Europe, still prepare and serve the beverage with an almost reverential care.

public edifices, are palaces. They remain the substantive evidence of the tremendous riches of Venice, reminders that this, in its medieval heyday, was the most brilliant, the most glittering, the most spectacular city in the world, the city that once "held the gorgeous East in fee." Its wealth and its palaces were built on trade monopolies in what were then rare foods: sugar, salt, pepper, spices, coffee. And the city that supplied these commodities to the rest of the European world made lavish use of them at home, establishing a subtle and ingenious school of cooking—a finished cuisine enriched by contributions from the lands brought under the control of Venice when her riches and power were at their height.

Of the three regions associated with Venice, only Veneto, where the city lies, has pure Italian cooking. The cooking of the Trentino-Alto Adige region, to the northwest, once owned by Austria-Hungary, is largely Austro-German. Still farther afield, Friuli-Venezia Giulia, which occupies part of the Dalmatian coast in the neighborhood of Trieste, offers overtones of Austrian, Hungarian, Slavic and Balkan cuisines on its menus. These influences are a natural consequence of the fact that Venice once controlled the entire Yugoslav coast and Trieste was once the Austro-Hungarian Empire's Adriatic seaport.

Today, the foreigner who visits Venice creates a demand for what he calls "Italian" food, and the demand is met. What he gets is Italian, certainly, but it is not necessarily Venetian.

Nevertheless, Venice has not abandoned all its culinary traditions to the demands of the tourist trade. It would be difficult to find a more representative Venetian menu than the meal I ate one September at the Colomba restaurant. It began with a white-fleshed Mediterranean fish, *orata*, cooked with mussels and crayfish, and seasoned with a mixture of curry, a touch of tomato extract, marjoram, nutmeg and capers. This was followed by *fegato alla veneziana*—well-peppered calf's liver sautéed with onions *(page 117)*. The combination of liver and onions is encountered in many parts of the world, but the Venetians claim to have invented it. The question is academic; it is a fact that while liver is often a coarse dish elsewhere, in Venice it is a delicate delight. Mine, happily, was accompanied by the *polenta* of the region—not the yellow *polenta* found in most other parts of northern Italy, but one of a fine white texture, made from the white maize grown in Friuli-Venezia Giulia.

My basic Venetian meal was accompanied by local wines—a white Casteller and a red Merlot, both from the Trentino-Alto Adige region. The white was light, dry and fruity, like a Rhine wine. The red was warm, with plenty of body, but slightly piquant. The wines from the Trentino-Alto Adige often reflect the tastes of its people, so long under Austrian rule. Veneto, the Friuli-Venezia Giulia and the Trentino-Alto Adige all produce a wide range of wines. The whole northeastern area, except for the high mountain wall to the north, which shields it from the cold winds, is remarkable wine country. The proprietor of the Apicio restaurant in the Hotel Metropole in Rome once invited me to a dinner at which he selected three of the finest wines produced near Venice: the excellent white Pusterla Valle d'Oro, the heartier white Vaspaiolo, and a strong rosé, Cerasuolo del Piave. Many of the wines from the neighborhood of Venice are exported. Among the very best travelers are Soave, Valpolicella and Bardolino *(all shown on page 77)*.

Commendatore A. Deana, owner of the Colomba and a lover of modern art, had filled the walls of his restaurant with contemporary paintings, and the cover of the menu was designed by the distinguished artist Giorgio de Chirico who happened to be lunching there the same day that I was present. The meal that I ordered, itself a work of art, lacked only two dishes to be the ideal, classic Venetian repast: *scampi* and *risi e bisi* (rice and peas), the most characteristic of all Venetian dishes *(page 117)*. For the latter, it was the wrong season. The true Venetian insists that the peas be young, fresh and tender, which means that *risi e bisi* is available only in spring; the purist also demands that the peas come from fields near the shores of the Venetian lagoon between Chioggia and Burano. The rice and peas are cooked in chicken or meat stock, and the dish has a definite liquid consistency; you can start an argument any time on whether *risi e bisi* is a vegetable dish or a soup. Whichever it is, a fork is usually supplied to eat it with, even in restaurants that list the dish with the soups.

Scampi are served in a seeming infinity of fashions: they can, for instance, be combined with other forms of seafood, in a *brodetto*, rolled in slices of ham, or boiled, cooled and served with a dressing of olive oil, lemon juice, salt and pepper. *Scampi* can be baked in the oven or fried, or—as I have grown to prefer them over the years—grilled in butter and garlic *(page 116)*. The American cook need not worry about not being able to buy genuine Venetian *scampi*: anything that can be done with them can also be done with American shrimp.

Scampi, extraordinary though they are, are imitated everywhere, but there is one seafood specialty of Venice that I have encountered nowhere else: oysters with caviar. The caviar comes not from Russia but from the sturgeon of the Po, Italy's largest river, which reaches the Adriatic in Veneto. The secret of preparing this dish is to give its two ingredients time to exchange flavors. You open the oyster, cover it with caviar and season it with lemon juice and pepper (some use cayenne pepper). Then put the top shell back on and return the oysters to ice or the refrigerator for several hours before serving.

Among the fish dishes of Venice, many are known by Venetian dialect names that sound strange even to other Italians: *sfogie in saòr* (sole with herb sauce); *sardoni a scotadeo* (fresh sardines spitted, roasted, basted and served with lemon juice); and *bisato in tecia* (eels with tomatoes and herbs, served with fried bread covered with Parmesan cheese). The Venetians do a great many other things with eels. The eel dish that bears the city's name, *anguilla alla veneziana*, is served with tuna and lemon juice. Another favorite is *anguilla marinata*, eels marinated in oil and vinegar *(page 117)*.

Salt or dried cod is one very popular variety of fish that seems somewhat out of place in a city on the ocean, where fresh seafood is always available. But the Venetian predilection for preserved cod is shared with all the southwestern European countries; it is found on the Basque coast of northern Spain and in Portugal, in southern France, in Sicily and in many other parts of Italy. The Normans—who knew of it from their Viking heritage—bestowed this dish on southern Europe; it was virtually their only contribution to Latin cooking. As a result, Venice provides many varieties of dishes that involve *stoccafisso* (the cod are imported from Norway, where they are suspended from racks of sticks for drying and hence are called "stick

Venice's menu, like Venice itself, arises from the sea. A favorite dish is shrimplike *scampi* with *risi e bisi* (rice and peas). Padua has squash-plant-flower fritters; Rovigo, beets; Vicenza, turkeys; Verona, golden bread cake with Italian cranberries; Treviso, *radicchio* (lettuce) for salads. Trentino-Alto Adige's diet is Austrian. Friuli-Venezia Giulia mixes Slavic dishes with Austrian.

fish"—in Norwegian, *stokkfisk*). *Baccalà* is a slightly different type of preserved cod, which has been salted and then slowly dried on rocks in the sun; it forms the basis of a number of Venetian dishes, including *baccalà mantecato* (creamed cod) and *baccalà alla vicentina* (dried cod cooked in milk and flavored with onion, garlic and anchovies, plus cinnamon and a scattering of other spices).

Fish may preoccupy the palates of dwellers on the coast, but even a short distance inland, the cuisine is dominated by rice—though seafood is often built into rice dishes, as in *risotto con scampi (page 116)*. For centuries Venice dominated the greater part of the Po Valley, which is rice country, and there is an endless list of Venetian rice dishes; most of them, like *risi e bisi,* are extremely moist. An exception is *riso ai gamberi*—boiled rice, light and dry, with a sauce of shrimp, garlic, olive oil, pepper and tomato sauce. "The people of Veneto, and especially the Venetians, like *risotto-all'onda* [wavelike risotto], a fashion of naming a dish that could occur only to a seafaring people," the Italian gastronome Giuseppe Mazzotti wrote in *Le Vie d'Italia* in 1965.

A phenomenon among Venetian rice dishes is *risi con la ua* (Venetian dialect meaning "rice with grapes"). Since fresh table grapes of the Malaga type are used, one might expect that sugar would then be added to produce a rich dessert. Not at all. The other ingredients are garlic, oil and parsley, and the finished dish is smothered under grated Parmesan cheese.

A gondolier propels his boat along one of the small canals of Venice, delivering vegetables to shops and restaurants. While motorboats now crowd the Venetian canals, gondolas still serve as delivery trucks and taxis—for riders who are in no rush.

Among other rice combinations are "white" and "black" rice. *Risotto bianco,* a hearty dish, is usually served with fish and is not to be confused with *riso in bianco* (rice in a broth)—called "white" because it contains no tomato and is recommended for dyspeptics. *Risotto nero,* or *risotto con le seppie,* is made with cuttlefish, whose "ink" dyes the rice black. This dish, Mazzotti writes, "causes the brows of novices to knit suspiciously, and their noses to wrinkle; nevertheless, at the second mouthful, they almost always allow themselves to be conquered by the rare flavor of this dish, alarming as it is to the eye."

The eye, in Italy, is much more likely to be beguiled than alarmed, and for visual charm there are few places that can rival the colorful cities once conquered and long ruled by the Venetian Republic. All are close to the culinary tradition of Venice; each has added local dishes and raw materials to the regional menu. Padua, where Galileo taught in a university started in 1222, contributed *fiori di zucca alla padovana,* fritters of squash-plant flowers, and *soare,* a sort of marmalade made from grape must (the juice before and during fermentation), pears and apples. But there are many good things in Padua, among them fine omelets, beefsteaks with mushrooms in wine sauce, and all manner of coffees. They range from coal black *espresso* to pale brown *cappuccino,* which is named for the color of the robes of Capuchin monks. Paduans also like *caffè alla Borgia,* which is coffee laced with apricot brandy, and sprinkled with cinnamon.

Rovigo, another of the old Venetian Republic cities, is the center of the area known as Polesine, from the Latin *Pullicinium,* meaning land that has emerged from the sea. More exactly, it is land built up from silt deposited by the Po and Adige Rivers—silt that has interposed 14 miles of rich alluvial soil between the present coast and the port of Adria (active from about 600 B.C. through the Fourth Century A.D.), which gave its name to the Adriatic. This area is naturally agricultural; from its sugar beets are produced 100,000 tons of sugar a year. Vicenza, whose 16th Century resident architect, Palladio, deeply influenced the work of such English masters as Christopher Wren, is a graceful city set in a handsome landscape. It is the center of turkey country. The town holds an annual fair that used to feature a cruel game in which blindfolded contestants tried to bash in a turkey's head with long staffs. Today, the worst fate a Vicenza turkey faces is to be served up *con sugo di melagrana* (with pomegranate sauce).

Everybody knows Verona as the city of Romeo and Juliet. There is even a Romeo and Juliet restaurant there, its walls decorated with frescoes telling the lovers' story. Guides in Verona, undeterred by the fact that the lovers were fictional, will show you Juliet's tomb and Romeo's and Juliet's houses. Verona has additional literary associations; in it the great medieval poet Dante Alighieri, banished from his native Florence, found sanctuary and in his honor there is a square in the city called the Piazza Dante and a splendid 18th Century-style café called the Caffè Dante. There one can sample a glory of Verona that all but rivals its Roman antiquities. This is its *pandoro,* the most popular cake of the whole Veneto region, a mouth-melting confection delicately flavored with vanilla. It goes well with a fruit dessert, *mirtillo,* that lingers in my memory from the famous Restaurant of the Twelve Apostles in Verona. The *mirtillo* is a tiny, tart, red berry that looks like a small cranberry and tastes like one, although its flavor is subtler

The *espresso* machine affords the quickest way of making the strong, dark coffee that Italians love. A battery of machines like this one can meet the demands of a large restaurant.

than that of the American variety. It is nonetheless distantly related to American cranberries and blueberries.

In the market of Verona, everything from persimmons to potatoes, from chestnuts to quail, is spread out under brightly striped umbrellas that are set up to protect the merchandise from the sun. Buxom market women adorn their hair with a leaf or two of lettuce. Shoppers munch *bombolini,* hunger-quelling *gnocchi* coated with bread crumbs fished by vendors out of bubbling pots of fat. And the appropriately named Piazza delle Erbe (Square of Herbs), in which the market is located, has for the foreigner the special attraction of typifying the continuity between past and present that is one of the characteristics of the contemporary Italian scene. The market stalls are grouped around a pre-Christian Roman fountain and a 16th Century Venetian column, all dominated by the medieval palaces that surround the Piazza delle Erbe.

Attractive as the market of Verona is, I prefer the markets of Treviso, which occupy a series of adjoining squares. In olden times the Doges and aristocracy of Venice moved in the summers to cooler Treviso, "the garden of Venice." The tradition of fine cooking and good living therefore took root in the latter city, and today many connoisseurs contend that the finest traditional food can be found only in Treviso. A walk through Treviso's markets might well begin behind the Piazza dei Signori (Gentlemen's Square), where there is an outdoor emporium devoted solely to mushrooms, chiefly the little orange ones that grow under the pines in the surrounding hills. Round a corner, and you are in the vegetable and fruit market. Turn another, and you reach the fish market, conveniently located alongside the canals, into which refuse is tossed. Such a method of disposing of garbage does not turn the canals into sewers as it does in Venice (where the small side canals tend to become stagnant, unaffected by the negligible tides). The Canals of Treviso served the purpose of carrying the fast-running streams from the mountains through the city to the sea, and they remain clean and pure even as they carry away the refuse from the fish market to the ravenous gulls, who wheel through the sky and dive down for it.

In the late fall and winter, the vegetable market of Treviso is gay with *radicchio,* a lettucelike plant that is found nowhere else in the world. A specialty of the Treviso district, it comes in two varieties, one from the environs of Treviso itself and the other from Castelfranco Veneto, in the southwestern corner of the province. Whichever the variety, *radicchio* is both pretty and edible. *Un fiore che si mangia* (a flower to eat) was a phrase used by a local poet to describe it; *re delle insalate* (king of salads) is another. The decorative quality of *radicchio* faces the buyer with a difficult choice: whether to keep it to look at or to eat it—a dilemma expressed in a local jingle: *"Se lo guardi, egli e un sorriso; / Se lo mangi e un paradiso: / Il radicchio di Treviso."* This might be translated (very freely): "If you keep it, that is nice; / Eat it, and it's paradise: / The *radicchio* of Treviso."

The Treviso *radicchio* is shaped rather like a delicate form of romaine lettuce and is a light red, almost a rose, with white veins. The Castelfranco variety has the form of a camellia and is pink, but not uniformly so, showing dark streaks against a light ground, and has a blander, sweeter taste. Some restaurants mix the two types together and call the result "Treviso salad," which infuriates the purists—and they are many—of Treviso. The two *radicchi* are quite distinct—in the local tradition, anyway—and should be kept separate, even on the table.

Tradition is high among the values of Friuli-Venezia Giulia. Stubbornly maintaining the ancient ways of a sober, hard-working and undemonstrative population, the Friuliese still make their own bread instead of buying it from a bakery, and concentrate their family life and their renowned hospitality around the *fogher*—the hearth or open stove. This often stands in the center of the kitchen, with a flared hood above that carries off smoke and odors and is surrounded by a beautifully wrought iron grill from which are suspended the pots, kettles, spits and other utensils needed for cooking over the exposed flame.

As basic and traditionally Italian as are the gastronomic values of Friuli-Venezia Giulia, there are also strong non-Italian influences in some parts of the northeast, which is bordered by Slav territory on the east and Germanic on the north in what was once the Austro-Hungarian Empire. Thus there are islands of Germanic cooking in Veneto, along with somewhat rarer instances of Hungarian and Balkan dishes.

The Trentino-Alto Adige was the Austrian South Tyrol before World War I, and—apart from the famous San Daniele prosciutto, air-cured like Parma ham—a typical menu recalls the German cuisine. Although some of the names have been Italianized, others have not changed at all: *schnecken-suppe* and *saure suppe* (snail soup and tripe soup); *wurstel* and *sauerbraten* (sausage and meat cooked in a vinegar sauce). *Strudel* and *Tiroler Krapfen* are a pastry and a cake widely known throughout the world by their German names. It may take a bit longer to recognize *crauti* as Italianized sauerkraut.

Another name of non-Italian origin found on the Alto Adige menu is *gulasch* (easily recognizable as goulash). This Hungarian dish presumably reached the Alto Adige via Austria, after having first invaded the Austrian cuisine. But the dish is also found in Trieste, on the Yugoslav border, not far from Hungarian territory.

Trieste is a town of gusty winds often so high and strong that the police must string ropes along the streets so that the pedestrians can cling to them and slowly pull themselves along, thus working up an appetite for the city's hearty cuisine, which owes a number of dishes to the Hungarians, including a mixture of two cheeses (Gorgonzola and *mascarpone*) creamed together and seasoned with crushed anchovy, caraway seeds, leeks and mustard. Trieste's geographical position, which opens it to invasion from many different cuisines, gives it a highly varied menu. I have a cookbook called *Trieste Cooking* that lists 1,182 recipes. The book claims that they are all dishes regularly served in Trieste, but their origins are diverse. Some of them are described by names too far removed to be taken seriously as anything more than faddish borrowings—e.g., "Portuguese butter" (with egg and tomato extract) and "Swedish jelly roll." But the many dishes with Balkan names and descriptions in the cookbook may be presumed to bear them honestly—artichokes or cucumbers Greek-style (with oil, lemon juice, celery, bay leaves and fennel seeds), *jota* (a rib-sticking soup of beans, corn meal and cabbage, to which some cooks add pork crackling—the crisp, smoked rind of the animal), or *gnocchi* with *powidl* (prunes).

When it comes to the Balkan influence in Italian food, the most famous single dish is not a specialty of Trieste but is found surprisingly far west—in

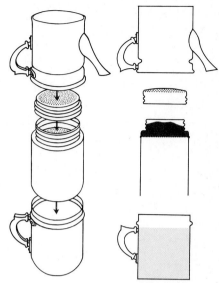

Italian coffee can be made at home in a drip pot, or *napoletana:* Fill the basket of the inner cylinder with finely ground Italian-roast coffee and attach filter; fill outer cylinder with water.

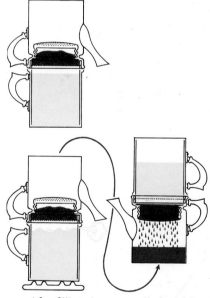

After filling the outer cylinder with water, put inner cylinder in it. Place the spouted vessel on top, spout pointing downward. Bring to a boil over low heat. Then turn the *napoletana* over, so that the spout points upward, and let the water drip through.

In a country restaurant near Treviso, chicken, quail and other game birds are roasted on a stove that stands clear of the wall, so that it may heat the room as well as cook. Called a *fogher*, its spits are moved at varying speeds by clockworks. The cook uses flaming lard to baste the birds.

the Trentino-Alto Adige. This is the so-called Elephant Platter, served at the Elefante hotel in Bressanone. It is derived from the nearly national Serbian dish *Balkanska plosca*, which features all sorts of meats heaped over a mound of seasoned rice—"a strange mixture of field and forest, of bitter and sweet, of coarse and delicate, of hot and cold, of damp and dry, of light and heavy." The words are those of Petrarch, who was talking about banquets in the 14th Century, but they apply equally well to the Elephant Platter as it is served at the Elefante.

Local lore does not tell how the dish came from Serbia to Bressanone, and in any case the management of the hotel that serves the Platter does not seem to be aware of its Balkan origin. But if it seems odd to find a Balkan dish so far afield, it is not much stranger than to find it in an Alpine setting bearing the name of an animal that exemplifies the tropical and the exotic. The Elephant Platter, to explain the matter, gets its name from an elephant named Solomon that reached Bressanone in the 16th Century, a period when, it is safe to say, no elephant had been seen within hundreds of miles (the Carthaginian invader Hannibal brought his war elephants into Italy in 217 B.C., and though nobody knows exactly where he crossed the Alps, it was almost certainly well west of Bressanone).

Solomon arrived in the fall of 1551. A gift from John III of Portugal to Maximilian of Austria, he was making his way overland from Genoa to Vienna, escorted by a retinue of handlers. At Bressanone, Solomon's companions learned that the Brenner Pass was blocked with snow, so they put up for the winter at the Heberge Hohen Feld, a hostelry to which no particular attention had been paid since its founding in 1420. Solomon put the

place on the map. When the snow melted, and Solomon moved on, the owner of the hotel changed its name to honor his most illustrious guest, and it has been the Elefante ever since.

The Elephant Platter served there is truly elephantine in proportions, and in fact consists of three platters. First comes an appetizer tray, laden with sardines, tuna fish, hard-boiled eggs with mayonnaise, prosciutto, salami, assorted sausages, sliced tomatoes, a selection of salads—a mammoth *antipasto*. The second course is a platter three feet long heaped with meat and vegetables; they may vary from time to time, but the rule is that there must be at least six different kinds of meat and 12 vegetable concoctions. One assortment I sampled included grilled steaks, hamburger, pork chops, mutton chops, lamb chops, veal steaks, grilled liver, boiled ham and fish roe— accompanied by sauerkraut, rice, potatoes (cooked five different ways), macaroni, spaghetti, peas, carrots, spinach, grilled tomatoes, beans, zucchini, lettuce and cucumbers. Whether anyone is still hungry, the third platter is completely irresistible; it offers a selection of cheeses, stewed fruits, cakes and fresh fruit.

If you have it in mind to go to Bressanone and order the Elephant Platter, take plenty of company with you. The hotel's cooks won't make the platter for fewer than four guests, and they prefer more. There is a local legend that one customer showed up alone, insisted on the Elephant Platter and ate it all by himself, on a bet; he won the bet, but died afterwards. The management of the Elefante takes a dim view of this story. "Of course he died afterwards," they say. "Everybody dies afterwards. He died a long time afterwards. Hardening of the arteries."

The kitchen of the 18th Century Villa Piovene, near Vicenza, is still in daily use and still looks much as it did when the house was built. The cook (*at sink in rear*), who has worked for the villa's owners for 50 years, accepts a gas range, but her best dishes are cooked at the open hearth.

A hand coffee grinder, a balance scale and an array of copper pans are part of the villa's collection of old kitchenware. During World War II the copper pans, adjudged unique as a collection, escaped confiscation by the Italian government. The collection has since been kept intact.

Even older than the kitchen itself is the kitchen sink— a 16th Century pink marble fountain originally carved for a nearby monastery and later adapted for use at the villa. The cook washes her pots, pans and dishes in the two wooden tubs, then stacks them in racks to dry.

113

To serve 6 to 8

2 pounds fish heads, bones and
    trimmings
3 cups water
1 cup dry white wine
⅔ cup sliced onions
2 celery tops with leaves
3 parsley sprigs
1 bay leaf
¼ teaspoon dried thyme
½ cup olive oil
2 pounds each of 3 kinds of white fish
    fillets or steaks—such as haddock,
    flounder, cod, perch, pollack,
    snapper, mackerel, bass or rockfish
    —cut into 2-inch serving pieces
⅛ teaspoon powdered saffron or
    crumbled saffron threads
1 cup coarsely chopped fresh tomato
    pulp (about 1 pound tomatoes,
    peeled, seeded and gently squeezed)
3 tablespoons finely chopped fresh
    parsley
1 teaspoon finely chopped garlic
½ teaspoon dried oregano, crumbled
1 teaspoon salt
Freshly ground black pepper
1 tablespoon freshly grated lemon
    peel

Zuppa di Pesce
FISH SOUP

When cooked, this dish does not provide as much liquid—for the number of people it serves—as a conventional soup might seem to require; it is more a dish of fish served in a seasoned liquid. It is nevertheless eaten as a soup, with a spoon.

In a 4- to 6-quart enameled or stainless-steel saucepan, combine fish heads, bones and trimmings with water and wine. Bring to a boil over high heat, skimming off any foam that rises to the surface. Add the onions, celery tops, parsley sprigs, bay leaf and thyme and return stock to a boil. Reduce

the heat and simmer uncovered for 20 minutes. Strain the stock through a fine sieve into a bowl or saucepan, pressing down hard with a spoon on the fish trimmings and vegetables to extract their juices before discarding them.

Heat the olive oil in a heavy 4- to 5-quart flameproof serving casserole until a light haze forms over it. Brown the fish in the oil over moderately high heat for only 2 or 3 minutes on each side. Tip the casserole and, with a bulb baster, remove all but 2 or 3 tablespoons of oil. Stir the saffron into the strained fish stock and add it, the tomatoes, 1 tablespoon of chopped parsley, garlic, oregano, salt and a few grindings of pepper to the casserole. Bring to a simmer, stirring gently, then reduce the heat, cover and cook 5 to 8 minutes, or until the fish is just firm and flakes easily when pierced with a fork. Be careful not to overcook. Taste and season with more salt and pepper, if needed, and sprinkle the top with the remaining chopped parsley and the grated lemon peel. Serve the soup from the casserole.

Some of the flavorful elements used to produce *zuppa di pesce* are shown here. Above are the makings for the soup stock. Shown at the left are steaks cut from three different fish—mackerel, bass and red snapper.

To serve 6 to 8

1 pound medium-sized fresh shrimp
   in their shells or thoroughly
   defrosted frozen shrimp
2 pounds fish heads and trimmings
2 quarts water
½ cup dry white wine
2 small onions, sliced
1 carrot, sliced
2 parsley sprigs
1 bay leaf
5 tablespoons butter
½ teaspoon finely chopped garlic
2 cups plain white raw rice, preferably
   imported Italian rice
4 tablespoons soft butter
½ cup freshly grated imported
   Parmesan cheese

Risotto con Scampi
BRAISED RICE WITH SHRIMP

Shell the shrimp carefully and save the shells. With a small sharp knife, slit each shrimp down the back and lift out the black or white intestinal vein. Wash the shrimp quickly under cold running water and dry them on paper towels.

In a 3- to 4-quart glass or enameled saucepan combine the shrimp shells, fish heads and trimmings, water and wine. Bring to a boil over high heat, removing the scum as it rises to the surface. Add the onions, carrot, parsley and bay leaf, reduce the heat and simmer partially covered, skimming the stock occasionally, for 30 minutes. Remove from the heat and strain the stock through a fine sieve into another saucepan, pressing down hard on the trimmings and vegetables with the back of a spoon to extract their juices before discarding them. Set the pan of strained stock over low heat and let it barely simmer.

In a heavy 8- to 10-inch skillet melt 1 tablespoon of butter over moderate heat. Toss in the shrimp and garlic and cook, stirring frequently, for 2 or 3 minutes, or until the shrimp are pink. Cover and set them aside.

Melt the remaining 4 tablespoons of butter over moderate heat in a heavy 3-quart flameproof casserole. Add the 2 cups of rice and cook, stirring constantly, for 2 or 3 minutes, or until the grains become somewhat opaque. Add 2 cups of the simmering stock and cook the rice uncovered over moderate heat, stirring occasionally, until almost all the liquid is absorbed. Add another 2 cups of stock and cook, stirring again, until it is absorbed. Then add 2 more cups of stock. When this is absorbed, the rice should be tender. If, however, the rice is still too firm, add more stock—½ cup at a time—and continue cooking and stirring until the rice is done.

With a fork, gently stir in the shrimp and garlic and the juice that will have accumulated in the skillet. Then stir in 4 tablespoons of soft butter and, finally, the freshly grated Parmesan cheese. Serve the *risotto con scampi* at once while it is creamy and hot.

To serve 6

2 pounds large fresh shrimp in their
   shells or defrosted frozen shrimp
8 tablespoons (1 quarter-pound stick)
   of butter
½ cup olive oil
1 tablespoon lemon juice
¼ cup finely chopped shallots or
   scallions
1 tablespoon finely chopped garlic
1 teaspoon salt
Freshly ground black pepper
4 tablespoons finely chopped fresh
   parsley, preferably the flat-leaf
   Italian type
Lemon quarters

Scampi alla Griglia
BROILED SHRIMP WITH GARLIC BUTTER

Shell the shrimp, but be careful not to remove the last small segment of shell or the tail. With a small sharp knife, slit each shrimp down the back and lift out the black or white intestinal vein. Wash the shrimp quickly under cold running water and pat them thoroughly dry with paper towels.

Preheat the broiler to its highest temperature. In a shallow flameproof baking dish or pan just large enough to hold the shrimp in one layer, melt the butter over low heat, and be careful not to let it brown. Stir in the ½ cup of olive oil, lemon juice, shallots, garlic, salt and a few grindings of pepper, add the shrimp and turn them in the butter and oil until they glisten on all sides. Broil them 3 to 4 inches from the heat for 5 minutes, then turn the shrimp over and broil them for 5 to 10 minutes longer, or until they are lightly browned and firm to the touch. Be careful not to overcook them. With tongs, transfer the shrimp to a heated serving platter, pour the sauce from the pan over them, and sprinkle with chopped parsley. Garnish with lemon quarters, and serve.

Risi e Bisi

BRAISED RICE AND PEAS

Bring the chicken stock to a simmer in a 2- to 3-quart saucepan and keep it barely simmering over low heat. In a heavy 3-quart flameproof casserole, melt 4 tablespoons of butter over moderate heat. Add the onions and cook, stirring frequently until they are transparent but not browned. Add the peas, rice and diced ham. Cook for a minute or 2. When the rice grains are buttery and somewhat opaque, add 2 cups of the simmering stock and cook uncovered for about 5 minutes, stirring occasionally, until almost all of the liquid is absorbed. Add 1 more cup of stock and cook, stirring, until this stock is almost absorbed. Then add another cup of stock. After this is absorbed, the rice and peas should be tender. (If not, add more stock—½ cup at a time—and continue cooking and stirring.) Now gently stir in soft butter and grated cheese. Serve at once while the rice is creamy and hot.

To serve 6

5 cups chicken stock, fresh or canned
4 tablespoons butter
½ cup finely chopped onions
2 cups fresh green peas (about 2 pounds unshelled)
1½ cups plain white raw rice, preferably imported Italian rice
¼ pound cooked smoked ham, diced (about 1 cup)
2 tablespoons soft butter
½ cup freshly grated imported Parmesan cheese

Fegato alla Veneziana

SAUTÉED CALF'S LIVER WITH ONIONS

Heat 2 tablespoons of olive oil in a heavy 8- to 10-inch skillet. Add the onions and cook over moderate heat, stirring frequently, for 7 or 8 minutes. Then stir in the sage and cook 2 or 3 minutes longer, or until the onions are limp and lightly colored. Set the skillet aside, off the heat.

Pat the liver strips dry with paper towels and season them with salt and a few grindings of pepper. In another large heavy skillet, heat the remaining 2 tablespoons of olive oil until a light haze forms over it. Drop in the liver strips and sauté them, turning them frequently, for 2 or 3 minutes, or until they are lightly browned on all sides. Stir in the onions and cook with the liver for 1 or 2 minutes. Transfer the liver and onions to a heated platter. Immediately pour the white wine vinegar into the skillet and boil this mixture briskly for a minute or 2, meanwhile scraping in any browned bits clinging to the pan. Pour the sauce over the liver and onions and sprinkle with the chopped parsley. Serve immediately.

To serve 4

4 tablespoons olive oil
1 cup thinly sliced onions
¼ teaspoon dried sage leaves
1 pound calf's liver, cut crosswise into ¼-inch strips
Salt
Freshly ground black pepper
2 tablespoons wine vinegar, preferably white
2 tablespoons finely chopped fresh parsley

Anguilla Marinata

MARINATED EEL

In a heavy 2- to 3-quart saucepan, heat 1 cup of olive oil. Add the onions, garlic, thyme, bay leaves, peppercorns and salt and cook over moderate heat, stirring frequently, for about 7 or 8 minutes, or until the onions are transparent but not brown. Pour in the vinegar and water, bring to a boil, reduce the heat and simmer the marinade uncovered for 20 minutes.

Meanwhile, brush the pieces of eel with lemon juice. Dip them into the flour and shake off the excess. Then heat 2 tablespoons of oil in a heavy 10- to 12-inch skillet until a light haze forms over it. Drop in 5 or 6 pieces of eel at a time and cook over moderately high heat for 4 to 5 minutes. Add more oil if needed. Transfer the eel to a shallow 9-by-12-inch glass, porcelain or enameled baking dish and pour over it the hot marinade. When it is at room temperature, cover the dish with plastic wrap and refrigerate for at least 24 hours. To serve, lift the pieces out of the marinade and arrange them on a serving plate. Moisten the eel with a little of the marinade before serving.

To serve 4 to 6

MARINADE
1 cup olive oil
4 cups thinly sliced onions (about 1 pound)
6 garlic cloves, sliced
½ teaspoon dried thyme
2 bay leaves, crumbled
8 peppercorns
1 tablespoon salt
1 cup wine vinegar, preferably white
1 cup water
2 pounds eel, cleaned and sliced into 3-inch pieces
¼ cup lemon juice
Flour
2 to 4 tablespoons olive oil

VII

Genoa
and Liguria

I

n the days when the great galleons toiled painfully home, beating their zigzag courses against the offshore breezes in the Gulf of Genoa, their first hint of land was the wind-carried scent of sweet basil from Liguria. The sailors knew then that the green hills above Genoa, carpeted with aromatic herbs, would soon heave into sight.

Genoa's maritime tradition helps account for the devotion of its people to herbs and vegetables, which were basic to Genoese cuisine in the days of the city's great navigators—men like Columbus and the admiral and statesman Andrea Doria—and continue to be basic today. "Genoese cooking seldom uses spices, only herbs, and a great variety of them," says Marchese Giuseppe Gavotti, chancellor and national secretary of the Italian Academy of Cooking at Savona, near Genoa. "It is the result of the sailors' yearning for fresh green foods when they return home."

The reason for that yearning is clear from a letter that Columbus wrote to his royal employers. It gives the ordinary seaman's shipboard diet as biscuit supplemented by such rations as salt meat and fish, lentils and chick-peas. History does not tell us whether the great Genoese captains shared their crews' limited fare while at sea. In port they ate well, even lavishly. Ostentatious banquets were given by Andrea Doria to promote his fortunes—he was an artful politician who supported Francis I of France in his invasions of Italy and then, when the French King proved ungrateful, shifted to the service of the Holy Roman Emperor Charles V. Charles V was the guest at one of Doria's most flamboyant feasts, staged on a specially built pier in 1533. When the gold and silver plates had been dirtied, they were thrown into the

The sea is the source of many superb Ligurian dishes. Displayed opposite are some of the region's prides: squid *(upper left)*, sea bream, a dentex and sea perch *(center)*, red mullet *(lower left)* and a mackerel *(lower right)*.

119

water—"where naiads and tritons were disporting themselves," according to contemporary accounts. A grandly careless gesture this, but hardly extravagant: fish nets were cunningly stretched underwater to retrieve the plates for another day.

As such forethought suggests, the Genoese admirals came from a society that had a respectful attitude toward money. The Genoese knew how to make money, and how to use and protect it; they were pioneers in such institutions as marine insurance and the bank check. They were characterized long ago in the Latin phrase *Genuensis ergo mercator*—a Genoese, therefore a tradesman. This fiscal singlemindedness may help explain why spices never became an important part of Genoese cooking. Like Venice, Genoa grew rich ferrying the priceless spices of the East to Europe. But while the merchants of Venice reserved plenty of their cargoes for their own cooking, the Genoese regarded the spices of far-off lands primarily as merchandise to be exchanged for gold.

Instead of spices, it was the herbs of their own hills that gave distinction to their daily diet. Thus the pungency of basil is the soul of the classic Genoese sauce, *pesto* (the body is cheese and garlic); the sharpness of sage and rosemary set off the smooth taste of Ligurian grilled lobster; marjoram is the subtle perfume in the *cima alla genovese (page 128)*, which has some of the better attributes of a meat loaf; and an unusual local herb, *scorzonera,* is essential to the showpiece Genoese salad, *cappon magro,* so elaborate that only a first-rate restaurant is capable of handling its preparation. Basil still flourishes in Liguria as nowhere else in Italy. It and other particularly tasty specialties of the Ligurian region—dill, cucumbers, tomatoes, asparagus— are grown under glass on hillside plots and shipped throughout Europe during the winter months.

But the produce of Liguria's farms is no more important than what grows in the sea itself. The principal source of staples for the tables of the region has always been the sea. Among the best-known products is the sea date (so called from its shape, which resembles that of the fruit), a mussel found in many parts of the world but, the local citizens claim, never so luscious as when it grows in the Gulf of La Spezia. The Emperor Frederick Barbarossa apparently agreed; he decreed in 1154 that whenever his Ligurian vassals waited on him in Rome, they should bring him a shield heaped with mussels. Even more of a delicacy is the sea truffle, eaten raw with lemon juice as an appetizer. But all the many varieties of Mediterranean fish are available in Ligurian waters, and they go into a number of dishes, from *ciuppi* and *zuppa di cozze (page 129),* two local versions of fish and mussel soup, to *bignè di pesci misti,* a mixed fish fry *(page 133).*

Such native produce, harvested from rich farms and a bountiful sea, became the foundation for a lusty cuisine. One of the typical *antipasti* of the Ligurian region is a simple combination of greens with a dolphin fillet, dried in the sun and the sea breeze. *Minestrone*—which the Genoese claim to have invented—contains more vegetables when served in Liguria than anywhere else. These characteristic dishes, and others as satisfying, appeared during the two Genoese meals I remember best.

La Santa restaurant in Genoa furnished the more distinguished of these repasts, though the place itself is located in a far from elegant part of town. If you take a taxi to La Santa, the driver will probably stop at the head of

a dark, narrow alley called the Vico Indoratori and suggest that you make the rest of your way to the restaurant on foot. Once into the Vico, a car cannot turn around, and prudent taxi drivers prefer to avoid traveling to the other end of the alley. Their caution is understandable. A few blocks beyond the restaurant, the Vico empties into a teeming warren that is not for the timid. This is the quarter near the docks, and here Genoa maintains in every way the traditions of a seaport. Today's sailors may no longer feel the same desperate yearning for fresh food, but long voyages stir other appetites, and Genoa, like many another seaport, does not disappoint them. Nor does the pleasant, impeccably respectable La Santa disappoint the visitor whose only appetite is for good food.

Here I first tasted *pesto (page 129)* on its home territory. *Pesto,* a sharp and pungent cheese paste, may appear on almost any dish in Genoa, but its favorite applications are three: as a floating, creamy green island on the surface of a thick *minestrone;* on *trenette,* the local variety of ribbon pasta; or, as I had it, on a potato *gnocchi,* which the people of Genoa call *trofie.*

The classic *pesto* contains two kinds of cheese—a little Parmesan and young, sharp Sardinian *pecorino* or *pecorino romano*—plus basil, garlic, olive oil and pine nuts (sometimes replaced by walnuts). All this is crushed into a paste with a marble mortar and wooden pestle (hence, *pesto*). To unaccustomed palates, the real *pesto* sometimes seems almost unpleasantly sharp, but it can be—and has been—altered to suit everyone's taste. There is excellent authority for changing the recipe; no two Ligurian towns make it the same way. The version served at La Santa was smoother than I had expected, and I was told this was true because the restaurant's regular recipe included cream.

After the *gnocchi* and *pesto,* La Santa proffered a piquant grilled lobster, served with a sauce like a thick mayonnaise, to which lobster coral (roe) had been added, along with a variety of local herbs; this produced a strange, somewhat Oriental flavor, reminiscent of certain dishes I had tried in Tunis. With it came a rice creation, seemingly a very simple dish, with only butter, cheese and stock added. The rice was exquisitely cooked, each grain separate and slightly crunchy; but the taste was so subtle that one realized that once again delicate herbs had gone into the cooking of the meat that provided the base of the stock.

With this I drank a regional white wine, Coronato, not very dry and a little thin. Coronato is one of the Ligurian wines most often mentioned favorably (along with those of the Cinqueterre), but the fact is that most Ligurian wine is not outstanding, and many Genoese prefer to drink wine from the vineyards of the adjoining Piedmont region rather than that made from their own grapes.

La Santa is a small place, where couples talk quietly at small tables lighted

The Ligurian coast, including the great seaport of Genoa, could be called a shrine of Italian cooking. The region claims credit for inventing two dishes that have understandably spread round the world—*minestrone* and ravioli. Furthermore, the Italian Academy of Cooking is located at Savona and the Museum of Spaghetti at Pontedassio. The local cuisine is a marriage of the products of the sea and those of the herb-growing back country.

121

by discreet, rose-shaded lamps. It contrasts sharply with the source of my second memorable meal in Genoa. Da Mario is a tremendous and popular restaurant, cheerful almost to the point of boisterousness, where hearty eaters come in large parties. It might easily be taken for a factory of mass-produced meals with little subtlety about them if it were not for the buffet at the rear, where most of the Genoese specialties are on mouth-watering display. Among the most tempting of these delicacies when I was there was the famous *cima alla genovese*—a sort of galantine or *roulade* of boned breast of veal stuffed with well-seasoned meats, hard-boiled egg, pistachio nuts, peas, spinach and, sometimes, truffles *(page 128)*.

Also on the sideboard was the impressive salad known as *cappon magro,* which means, roughly, "fast-day capon." Since it contains no capon, it might be classified with one of those joking names like "Salisbury steak" (an American euphemism for a large patty of ground meat) or "Scotch woodcock" (eggs served on toast spread with anchovy paste). But *cappon magro* is certainly not like these dishes of relatively inexpensive food given a fancy name. There is nothing poor about *cappon magro*—"a dish worthy of Homeric heroes," in the words of the writer Achille Noli. Just as capon is considered a luxurious repast, so is *cappon magro,* though it is acceptable to Roman Catholics on days of abstinence, since it contains no meat.

Signor Noli also suggests that if you are not a Homeric hero but a "weakling of the stomach or a convalescent, content yourself by caressing this dish with an avid eye." It is indeed something to look at, almost as much a work of architecture as an example of the culinary art, since the splendid boiled vegetables and pickled fish of which it is chiefly composed are built up into an imposing dome of a number of different-colored layers, the whole swathed in rich green sauce.

All sorts of liberties are allowed with the ingredients for this dish, except one: the herb *scorzonera* is never omitted. The word *scorzonera* was brought to Liguria by Spaniards from Catalonia (where the herb also grows); in the local Catalan dialect it was spelled *escorso,* literally "vipers," because of the belief that it was an antidote against snakebite.

We did not go hungry; the case was quite the contrary. We started with a dish I had never tasted—*bianchetti,* composed of incredibly tiny, just-hatched anchovies or sardines, about a quarter of an inch long, white and semitransparent. They were floured, fried in hot oil and coated with chopped parsley that had been fried quickly in hot oil. The sauce consisted simply of olive oil and lemon juice, but these delicately flavored, carefully prepared fish happily required nothing more elaborate.

The next dish was the Genoese variety of *minestrone* with *pesto.* When *pesto* is served with *minestrone,* it is added at the last moment, floated on a soup the Genoese prefer to be thick. The *minestrone* I had at Da Mario contained peas, potatoes, oil, garlic, a little onion and a few herbs. But *minestrone alla genovese* can be much more elaborate. One recipe I have also includes squash, cabbage, zucchini, *fava* beans, red beans, string beans, ripe peeled seeded tomatoes, diced eggplant and celery, plus a choice of several varieties of small pasta to thicken the soup—*cannoliochi* (small *cannoli,* or tubes of pasta stuffed with chopped meat and herbs), *ditalini* (little fingers) or *penne* (feathers).

The *minestrone* was followed by two dishes based on the dried codfish

Genoese use both the curly-leafed parsley *(bottom)* familiar to American cooks and the more pungent flat-leafed Italian parsley *(top)* to season fish dishes.

that the Normans popularized during their forays and settlements throughout the Mediterranean region. One was *stoccafisso* (dried cod) fritters; the other was *baccalà*, for which the fish was washed, left to soak in milk for several hours, then cooked very slowly in oil.

We now arrived at a famous Genoese dish—vegetable tart. In a puff-paste crust, this contained artichokes melted into a delicious creamy mixture, with which were combined hard-boiled eggs and squash. A renowned variation of this vegetable dish is the Easter tart—*torta pasqualina*. Along with the artichokes and eggs, this one is filled with spinach and *prescinseua*— sour cheese made from milk curds—mixed with milk, though other combinations are also used.

The meal at Da Mario ended with *latte dolce,* a dessert made of whipped cream, ordinary cream and a suspicion of lemon. It was accompanied by an unnamed white wine of the region, agreeable and not too dry, and *rossese,* supposed to have been Napoleon's favorite red wine, which comes from Dolceacqua, near Imperia. It is warm, with plenty of body, but not heavy, and has a slight aftertaste of pepper.

There are many other good things on the Ligurian menu, among them *vitello all'uccelletto,* a roast lean veal flavored with sage, which gives it the characteristic taste of game; and *riso arrosto alla genovese,* a *timbale* of rice, sausage, peas, artichokes, mushrooms, cheese and onion browned in an oven. In fact no repast, no matter how splendid, can include everything of note. Omitted from our magnificent Genoese meals was perhaps the best-known of all local dishes—ravioli *(page 130).* The legend is that ravioli developed on shipboard as a means of employing leftovers on long voyages, when every scrap of fresh food counted. Whatever remained after a meal was combined, chopped up together, stuffed into envelopes of dough and served at the next repast. This was called *rabiole,* a dialect term for leftovers—things of little value.

As the Genoese make it today, ravioli belies any such humble origin. One hearty recipe for *ravioli alla genovese* calls for a stuffing made from lean veal, breast of pork, calf's brains, sweetbreads, egg, bread crumbs soaked in milk, and grated Parmesan cheese, seasoned with chopped chard and sometimes nutmeg. Not all fillings are as complex as this one, but whatever mixture is used, it is stuffed into envelopes made with fine white flour, lukewarm water and egg.

It is appropriate that the province of Liguria, which can claim credit for inventing a species of pasta that is now eaten all over the world, is also the site of Italy's Spaghetti Museum, located at Pontedassio. On display there are ancient and modern machines for making pasta, as well as documents concerning various forms of pasta going back to the 13th Century, including Papal bans regulating the quality of the different pastas. One of the documents preserved in Pontedassio is a 16th Century book by one Giovanni da Vigo, a physician who, whatever his talents, would perhaps attract few Italian patients today. He warned his readers that "pasta should be eaten very rarely and flavored only with pepper and rue"—an herb with a strong smell, a bitter taste and a medieval reputation as a sovereign preventive of infectious disease. Fortunately for lovers of good food, the good doctor's advice has been ignored, and all sorts of herbs, from Liguria and elsewhere, help to make pasta a worldwide favorite.

Together with clams and mussels, eels form part of many a succulent Ligurian meal. The larger eels *(capitoni)* are a traditional Christmas Eve specialty.

Lamp-and-Spear Fishing

A few miles north of La Spezia on the Ligurian coast are the Cinqueterre ("five lands")—Monterosso, Vernazza, Corniglia, Manarola and Riomaggiore. In each of these five fishing villages of the Cinqueterre are families who live on vegetables grown on the steep hillsides and on fish from the sea. The men use nets to catch anchovies and spears to take larger fish. Rowing offshore at night, they use gas lamps attached to the sterns of their boats to attract their catches (*following pages*).

The village of Vernazza (*right*) clings to an outcrop overlooking the Gulf of Genoa. Whether farmers or fishermen, most people— like the woman above carrying produce to market— labor much as they have done for centuries, although some run shops and cafés that cater to tourists.

In early morning, a fisherman shakes out his net, which holds a catch of a red mullet and two *cicale,* a species of shrimp.

Toward dusk, Agostino Villa of Vernazza emerges from his modest house for a night of offshore fishing, carrying his gas lamp, or *lampara*. Light from the gas mantles of the *lampara* draws both anchovies and larger fish into the nets let down from the boats or within easy striking distance of the fishermen's formidable 12-foot, nine-pronged spears.

At sunset, the fishermen of Vernazza row their boats into shallow water and wait for the large fish to appear. The first arrive at dark, and the fishing will go on almost until midnight. Other fishermen go into deeper water, using *lampare* to attract schools of anchovies; when the water is swarming with the little fish, the men cast their nets to lift them into their boats.

A sea bream impaled on his long spear, Villa prepares to haul his catch aboard.

To serve 6 to 8

3 slices white bread, crusts removed
⅔ cup milk
2 tablespoons butter
½ cup finely chopped onions
¼ pound boneless pork, ground twice
¼ pound boneless veal, ground twice
¼ pound fresh pork fat, ground twice
1 small calf's sweetbread, blanched
   10 minutes and finely chopped
⅓ cup freshly grated imported
   Parmesan cheese
½ cup thoroughly squeezed and
   firmly packed defrosted frozen
   chopped spinach, or ½ pound
   fresh spinach, cooked, squeezed dry
   and chopped
¼ teaspoon dried marjoram
¼ teaspoon dried thyme
1 tablespoon salt
1 egg, lightly beaten
½ cup shelled pistachio nuts
1 cup fresh or defrosted frozen peas
A 4- to 5-pound breast of veal
   (ask the butcher to bone it and
   cut into it a pocket for stuffing)
3 hard-cooked eggs, peeled
Bones and trimmings from the breast
   of veal, if available
1 onion, cut in half
3 whole garlic cloves
1 carrot, peeled
1 bay leaf
2 parsley sprigs
2 to 3 quarts fresh or canned chicken
   stock, or water, or a combination of
   stock and water
Freshly ground black pepper

Cima alla Genovese
COLD BRAISED STUFFED BREAST OF VEAL

Soak the white bread in the milk for about 10 minutes. Meanwhile, melt the 2 tablespoons of butter in a small skillet, and over moderate heat cook the chopped onions in the butter for 7 or 8 minutes, stirring often, until they are transparent but not brown. Transfer the onions to a large bowl, and add the ground pork, veal, pork fat, chopped sweetbread, grated Parmesan cheese, chopped spinach, marjoram, thyme, salt and the egg. Knead the ingredients with your hands or beat them with a wooden spoon until they are well mixed and fluffy. Squeeze the soaked bread dry and mix it in with the other ingredients. Gently fold in the shelled pistachio nuts and peas.

Spread about half of this stuffing evenly in the veal pocket and on top of the stuffing arrange the hard-cooked eggs lengthwise in a row. Spoon in the rest of the stuffing, covering the eggs completely. Sew up the opening of the pocket with strong kitchen thread.

Place the veal bones and trimmings (if available), onion halves, garlic, carrot, bay leaf and parsley in a large soup pot and lay the stuffed veal on top of them. Add enough stock or water to cover the meat completely, and grind in a little black pepper. Bring to a boil, reduce the heat, cover the pot and simmer as gently as possible for 1¼ hours, or until the veal is tender when pierced with the tip of a sharp knife. Transfer the veal to a large, heavy, shallow baking dish and let it cool to room temperature. Refrigerate until the meat is thoroughly chilled. Serve cold, cut into ¼-inch slices.

Boned breast of veal enfolds eggs, pistachio nuts, vegetables and ground meats.

Zuppa di Cozze
MUSSEL SOUP

If the amount of liquid called for in the ingredients sounds insufficient for a soup, do not worry. The shellfish produce their own liquid when cooked, and the dish, although served as a soup, is actually more like mussels in a seasoned liquid.

Scrub the mussels with a stiff brush or soapless steel-mesh scouring pad under cold running water. With a small, sharp knife cut off their "beards" —the very strong, black, ropelike tufts on their shells with which they attach themselves to their anchorages in the sea.

Combine the chopped onions, celery and garlic on a cutting board and chop them into very small pieces. (This mixture is called a *battuto;* when cooked, it is called a *soffritto.*) Heat the ½ cup of olive oil in an enameled or stainless-steel 3- to 4-quart saucepan. Over moderate heat, cook the chopped vegetables in the oil with the basil and a few grindings of pepper.

Stirring frequently, cook the *soffritto* for 8 to 10 minutes, or until it is lightly colored. Pour in the white wine and boil it briskly to reduce it to about ¼ cup. Then add the chopped tomatoes and their liquid and simmer uncovered over low heat, stirring frequently, for about 20 minutes. Drop in the mussels, cover the pan, and cook over high heat, shaking the pan from time to time so that the mussels cook through evenly. At the end of 10 minutes, the mussels should all be open; if not, cook a few minutes longer.

To serve, ladle the mussels, shells and all, into individual soup bowls and spoon the soup over them. (You might find that an extra dish or bowl on the table will be useful for the shells of the mussels.) Sprinkle each serving with grated lemon peel and accompany with hot, crusty Italian bread, which you can dip into any remaining seasoned broth.

To serve 4

4 dozen small mussels in their shells
¼ cup coarsely chopped onions
¼ cup coarsely chopped celery
1 teaspoon coarsely chopped garlic
½ cup olive oil
1 tablespoon finely chopped fresh basil or 1 teaspoon dried basil
Freshly ground black pepper
½ cup dry white wine
2 cups canned Italian plum or whole-pack tomatoes, chopped but not drained
2 teaspoons freshly grated lemon peel

Pesto alla Genovese
BASIL, GARLIC AND CHEESE SAUCE

TO MAKE THE PESTO IN A BLENDER, combine the coarsely chopped fresh basil (or fresh parsley and dried basil), salt, pepper, garlic, pine nuts or walnuts and 1 cup of olive oil in the blender jar. Blend them at high speed until the ingredients are smooth, stopping the blender every 5 or 6 seconds to push the herbs down with a rubber spatula.

The sauce should be thin enough to run off the spatula easily. If it seems too thick, blend in as much as ½ cup more olive oil. Transfer the sauce to a bowl and stir in the grated cheese.

TO MAKE THE PESTO BY HAND, crush the coarsely chopped fresh basil (or fresh parsley and dried basil) with a mortar and pestle or place in a heavy mixing bowl and crush with the back of a large wooden spoon until the herbs are smooth and almost pastelike. Work in the salt and pepper, garlic, and pine nuts or walnuts, and then add the olive oil ½ cup at a time, continuing to crush the herbs. When the sauce is thin enough to run off the pestle or spoon easily, mix in the grated cheese. Serve the *pesto* thoroughly mixed into hot drained pasta that has been tossed first with a few tablespoons of soft butter.

NOTE: Often in Italy the *pesto* is thinned further by adding to it 1 or 2 tablespoons of the hot spaghetti water before mixing it with the pasta.

To make about 1½ to 2 cups

2 cups fresh basil leaves, stripped from their stems, coarsely chopped and tightly packed; or substitute 2 cups fresh flat-leaf Italian parsley, coarsely chopped, and 2 tablespoons dried basil leaves
1 teaspoon salt
½ teaspoon freshly ground black pepper
1 to 2 teaspoons finely chopped garlic
2 tablespoons finely chopped pine nuts or walnuts
1 to 1½ cups olive oil
½ cup freshly grated imported *sardo, romano* or Parmesan cheese

To make about 45

Ravioli

1 cup *ricotta*
½ cup farmer cheese, rubbed through
  a fine sieve
¾ cup freshly grated imported
  Parmesan cheese
2 teaspoons grated onion
3 egg yolks
1½ teaspoons salt
Pasta dough *(page 44)*

In a large mixing bowl, combine the 1 cup of *ricotta*, the farmer cheese, the ¾ cup of grated Parmesan cheese, grated onion, 3 egg yolks and 1½ teaspoons of salt and carefully stir them together until they are well mixed. Set aside until you have rolled out the dough.

Divide the pasta dough (prepared according to the recipe on page 44) into four pieces and roll out the first one quarter of the dough to make it as thin as possible. Cover the rolled pasta with a damp towel to prevent its drying out, and roll out the second quarter of dough to a similar size and shape. Using the first sheet of rolled-out pasta as a sort of checkerboard, place a mound of about 1 teaspoon of the cheese-and-egg-yolk mixture every 2 inches across and down the pasta. Dip a pastry brush or your index finger into a bowl of water and make vertical and horizontal lines in a checkerboard pattern on the sheet of pasta, between the mounds of cheese filling. Be sure to use enough water to wet the lines evenly (the water will act as a bond to hold the finished ravioli together). Carefully spread the second sheet of rolled-out pasta on top of the first one, pressing down firmly along the wetted lines.

With a ravioli cutter, a pastry wheel or a small, sharp knife, cut the pasta into squares along the wetted lines. Separate the mounds of ravioli and set

1 Space little mounds of cheese or meat filling 2 inches apart on a sheet of pasta. Then with a brush dipped in water draw straight lines between the mounds.

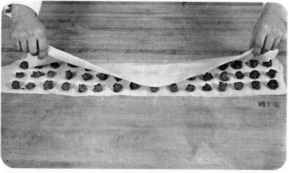

2 Now place a second sheet of pasta evenly over the first sheet. Work quickly; the sheets must remain damp and pliable or they will crack when pressed into shape.

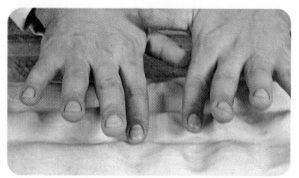

3 Press down between the mounds to form the ravioli envelopes. The wetted areas of the pasta sheet will act as a bond to seal the fillings into the envelopes.

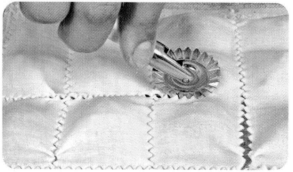

4 With a ravioli cutter *(above)* or a knife separate the envelopes from each other. The ravioli is now ready to be cooked in salted boiling water.

them aside on wax paper. In the same fashion, roll out, fill and cut the 2 other portions of dough.

To cook, drop the ravioli into 6 to 8 quarts of rapidly boiling salted water and stir them gently with a wooden spoon, to keep them from sticking to one another or to the bottom of the pot. Boil the ravioli for about 8 minutes, or until they are tender, then drain them thoroughly in a large sieve or colander. Serve the ravioli with tomato sauce *(page 47)* or add butter and freshly grated imported Parmesan cheese, and gently stir them all together immediately before serving.

MEAT FILLING FOR RAVIOLI: Melt the 3 tablespoons of butter in a small skillet and cook the onions, stirring frequently for about 7 or 8 minutes, or until they are soft and transparent but not brown. Add the ¾ pound finely ground raw veal and cook, stirring constantly, until the veal loses its red color and any accumulating liquid in the pan cooks completely away. Transfer the entire contents of the skillet to a mixing bowl and stir in the chopped spinach, grated Parmesan cheese and a pinch of nutmeg. In a separate bowl, beat the eggs lightly and add them to the onion, veal and spinach mixture. Taste and season with salt.

MEAT FILLING

3 tablespoons butter
4 tablespoons finely chopped onions
¾ pound finely ground raw veal
1 ten-ounce package frozen chopped spinach, defrosted, thoroughly squeezed and chopped again, or ¾ pound fresh spinach, cooked, squeezed and chopped
½ cup freshly grated imported Parmesan cheese
Pinch of ground nutmeg
3 eggs
Salt

Topped with a masking of tomato sauce and a sprinkling of Parmesan cheese, the completed squares of ravioli stand ready to be brought to the table.

131

Fresh from the broiler, spinach *gnocchi* balls are delicate in taste and texture.

Gnocchi Verdi

SMALL SPINACH DUMPLINGS

To serve 4 to 6

4 tablespoons butter
2 ten-ounce packages frozen chopped
    spinach, thoroughly defrosted,
    squeezed completely dry, and
    chopped very fine (about 1½ cups),
    or 1½ pounds fresh spinach,
    cooked, squeezed and chopped
¾ cup *ricotta* cheese, or substitute
    whole-curd cottage cheese, rubbed
    through a sieve
2 eggs, lightly beaten
6 tablespoons flour
¾ cup freshly grated imported
    Parmesan cheese
½ teaspoon salt
½ teaspoon freshly ground black
    pepper
Pinch of ground nutmeg
6 to 8 quarts water
1 tablespoon salt
4 tablespoons melted butter

In an 8- to 10-inch enameled or stainless-steel skillet, melt 4 tablespoons of butter over moderate heat. Add the chopped fresh or frozen spinach and cook, stirring constantly, for 2 to 3 minutes, or until almost all moisture has boiled away and the spinach begins to stick lightly to the skillet. Add the ¾ cup of *ricotta* and cook, stirring, for 3 or 4 minutes longer.

With a rubber spatula, transfer the contents of the skillet to a mixing bowl and mix in the 2 lightly beaten eggs, 6 tablespoons of flour, ¼ cup of the grated cheese, ½ teaspoon salt, pepper and nutmeg. Refrigerate for 30 minutes to 1 hour, or until the *gnocchi* mixture is quite firm.

Preheat the broiler. Bring the 6 to 8 quarts of water and 1 tablespoon of salt to a simmer over moderate heat in a large soup pot or saucepan. Flour your hands lightly and pick up about 1 tablespoon of the chilled *gnocchi* mixture at a time. Shape the tablespoonfuls into small balls about 1½ inches in diameter. Gently drop the balls into the simmering water and cook them uncovered for 5 to 8 minutes, or until they puff slightly and are somewhat firm to the touch. With a slotted spoon, lift the *gnocchi* out of the water and set them aside on a paper towel to drain.

Pour 2 tablespoons of the melted butter into a shallow 8-by-12-inch flameproof serving dish and swirl the butter around until the bottom of the dish glistens. Arrange the *gnocchi* in the dish in one layer ¼-inch apart, dribble the remaining 2 tablespoons of melted butter over them, and sprinkle with the remaining ½ cup of grated cheese. Set under the broiler, 3 inches from the heat, for 3 minutes, or until the cheese melts.

Serve the *gnocchi* at once, directly from the flameproof dish. Serve additional grated cheese separately, if you wish.

132

Lingua di Bue Brasata
BEEF TONGUE BRAISED IN RED WINE

To serve 4 to 6

Cover the tongue with cold water in a large pot or kettle. Bring to a boil, partially cover the pot, reduce the heat and simmer for 2 hours. Remove the tongue from the water and place it on a cutting board. When it is just cool enough to handle, skin the tongue with a small sharp knife, cutting away the fat, bones and gristle at its base.

Preheat the oven to 350°. In a heavy 10- to 12-inch skillet, heat the oil until a light haze forms over it. Add the tongue and brown it on all sides. Now melt the butter in a heavy flameproof casserole. When the foam subsides, add the onions, carrots and celery and cook them over moderate heat, stirring frequently, for 8 to 10 minutes, or until they are lightly colored. Pour in the wine and boil it briskly, to reduce it to ¼ cup. Place the tongue on top of the vegetables and add the beef stock, parsley and bay leaf. If the stock does not rise ⅓ of the way up the side of the tongue, add more stock or water. Bring to a simmer, cover, and place in the middle of the oven for 1½ hours, or until the tongue is tender and can be easily pierced with the tip of a knife. Transfer the tongue to a heated platter and carve it into thin slices. Strain the braising liquid and serve as a sauce.

A 3-pound fresh beef tongue
¼ cup olive oil
4 tablespoons butter
1 cup finely chopped onions
½ cup finely chopped carrots
½ cup finely chopped celery
½ cup dry red wine
2 cups beef stock, fresh or canned
2 parsley sprigs
1 bay leaf

Bignè di Pesci Misti
DEEP-FRIED SEAFOOD

To serve 4

Stir the flour, warm water, 3 tablespoons of oil and ½ teaspoon of salt together in a large mixing bowl until they have combined to make a smooth cream. Do not beat or overstir. For best results, set the finished batter aside at room temperature and let it rest for about 2 hours, although it may be used at once if it must. The egg white should be beaten vigorously with a whisk or rotary beater until it is stiff and then folded into the batter just before the batter is used.

Bring 1 quart of water to a boil in a 3- to 4-quart saucepan and in it simmer the squid, covered, over moderate heat for 20 minutes. Drain the squid through a sieve or colander and lay the pieces on paper towels. Shell and devein the shrimp *(page 116)*, leaving the tails on. Wash the shrimp and the smelts quickly under cold running water, dry them and set them aside with the squid. Salt and pepper the squid, shrimp and smelts.

Heat 3 to 4 inches of oil or shortening in a deep-fat fryer to 375°. Preheat the oven to 250° and line a large shallow baking dish or baking sheet with paper towels. Deep-fry the shrimp, smelts and squid separately, first dropping 5 or 6 pieces into the batter (into which you have just folded the beaten egg white). When they are well coated, lift them out one by one with tongs or a slotted spoon. Hold the pieces over the batter bowl for a second to let the excess batter drain off before placing them in the hot oil. Deep-fry the seafood, turning the pieces once or twice, for 5 or 6 minutes, or until golden brown. With tongs, transfer the browned pieces to the lined baking dish or baking sheet to drain. When you have fried the first batch, place the baking sheet or dish in the oven to keep the fried seafood warm. Then dip the next batch into the batter and deep-fry it. As soon as the last piece is fried and drained, arrange the seafood on a napkin-lined platter and serve it, garnished with lemon quarters.

BATTER
1 cup all-purpose flour, sifted before
    measuring
¾ cup lukewarm water
3 tablespoons vegetable oil
½ teaspoon salt
1 egg white

1 quart water
1½ pounds squid, cut in ½-inch
    rings
½ pound medium fresh shrimp in
    their shells or frozen shrimp,
    defrosted
½ pound smelts, cleaned and heads
    removed
Salt
Freshly ground black pepper
Vegetable oil or shortening for
    deep-fat frying
Lemon quarters

VIII

Milan and Lombardy

The tall Lombardy coffee cake known as *panettone*, a delight made with raisins and candied fruit, adorns a table of the Caffè Motta, hard by the soaring Milan cathedral. *Panettone* accompanies many Italian breakfasts, but the cake's association with Milan is especially strong.

Milan moves almost with the frenzied step of Manhattan," the travel writer Horace Sutton once reported, and even to the casual tourist, the dynamic tempo of Italy's commercial center is inescapable. But once out of the traffic and into the kitchen, the rush is forgotten. The traditional characteristic of Milanese cooking, still dominant, is that it takes its time. "The prevailing usage is slow cooking, over a low steady fire," Ottorina Perna Bozzi counsels in *Vecchia Milano in Cucina (The Cooking of Old Milan)*. "Only fried dishes, *scaloppine*, and soups are ordinarily cooked over a high flame. Boiled dishes should be simmered; roasts should not be cooked rapidly, but you should wait until, at the end of its cooking, the meat takes on a golden-brown color. How else can you achieve that magnificent thick meat gravy? The principal basis of Milanese cooking is that everything should be cooked slowly, in a covered dish, for a long time." She could have been talking about *manzo brasato alla lombarda (page 142)*, beef lovingly braised in stock and red wine; it spends three hours acquiring its special, spicy juiciness.

The seeming incompatibility between the bustle of modern Milan and the leisurely pace of Milanese cooking habits stems from the fact that the culinary traditions of the city and the surrounding region of Lombardy are much older than the preoccupation with business. The great French novelist Stendhal described the Milan of the early 1800s—which he loved—as a much more tranquil place than it is today. "The *arte di godere*, the art of enjoying life," wrote Stendhal in his diary, "appears to me here to be two centuries ahead of Paris." And he added later, in the same day's entry, "I went to drink a delicious cup of iced coffee and cream, superior, in my opinion, to anything to be found in Paris, and returned to write this."

The happy origins of the local cuisine are much older than Stendhal's era. In the 14th Century one Galvaneo Fiamma, after being invited to the wedding feast of Violante Visconti and the Duke of Chiarenza in 1368, showed himself an ungrateful guest when he stigmatized the Visconti family as heavy eaters—*magni comestores*. He had justification for the charge; he had been served a 50-course dinner. Plutarch relates that Julius Caesar introduced the dish of asparagus with butter into Classical Roman cooking after he was conquered by it in Lombardy. A certain fascination with food has long been exhibited by artists of the region. It was a native of Milan, Giuseppe Arcimboldi, who distinguished himself in the 16th Century by painting human likenesses composed of food: heaped-up fruit, vegetables, shellfish or fish. And in Bergamo in the 16th Century a whole school of painting developed that was devoted to the subject of food.

Well entrenched as are the old Lombard traditions, they must now withstand increasing pressure from new customs. What is locally called "the economical cuisine"—cooking done on modern stoves to save time as much as money—threatens to drive out the old-fashioned ways. The cheery Milanese kitchen, with its wood-burning stove made of bricks, and its open hearth where the daily batch of *polenta* simmers in a copper kettle and a spitted roast turns slowly, may soon be only a nostalgic memory. But the wealth that Milan derives from its industrial and commercial activity could save its cuisine; affluence has made it a bourgeois city, and bourgeois societies have usually liked to eat heartily and well.

The Milanese do now. In the homes of Lombardy (and in the more conscientious restaurants) the unhurried cuisine, based on the lavish use of butter, has so far managed to survive. It is rich but not cloying. Centuries of practice have taught Milanese cooks how to avoid the potential dangers of this style of cooking. The result is "tasty, refined and aromatic," in the opinion of the gastronome Signora Bozzi, who proves her point by extolling the merits of many of the Milanese products: succulent sausages, stuffed turkeys, salami from the Brianza area, rich, nourishing broths, whipped cream, fruit pickles, superb sweets and candies. The late French expert Léon Daudet agreed: "This healthy and even delicious cooking is the result of exercising judgment, as well as of finesse in taste." The style need not consume enormous amounts of time; the principle is sufficiency. For example, *peperonata*, a piquant dish of peppers, onions and tomatoes braised in butter and oil *(page 142)*, is cooked long enough for all the vegetables to absorb all the liquid in the pan—but the whole process normally takes no more than about half an hour.

It is not surprising that Frenchmen today have taken to Milanese cooking even as the French did in Stendhal's day, for the cuisine has many points in common with the classical French cuisine, including the Gallic fondness for butter. Over the years, the Milanese have been much influenced by French culinary traditions and practices. Many foods in Lombardy are known by names closer to French than to Italian—the English word "artichoke," for example, is *carciofo* in Italian, but in the dialect of Lombardy it is *articiocch*, a close relative of the French word *artichaut*. Celery is *sedano* in Italian, *céleri* in French, and *sèller* in the Lombard dialect.

French cooking appears to have had more influence on the Milanese than that of Austria, which exercised political dominion over the area for centuries. Because the Milanese lived long under the Habsburg Emperors, there has been a tendency to see in the heartier aspects of local cooking not the natural effect of an appetite-whetting northern climate, but an artificial situation: the result of baroque Austrian culinary tastes imposed on the good Italians of Lombardy.

The most frequently cited example of this influence is the common dish known as *costoletta alla milanese*, veal cutlet dipped in egg and bread crumbs and fried in butter. Proponents of the theory that Milanese cooking is essentially Austrian have declared to me that this is nothing more nor less than the famous *Wiener Schnitzel*. But *costoletta alla milanese* is not the same as *Wiener Schnitzel*. For one thing, the Milanese *costoletta* comes from the part of the animal known to Americans as the rib roast, while the meat for the *Wiener Schnitzel* comes from the heel or round. A further distinction is the fact that the Milanese dish is fried in butter, the Viennese in lard.

Apart from such technical differences, the dish actually originated in Milan and traveled to Vienna, not the other way; it had been familiar in Milan long before the Austrians arrived. A still extant menu of a Milanese banquet served in 1134 lists *lombolos cum panitio*, breaded veal chop. It was the Austrian General Joseph Radetzky who, as he reported in one of his letters, discovered the delicacy in Milan in the 19th Century and introduced it to Vienna. It is only one among many great dishes Milan has given the world. Another one, *osso buco*, made its way to Vienna and beyond; its reputation now reaches around the globe. *Osso buco (page 144)* is a segment of veal shin bone with the meat adhering to it, and the marrow left in. It is cooked in wine and stock, with onions and tomato, and usually served bedded on rice; it takes two and a half hours in the preparation.

Rice, with *polenta*, is ubiquitous in Lombardy. The Po Valley is one of the great rice-growing areas of the world, and the Po flows all the way across the region from west to east. Probably the most common rice dish is *risotto alla milanese (page 144)*, the distinctive feature of which is its saffron color and flavoring. It takes about an hour to cook, a long time for rice. *Alla milanese*, in fact, may often indicate the presence of rice: *minestrone alla milanese* contains rice, but the ordinary green-vegetable-and-tomato *minestrone* that you may be served in Milan does not. Another soup, humble, hearty and undeservedly obscure outside Italy (but well known to most Italians), originated in Lombardy. This is *zuppa alla pavese*—bouillon with a little raft of toast floating in it, carrying a poached egg sprinkled with grated Parmesan cheese *(page 145)*.

There is much else to tease, tantalize and gloriously satisfy the taste buds on all levels of sophistication in the cooking of Lombardy. Beef stewed slowly in a sauce of tomatoes and other vegetables, called *stufato*, makes a hearty meal. On a higher level *busecca*, tripe boiled with vegetables and flavored with spices, is an excellent dish and wholly different from the more famous *trippa alla fiorentina (Recipe Booklet)* and *trippa alla romana*. *Agoni al burro e salvia* is a mixture of little fish cooked in butter and flavored with sage, while *tinca carpionata* is a mixture of fried fish marinated in vinegar, wine, sage, garlic and onion and seasoned with pepper. For the still more sophisticated are *faraona alla creta*, guinea hens roasted in clay to keep the

Lombardy, richest of the regions of Italy, predictably offers a cuisine based on butter from highly productive dairy farms and rice from the well watered Po River Valley. The region originated a number of fine cheeses, among them Gorgonzola from the area about that town and the mild, creamy Bel Paese.

The features of *The Gardener,* a
fanciful painting by Giuseppe
Arcimboldi, are built up from an
arrangement of fruits and vegetables.
The artist, a 16th Century Milanese,
specialized in such portrait fantasies.

aroma of spices in the meat and *polenta e öséi,* little birds roasted in a rich
sauce and served with slices of *polenta.* The idea is to take a bite of *polenta*
and then a bite of crunchy bird, bones and all.

But for the casual visitor who simply passes through, the food most likely
to be associated with Milan is not a soup or a meat dish or even rice but
panettone (page 143). The traveler doesn't even have to get off the train to
make acquaintance with this light egg-yellow cake, studded with raisins
and candied fruit peel; he can buy a neatly packaged *panettone,* in any
convenient size, from window-to-window vendors. This is just about the
best possible accompaniment for breakfast coffee—a distinct improvement, in my opinion, on the French *brioche.* It is sometimes suggested
that its dome-shaped top is intended to recall the cupolas of Lombardy
churches, but since this is the shape that results naturally from cooking
dough with yeast in a cylindrical cake tin, the explanation seems gratuitous.

Another legend connected with the origin of *panettone* sounds much
more believable. According to one version of the story, *panettone* was
originally called *pan de tonio,* Tony's bread. Tony was a 15th Century
baker in the Milanese quarter of Borgo delle Grazie, whose greatest asset

was not his business but his nubile daughter, Adalgisa. A young man of good family named Ughetto della Tela wanted to marry her, but he thought the chances were slim that his family would accept the daughter of an impecunious commoner. A wealthy man, on the other hand, might be forgiven his daughter's lack of blue blood. So before Christmas, to provide the baker with the best of makings for the traditional Yule cake, Ughetto sold his hunting falcons. He used the money to buy Tony the finest flour, eggs and butter; he went further and paid for the ingredients of a previously unknown improvement, sultana raisins and lemons (to produce a candied peel). The investment paid off; it started Tony's business on a boom that eventually made Tony a wealthy man and Adalgisa an acceptable daughter-in-law for the haughty but money-loving relatives of the wise young Ughetto—to the gustatory happiness of later generations.

Today, nearly all of Italy eats *panettone*, especially at Christmas but throughout the year as well. The Motta and Alemagna companies of Milan, the two biggest producers of this cake, sell about 200 million packages of *panettone* in Italy each December. A relative of *panettone* also plays a holiday role in Lombardy, at Easter, when a bun called *colomba* (dove), made of the same dough (but with the addition of toasted almonds), is eaten. This custom dates back to 1176, when two doves are supposed to have landed near the Milanese army standards during the battle of Legnano between the forces of the Lombard League and the army of the Holy Roman Empire. The Milanese saw in this a sign of divine protection and, supported by Pope Alexander III, their forces defeated those of the Holy Roman Emperor Frederick Barbarossa. In the church of San Simpliciano, the anniversary of the battle is still celebrated by a special mass during which two live doves are released from the altar.

Among other Lombard sweets are two specialties of Cremona (famous as the place where the Stradivarius, the Amati, the Guarnieri and other great violins were made). *Mostarda*, candied fruits in a mustard syrup, may sound somewhat alarming, but the effect is much like chutney. It makes an excellent accompaniment for boiled meat. The other is *torrone*, a rich almond-flavored dessert particularly popular during the Christmas holiday season. It takes its name from the 13th Century campanile of Cremona, the Torrazzo. A fruit dessert that is a specialty of the Milanese is *pere ripiene*, pears stuffed with Gorgonzola cheese *(page 145)*.

Those who like to end their meal with cheese rather than sweets are well taken care of in Lombardy. Peck, one of the most famous cheese shops in Italy, is in Milan. It displays hundreds of varieties of domestic and imported cheeses, along with cheesecake and other products made from them. Many of Peck's wares, such as Gorgonzola, are locally produced. The town of Gorgonzola, for which the cheese is named, lies a little northeast of Milan. The Gorgonzola produced there is made exclusively from fresh cow's milk, uncooked, but curdled with calf's rennet. Successive layers of cold curdled milk are poured into prepared forms to set, and the cheeses are then ripened for two to three months.

Another Italian cheese widely known abroad is also a product of Lombardy—the yellow creamy Bel Paese. And so much Parmesan-type cheese (*grana lodigiano*) is made in the town of Lodi that the novelist Alexandre Dumas, noted as a lover of good food and a traveler, maintained that the best Parmesan comes from Lodi and not from its Parma homeland. But Alexandre Dumas *fils,* son of the writer who praised *grana lodigiano,* preferred another cheese from the same town—*mascarpone,* a fresh cream cheese eaten for dessert, sometimes with maraschino and sugar, sometimes with powdered chocolate. Also to be sought in the cheese counter are *stracchino* and *taleggio,* which share proud places among the great, world-famous cheeses of all Italy.

Nothing brings out the flavor of wine better than cheese, and nature usually arranges it so that good cheese country is also good wine country. Nature, however, slipped up somewhat in the case of Lombardy; it is not one of the top wine-producing regions. In only two areas is wine grown extensively. One is the Valtellina Valley, whose best wine is probably Sasella, bright ruby in color, with a perfume that recalls roses. Inferno, with a nutty after-taste, is also an agreeable Valtellina wine. The other wine district is on the shores of Lake Garda; its most interesting wine is perhaps Chiaretto del Garda, rosé with a slightly sharp almond taste. The traveler in Lombardy who is a collector of curious names may be tempted to try Sangue di Giuda, blood of Judas, but should be warned that it is a sweet, sparkling red—and that sweetness, sparkle and redness are a treacherous combination, which perhaps explains the name.

What Lombardy does offer in the way of outstanding beverages is a widely known apéritif, Campari. In 1867, Gaspare Campari opened a café near the Duomo, Milan's cathedral. It quickly became an elegant rendezvous for Milanese high society. Gaspare experimented and served several homemade apéritifs. But the rather bitter scarlet drink known all over the world today appeared only about 1890. It was developed by Gaspare's son Davide, who went to France to study the art of apéritif-making. By 1892, the Campari family had established a factory in Sesto San Giovanni to make bitter Campari in quantity. The family company later added Campari cordial and Campari soda. With a Campari named Guido still at its head, the company now has a plant in Rome, along with an import-export division that has carried the product all over the world.

Among the oldest and most famous of Italian exports, of course, is opera —which in Milan is intimately associated with food. Today, there is an excellent restaurant right next door to La Scala, perhaps the world's best-known opera house, but the connection of food with opera in Milan has always been more than casual. Before La Scala opened in 1778, Milanese opera buffs attending the performances at the old Ducal Opera House took their dinners right along with them; the food was heated up in a restaurant inside the theater building. As H. V. Morton describes them in his *A Traveler in Italy,* the boxes had sitting rooms with fireplaces where you could play cards if you were bored with the performance. The Grand Duke's box even had its own bedroom. At La Canobbiana, another opera house that opened in Milan in 1779, the management served whole dinners, including steaming plates of soup and *manzo brasato alla lombarda,* or steaks, while the opera was in progress. The 19th Century French romantic composer Hector Berlioz complained in his memoirs that he could not hear the opera against the noise of the clattering dishes at the Ducal Opera House; while at La Canobbiana, according to Morton, "only during a popular aria was the rattle of knives and forks stilled; then a reverent silence was absolute."

In a Cremona factory, wooden paddles blend mustard and other seasonings with fruit to make *mostarda*, a Lombardy relish resembling chutney.

CHAPTER VIII RECIPES

Manzo Brasato alla Lombarda
BEEF BRAISED IN STOCK AND RED WINE

To serve 6

1 teaspoon finely chopped garlic
1 teaspoon dried oregano, crumbled
½ teaspoon salt
¼ teaspoon freshly ground black pepper
8 to 10 half-inch pieces of lean bacon
3 pounds beef rump or bottom round, securely tied

3 tablespoons butter
1 tablespoon olive oil
½ cup coarsely chopped onions
¼ cup coarsely chopped carrots
¼ cup coarsely chopped celery
½ cup dry red wine
2 cups beef stock, fresh or canned
1½ cups drained canned whole-pack tomatoes, coarsely chopped
1 bay leaf

Preheat the oven to 350°. Mix the finely chopped garlic, oregano, salt and pepper together and roll the pieces of bacon in the mixture. Then, with a small sharp knife make deep incisions in the beef and insert the pieces of lean bacon in the openings.

In a heavy 10- to 12-inch skillet melt 1 tablespoon of butter with the olive oil over moderate heat and brown the beef, turning it from time to time so that it browns on all sides.

Melt the remaining 2 tablespoons of butter over moderate heat in a heavy casserole that is just large enough to hold the beef comfortably. Combine the coarsely chopped onions, carrots and celery on a cutting board and chop them together into very small pieces. (The resulting mixture is called a *battuto;* when cooked, it is called a *soffritto.*) Stir this mixture into the butter in the casserole and cook, stirring often, for 10 minutes, or until the *soffritto* is soft and lightly colored. Place the beef on top of the *soffritto.*

Discard most of the fat from the skillet, pour in the red wine and boil it briskly over high heat, stirring and scraping in the browned fragments that cling to the bottom and sides of the pan. When the wine has been reduced to ¼ cup, add it to the casserole with the beef stock, chopped tomatoes and bay leaf. The liquid should come about a third of the way up the side of the beef; if it doesn't, add more stock. Bring the casserole to a boil over high heat, cover it tightly and braise in the middle of the oven for about 2 hours, or until the meat is tender when pierced with a sharp knife.

To serve, transfer the beef to a carving board, cut off the strings, and slice the meat. Arrange the slices, slightly overlapping, in a row on a heated platter. Strain the braising sauce from the casserole through a fine sieve into a serving bowl, pressing the vegetables dry with the heel of a wooden spoon before discarding them. Skim as much fat as possible from the surface of the sauce, taste and season it with more salt and pepper, if needed. Moisten the slices of beef with a little of the braising sauce before serving them. Serve the rest of the sauce separately in a sauceboat.

Peperonata
BRAISED SWEET PEPPERS WITH TOMATOES AND ONIONS

To serve 6

2 tablespoons butter
¼ cup olive oil
1 pound onions, sliced ⅛ inch thick (about 4 cups)
2 pounds green and red peppers, peeled by blanching first, seeded and cut in 1-by-½-inch strips (about 6 cups)
2 pounds tomatoes, peeled, seeded and coarsely chopped (about 3 cups)
1 teaspoon red wine vinegar
1 teaspoon salt
Freshly ground black pepper

In a heavy 12-inch skillet, melt the 2 tablespoons of butter with the ¼ cup of olive oil over moderate heat. Add the onions and cook them, turning frequently, for 10 minutes, or until they are soft and lightly browned. Stir in the peppers, reduce the heat, cover and cook for 10 minutes. Add the tomatoes, vinegar, salt and a few grindings of black pepper; cover the pan and cook for another 5 minutes. Then cook the vegetables uncovered over high heat, stirring gently, until almost all the liquid has boiled away.

Serve the *peperonata* as a hot vegetable dish, preceding or along with the main course, or refrigerate it and serve it cold as part of an *antipasto* or as an accompaniment to cold roast meats or fowl.

Panettone

COFFEE CAKE

Sprinkle the 3 packages of yeast and 1 teaspoon of the sugar over ⅓ cup of lukewarm water. Be absolutely sure that the water is lukewarm (110° to 115°)—neither too hot nor too cool to touch. (If the water is too hot, it will kill the yeast; if too cold, the yeast will not be activated.) Let the yeast and sugar stand 2 or 3 minutes, then stir them together to dissolve them completely. Set the cup in a warm, draft-free place, perhaps in a turned-off oven, for 3 to 5 minutes, or until the yeast bubbles up and the mixture almost doubles in volume. If the yeast does not bubble and the mixture remains constant in size, this means that the yeast is inactive. Discard and begin again with 3 more packages.

With a rubber spatula, transfer the yeast mixture to a large mixing bowl. Stir in the 6 egg yolks, vanilla, lemon peel, salt and the rest of the ¼ cup of sugar. Then add 1½ cups of flour, ½ cup at a time, stirring the mixture constantly with your hand until the dough is sticky and soft but has enough body to be gathered into a rough ball. If necessary, add a little more flour. Divide the soft butter into three pieces and mix one piece at a time into the dough, which should then become heavy and stringy and fall from your hands in large blobs. Gather it together again in one mass.

Now add ½ to 1 cup more flour, a little at a time, mixing it in with your hands. When the dough is firm and, although oily, no longer sticky, knead it on a floured board for about 10 minutes, or until the dough is smooth and shiny and its surface is blistered. Then shape it into a ball. Place the ball in a large, clean bowl and sprinkle the top with a little flour. Cover the bowl with a plate or pot lid and set it in a warm draft-free spot (here again, an oven with the heat turned off is ideal). In 30 to 45 minutes the dough should rise to double its bulk.

Preheat the oven to 400°. Punch the dough down with your fists and gently knead in the diced candied citron and the white and dark raisins. Handle the dough as little as possible after you have added the raisins and citron or it will discolor. Shape the dough into a ball again, place it on a buttered baking sheet and cut a cross on the top of the ball. Generously butter one side of a strip of heavy brown paper about 25 inches long and 5 inches wide. Wrap the ball of dough loosely in the paper, buttered side in, so that the paper surrounds the dough in the pan like a collar. The collar should measure about 6 to 8 inches across. Fasten the ends of the paper in place around the dough with string, a pin or a paper clip and set the wrapped dough in a warm place to rise again.

When the dough has again doubled in bulk (after about another 15 minutes), brush the top of the dough with some of the melted butter and bake the *panettone* on the middle shelf of the oven for 10 minutes. Then reduce the oven temperature to 350°, brush the top of the *panettone* with more of the melted butter, and bake for 30 to 40 minutes longer. When done, the top should be crisp and golden brown. Brush again with melted butter about 15 or 20 minutes after the baking process begins.

When the *panettone* is done, cool it on a wire cake rack, removing the paper when the cake is cool enough to handle. To serve, cut the *panettone* into thick wedges. *Panettone* stays fresh a long time, if carefully wrapped in aluminum foil, and is an excellent accompaniment to coffee or wine.

To make 1 loaf

3 packages active dry yeast
¼ cup sugar
⅓ cup lukewarm water
6 egg yolks
1 teaspoon vanilla extract
½ teaspoon freshly grated lemon peel
½ teaspoon salt
2 to 3 cups flour
8 tablespoons (1 quarter-pound stick) soft butter
⅓ cup diced candied citron
¼ cup white raisins, rinsed and drained
¼ cup dark raisins, rinsed and drained
2 tablespoons melted butter

To serve 6 to 8

4 tablespoons butter
1½ cups finely chopped onions
½ cup finely chopped carrots
½ cup finely chopped celery
1 teaspoon finely chopped garlic
6 to 7 pounds veal shank or shin,
    sawed—not chopped—into 8
    pieces, each 2½ inches long, and tied
    with string around their
    circumference
Salt
Freshly ground black pepper
Flour
½ cup olive oil
1 cup dry white wine
¾ cup beef or chicken stock, fresh
    or canned
½ teaspoon dried basil
½ teaspoon dried thyme
3 cups drained canned whole
    tomatoes, coarsely chopped
6 parsley sprigs
2 bay leaves

GREMOLATA

1 tablespoon grated lemon peel
1 teaspoon finely chopped garlic
3 tablespoons finely chopped parsley

To serve 6 to 8

7 cups chicken stock, fresh or canned
4 tablespoons butter
½ cup finely chopped onions
⅓ to ½ cup chopped uncooked beef
    marrow (optional)
2 cups plain white raw rice, preferably
    imported Italian rice
½ cup dry white wine
⅛ teaspoon powdered saffron or
    saffron threads crushed to a powder
4 tablespoons soft butter
½ cup freshly grated imported
    Parmesan cheese

Osso Buco
BRAISED VEAL SHANKS

Choose a heavy shallow casserole or Dutch oven that has a tight cover and is just large enough to snugly hold the pieces of veal standing up in 1 layer. Melt the butter in the casserole over moderate heat and when the foam subsides, add the chopped onions, carrots, celery and garlic. Cook, stirring occasionally, for 10 to 15 minutes, or until the vegetables are lightly colored. Remove the casserole from the heat.

Season the pieces of veal with salt and pepper, then roll them in flour and shake off the excess. In a heavy 10- to 12-inch skillet, heat 6 tablespoons of olive oil until a haze forms over it. Brown the veal in the oil over moderately high heat, 4 or 5 pieces at a time, adding more oil as needed. Transfer the browned pieces to the casserole and stand them side by side on top of the vegetables.

Preheat the oven to 350°. Now discard almost all of the fat from the skillet, leaving just a film on the bottom. Pour in the wine and boil it briskly over high heat until it is reduced to about ½ cup. Scrape in any browned bits clinging to the pan. Now stir in the stock, basil, thyme, tomatoes, parsley sprigs and bay leaves and bring to a boil, then pour it all over the veal. The liquid should come halfway up the side of the veal; if it does not, add more stock. Bring the casserole to a boil on top of the stove. Cover and bake in the lower third of the oven, basting occasionally and regulating the oven heat to keep the casserole simmering gently. In about 1 hour and 15 minutes the veal should be tender; test it by piercing the meat with the tip of a sharp knife. To serve, arrange the pieces of veal on a heated platter and spoon the sauce and vegetables from the casserole around them. Sprinkle the top with *gremolata*—a piquant garnish made by mixing the grated lemon rind and chopped garlic and parsley together. *Osso buco* is traditionally served with *risotto alla milanese (below)* or plain buttered pasta.

For a more elegant version of *osso buco*, remove the casserole from the oven when the meat is tender and increase the oven temperature to 450°. With tongs, carefully transfer the veal to a large ovenproof platter, being careful not to lose the marrow in the bones on the way. Place the platter in the top third of the oven and bake the veal for 5 to 10 minutes, or until it is deep brown and brightly glazed. Meanwhile, strain the contents of the casserole through a fine sieve into a 2- to 3-quart saucepan, pressing down hard on the vegetables with the back of a spoon to squeeze out their juice before discarding them. Boil the braising liquid over high heat, stirring frequently, until it has reduced to about half its original quantity. Taste and season it with salt and pepper if needed. Pour the reduced sauce over the glazed veal and sprinkle the top with *gremolata*.

Risotto alla Milanese
BRAISED RICE WITH SAFFRON

Bring the chicken stock to a simmer in a 2- to 3-quart saucepan and keep it barely simmering over low heat. In a heavy 3-quart flameproof casserole, melt 4 tablespoons of butter over moderate heat. Cook the onions in the butter, stirring frequently, for 7 or 8 minutes. Do not let them brown. Stir in the optional marrow, then add the rice and cook, stirring, for 1 or 2 minutes, or until the grains glisten with butter and are somewhat opaque. Pour in the wine and boil it until it is almost completely absorbed. Then add 2 cups of the simmering stock to the rice and cook uncovered, stirring occasionally, until almost all of the liquid is absorbed. Add 2 more cups of stock and cook, stirring occasionally. Meanwhile, stir the saffron into 2 cups of stock and let it steep for a few minutes. Then pour it over the rice. Cook until the stock is completely absorbed.

By now the rice should be tender. If it is still firm, add the remaining stock—½ cup at a time—and continue cooking and stirring until the rice is soft. Stir in 4 tablespoons of soft butter and the grated cheese with a fork, taking care not to mash the rice. Serve at once while the rice is creamy and piping hot.

Zuppa alla Pavese
CHICKEN SOUP WITH POACHED EGGS

In a heavy 8- to 10-inch skillet, melt the butter over moderately low heat and in it cook the bread, turning frequently, for 4 or 5 minutes, or until the slices are golden brown on both sides. Place 1 slice of bread in each of 4 individual soup bowls. Bring the chicken stock to a simmer in a small saucepan, and let it simmer slowly while you prepare the eggs.

Bring 2 inches of water to a simmer in a 10- to 12-inch skillet. Break 1 egg into a saucer. Holding the dish as close to the water as possible, slide the egg into the skillet. Gently lift the white over the yolk with a wooden spoon. Following the same procedure and keeping the water at a slow simmer, break the 3 other eggs into the saucer 1 at a time and slide them into the water. Try to keep them separate. Poach the eggs for 3 to 5 minutes, depending on how firm you want them. Then remove them from the water with a slotted spatula or spoon and place 1 egg on top of the fried bread in each soup bowl. Sprinkle the eggs with grated cheese and pour the stock around it. Serve the soup at once.

To serve 4

4 tablespoons butter
4 slices of Italian bread, each ½ inch thick
3 cups chicken stock, fresh or canned
4 fresh eggs
2 tablespoons freshly grated imported Parmesan cheese

Pere Ripiene
PEARS STUFFED WITH GORGONZOLA CHEESE

With a small sharp knife, peel the pears and cut them in half lengthwise, leaving a stem attached to one of the halves of each pear. Remove the cores and scoop a scant tablespoon of pulp out of each of the pear halves. To prevent the fruit from turning brown, paint each section of pear inside and out with a pastry brush dipped in lemon juice.

Cream the Gorgonzola cheese and softened butter together by beating them against the side of a small bowl with a wooden spoon until they are soft and fluffy. Fill the hollows of the pears with 1 tablespoon of the cheese-and-butter mixture and carefully press the two halves of the pear back together again. Roll the pears around in the crushed nuts, then arrange them on a serving plate. Chill the pears for about 2 hours, or until the cheese stuffing is firm.

To serve 4

4 small firm ripe pears
1 tablespoon lemon juice
2 ounces imported Gorgonzola cheese (about ¼ cup), at room temperature
2 tablespoons soft unsalted butter
2 tablespoons crushed walnuts, pistachio or pine nuts

Glory of a Lombardian Kitchen

OSSO BUCO

1 Start by cooking carrots, onions, celery and garlic in melted butter.

3 After browning the shanks in a large skillet, put them in the casserole with the cooked vegetables.

RISOTTO ALLA MILANESE

1 Cook onions in butter, and add beef marrow, keeping rice at hand.

3 Next gradually pour wine and stock over the rice and cook until the grains are soft, but still holding their shape.

2 Next tie the meat of each veal shank to its bone, so that they will not part while they are being cooked.

4 Pour heated stock and wine over the mixture of meat and vegetables and place the dish in the oven to be braised.

2 Pour the rice in with the onions and stir until the rice becomes thoroughly coated with the butter.

4 Finally, stir in two tablespoons of butter and the Parmesan cheese. The rice should have a puddinglike texture.

Accompanied by a decanter of red wine, the completed *osso buco* sits amid *risotto alla milanese*. There is a special spoon for removing the marrow, which some consider the best part of the dish, from inside the bone.

IX

Turin
and Piedmont

At a Piedmontese restaurant, guests sit down to a traditional serving of *bagna cauda,* a hot dip that can be a full meal. Raw vegetables such as celery, peppers, lettuce and tomatoes are dipped in a warmed sauce of crushed anchovies, butter, garlic and olive oil.

With its largely precipitous terrain, Piedmont should be a stronghold of hearty, simple, muscle-building mountain cooking—and in great measure it is. But that is not the whole story. The Piedmontese also cherish a tradition of lavish, sophisticated cuisine developed by the aristocratic families of a region that had the good luck to be less frequently fought over than most parts of Italy. Upper-class Piedmontese, blessed with long periods of peace, had more time and more money to devote to the pleasures of the table.

"Piedmont gave birth to Italy," its inhabitants say, recalling that when Italy was united in 1861 as a single kingdom, its first ruler, Victor Emmanuel II, came from Piedmont's House of Savoy. "Piedmont gave birth to gastronomic Italy," a local writer has added, a bit of editing not likely to be accepted by the inhabitants of other regions. But all agree that Turin, the capital of Piedmont, added a carefully studied court cuisine to the indigenous mountain cooking and gave the region's dishes a subtlety not usually found in mountainous areas. The Piedmontese are not unaware of this dual blessing; as a rule, cooking schools are rare in mountain country, where the art is passed on not from teacher to pupil, but from mother to daughter. Piedmont, however, possesses two excellent culinary academies, one at Cocconato and the other at La Morra. A good example of the two influences of simplicity and sophistication working upon each other is *trotelle alla savoia (page 158)*—trout baked on a bed of mushrooms—a dish that is simultaneously simple, sophisticated, delicate and robust.

In the end, the two culinary traditions have turned out to be complementary. The sophistication and subtlety are sometimes disguised; the

149

heartiness of the fare is apparent. The chief agricultural products of the plain in Piedmont are grains (mountaineers everywhere in the world are heavy consumers of cereals). Piedmont is the greatest rice-producing area of Italy. The streams that run off the mountains are diverted to flood the fields in which rice is cultivated, just as in the Far East. (The picturesque scenes in the classic Italian film, *Bitter Rice,* were photographed in this region, and that is how rice is still handled here: seasonal laborers—including many young girls—bring in the crop by hand, though not all the girls look like Silvana Mangano, the star of the film.)

Since it involves the flooding of fields, rice culture has had its side effects on the Piedmont menu. Carp are bred in the relatively still water that irrigation brings to the rice fields. Frogs also grow there, to be used in soup or for a favorite local dish, *rane dorate*—skinned frogs dipped in flour and fried in olive oil. Piedmont makes a great variety of dishes with its rice, but the best of them all, *riso al limone* (boiled rice with lemon), is one of the simplest *(page 159)*.

The bread sticks called *grissini,* the most famous wheat product of the region, not only have penetrated almost every part of the world, but have been accepted abroad as so typical a product of Italy that they have lost their local label and are known everywhere simply as "Italian." Actually, the bread sticks are purely Turinese, and Napoleon, who was very fond of them, knew it; he always referred to them as "those little Turinese sticks." A thicket of them is likely to bristle from a water glass on the table of any Italian restaurant in the world. There is no point in learning to make them; you can buy them ready-to-eat in almost any city on earth.

The great gift of the mountain country to the cities of the plain is the masterly use of the truffle, always held in high esteem by gourmets. Truffles have been called the "*sancta sanctorum* of foods," "the diamonds of the table," and "a poetic mystery of the gastronomic world." The truffle is an unusual fungus. Having no chlorophyll, it must live in symbiotic partnership with some other growing thing that does possess chlorophyll. Truffles grow underground in the root systems of trees—and only certain kinds of trees. In Piedmont truffles grow chiefly under oaks, chestnuts, willows, hazels and poplars, at an altitude of between 1,300 and 1,950 feet. Since no part of the truffle appears above the ground, men have never learned how to spot them, but dogs can be taught to sniff them out. At Rodi, there is even a "university" for truffle hounds. Once the dog has found a truffle, the hunter then delicately eases the treasure out of the ground with a curved iron tool. Truffles are often gathered at night, with the aid of a small flashlight. Some truffle hunters say that this is done because the odor is stronger at night, but the real purpose probably is to conceal the location of the truffles from prying neighbors. Truffle hunters do not like to be watched because, when a truffle is taken, another will grow in the same spot. A neighbor who knows the spot may come secretly and harvest the second truffle.

The Piedmont truffle is of a special rare whiteness. Black truffles are sometimes found, but the most prized are the white ones peculiar to the region, especially the Langhe area south of Alba. The white truffle has a stronger flavor than the black variety, and is at its best between the months of November and February.

Truffles appear most often as taste provokers—with capon, with veal, even with lobster. There are also any number of dishes in which the truffle stars as the main ingredient—for instance, truffles cooked in Asti Spumante wine, with a very thin layer of Parmesan cheese, seasoned with olive oil, lemon juice, salt and pepper and cooked until the cheese has melted into the truffles, and then served with slices of lemon.

Parmesan cheese on a very thinly sliced truffle offers one of the few cases where a Piedmontese cook would need—or even want—to look outside his own region for cheese. Among the better local products are Robiole (a spicy, creamy cheese made especially well at Roccaverano and Murazzano), and the *toma veja* of the Gressoney Valley, a heavy cheese with a crust that takes on a reddish tint from the bacteria used in its fermentation. Of *toma veja* and other cheeses, a local saying goes: "It has three virtues: it sates hunger, it quenches thirst, and it cleans the teeth."

Fontina, named for Mount Font, at Quart, in the Valle d'Aosta, dominates them all. *Fontina* is a cheese of venerable age. As long ago as 1477 Pantaleone da Confienza wrote in his *Summa Lacticiniorum (Encyclopedia of Dairy Products):* "Valle Augusti casei boni sunt"—in the Valley of Augustus (the Valle d'Aosta) the cheeses are good. The rich yellow *fontina*, which comes in great cartwheels, is made with infinite pains. The process starts with the selection of the cows whose milk will be used; they must descend from both of the two local breeds of cattle. The method of curdling and the handling of the cheese is minute and detailed, and temperatures have to be carefully controlled throughout its production. The final touch is added by aging the cheeses for three to five months in well-aired cellars of stone and lime, at a height of nearly 10,000 feet.

Fontina cheese is the basis for *fonduta (page 156),* perhaps the most famous single dish specifically identified with Piedmont. *Fonduta* utilizes *fontina* and white truffles. Indeed, truffles make *fonduta* especially *piemontese* instead of merely Alpine. A cousin of *fonduta,* fondue, is found in both the Swiss and French Alps. But neither the Swiss nor the French fondue contains truffles, and there are other differences as well. *Fonduta* is both richer and quieter. In Piedmont, the melted cheese that is the basis for both *fonduta* and fondue is mixed with cornstarch, milk and egg yolks, none of which goes into fondue. There is nothing alcoholic in *fonduta;* Swiss fondue, by contrast, contains white wine and the white cherry brandy called kirsch. In France and in Switzerland, the fondue is placed bubbling on the table, with a flame beneath it, and the eaters spear lumps of bread on their forks, turn them in the common pot to coat the bread with the unctuous paste, and then gingerly insert the almost scalding result into their mouths. In Piedmont the *fonduta* is not allowed to come to a boil, and is served in a bowl covered with a layer of white paper-thin truffles. Usually the bread comes already dipped in the melted sauce, though sometimes the hot cheese is poured over rice or onto slabs of the corn-meal porridge known as *polenta*.

Other dishes in which *fontina* is prominently involved are *polenta* pudding (which is not a dessert, but alternate layers of well-peppered *polenta* and *fontina* cheese, baked in an oven); *polenta* on the spit—alternate cubes of *polenta* and *fontina* speared on cocktail sticks, dipped in beaten egg, rolled in bread crumbs, and fried in very hot oil; *fontina* soup—layers of toast and cheese in bouillon; and *fontina* salad (with yellow peppers, green olives, fresh cream, mustard and condiments).

Piedmont is covered by steep hills and mountains that abound in goat, chamois, white hare and wild boar. Carp are raised in the paddies around Vercelli and Novara, which also produce most of the Italian rice. The Langhe Valley around Alba yields white truffles and also Barolo, one of the finest wines in Italy. Good *grappa* (brandy) is produced at Cuneo and at Turin—a city that not only invented the now-ubiquitous Italian bread stick, but has managed to make itself the vermouth capital of the world.

The British writer Thomas Carlyle once declared that the French are such remarkable cooks that they would probably be capable of making a tasty dish of thistles. The Piedmontese have done it. While it is true that the cardoon, Piedmont's edible white thistle, is a very special variety of the plant, the thistle may not be so far removed from the kitchen as Carlyle thought. One way to treat cardoons is to dip them in beaten egg, roll them in flour, and fry them in oil, finishing them afterward in the oven, doused with butter and sprinkled thickly with grated Parmesan cheese. But their most characteristic appearance is with one of the most renowned and most localized of Piedmont specialties, *bagna cauda* (in dialect, *bagna caôda*), which means "hot sauce" *(page 157)*. This is a hot dip for cold vegetables, and in Piedmont the vegetable that is most popular for dipping into *bagna caôda* is the cardoon. However, those who have no edible thistles on hand can substitute celery, fennel, peppers, cauliflower or cabbage. One basic recipe for the dip includes butter, cream or olive oil, garlic and anchovies, but there are many variations: one requires chopped white truffles; others call for roasted walnuts or a glass of Barbera wine.

Searching for even more substantial mountain fare in the almost inaccessible upper reaches of the Valle d'Aosta, hunters come upon animals that have disappeared or become rare elsewhere in Europe: the wild goat, no longer found anywhere else in the Alps; the chamois, less rare in Piedmont than in France or Switzerland (there is a town named Chamois in the Italian Valtournanche, 5,450 feet up); the white hare and the wild boar. If you want to taste the wild goat or the chamois, you must do so on the spot. The former may be too gamy to appeal to all tastes, but chamois, as the Piedmontese cook it, is worth the trip. It is braised in Gattinara wine and then laced with a glass of *grappa,* or brandy. Among the ingredients for the seasoning and gravy are garlic, carrots, celery, thyme, juniper, parsley, bay leaf, onions, cloves, cinnamon, olive oil and tomato extract.

The Piedmontese version of the solid mountaineer diet is influenced in the high country regions by the fact that few families have ovens, so that home baking and roasting are of limited importance. When a Piedmontese feels a hankering for meat on a large scale, he is not likely to choose a roast. He prefers *bolliti misti* (mixed boiled meats)—beef, tongue, chicken, sausage and veal, cooked together and served with green sauce *(page 156)*. Another Piedmontese specialty is a stew called *finanziera di pollo,* made of chicken giblets, sweetbreads, mushrooms and truffles cooked in a thick meat sauce. But the Piedmontese are perhaps fonder of the pastas of their region. One is *agnolotti,* ravioli made with egg and stuffed with minced meat and chopped vegetables and served with a meat sauce, melted butter and grated cheese. Another is *gnocchi alla fontina,* little dumplings of semolina boiled in spiced milk in which *fontina* cheese has been melted, rolled in bread crumbs and egg, and fried.

Sugar is a high-energy, high-calorie food that enters strongly into many mountain diets. The sweet tooth of Piedmont is served by *dolce torinese,* a rich chocolate dessert containing almonds and butter cookies, served cold *(page 159);* by Piedmont pudding, a creamy lemon-flavored dessert; and by the fine candied chestnuts of Chiusa di Pesio, praised four centuries ago by the outspoken satirist Pietro Aretino.

After their solid food, mountaineers are apt to like a swig of strong drink—usually *grappa*. A noted admirer of the Italians, Ernest Hemingway, writing in *A Farewell to Arms* against a background of north Italian mountain country, often referred to Geverose, a fiery brandy that comes in several varieties. Among others, there is Grappa Piemonte Stravecchia from Cuneo, and Grappa delle Langhe, from Alba, which is distilled from *moscato* or Barolo grapes.

Barolo, rated by some connoisseurs as the greatest wine in Italy, is the product of a great wine-producing region and of superlative grapes. The region is the Langhe Valley, one of the 14 that radiate from Cuneo like the spokes of a wheel, each a compartment, each boasting its own specialties. This valley alone annually produces 700,000 gallons of wine, a commodity highly important to the economy of Piedmont.

The grape is Nebbiolo, which imparts an aroma of violets to the wine made from it (in the Langhe Valley, at least; Nebbiolo vines transplanted to the Vercelli region, where they are rebaptized *"spanna,"* are less likely to have the bouquet). By common consent, Barolo stands at the head of the wines made from the Nebbiolo grape; it is full-bodied, but a little rough when young. The violet aroma is a mere whisper, followed by a slightly resinous aftertaste. Wine from Barolo country was praised by Julius Caesar when he stopped at La Morra, in the Langhe region, and digressed from recounting his military exploits against the Gauls long enough to note that here he had been served a marvelous wine.

Two other Langhe wines made from the same grape are Barbaresco, the "younger brother" of Barolo, less rugged and lacking the Barolo rasp (an omission that pleases many winebibbers); and Nebbiolo, lighter than Barbaresco, as Barbaresco is lighter than Barolo. Nebbiolo, named for the grape, because closest to it, has the most pronounced violet fragrance of all.

From Piedmont also comes vermouth, the great *aperitivo* of Italy. The vermouth of the region is essentially a straightforward concoction of blended wines, spirits, herbs and bitters, but the name of the drink has a curious origin. Although Italy and France are the two most notable vermouth countries, the root of the word is Germanic. It comes from *Wermut*, the German word for wormwood, which is used in making absinthe, and appears in some vermouth formulas—including the Italian one.

Italian vermouth was first produced commercially by Benedetto Carpano, who made it in 1786 in his shop in the Piazza Castello, in Turin; but he was far from being the inventor of the drink. Pliny and Cicero mention aromatic wines in their works, and during the Middle Ages such drinks—usually made at home—were used for medicinal purposes. Some people, especially the manufacturers, still contend that there are healthful virtues embodied in vermouth. They support the claim by pointing out that some of the herbs, such as quinine and wormwood, are used in medicine. Some extremely bitter apéritifs certainly have an almost medicinal taste, which is said to exercise a salutary effect on hangovers. A drink of vermouth may also aid the digestion by stimulating the flow of gastric juices, and there are people who maintain that the relaxing effect created by the social act of taking a leisurely drink before the meal gives the stomach time to rest before the onslaught ahead of it. The comfortable sensation that may follow a glass of vermouth probably can be attributed to its alcohol content, which is about 30 to 32 proof, roughly one third the strength of whiskey. The alcohol

In the countryside near Alba, Pasquale Taricco, a truffle gatherer, gloats over a large specimen unearthed by one of his dogs. On an average day, he finds 15 to 20 of these precious and aromatic fungi. Local restaurants use a special grater (*bottom*) to shave slices of truffle to be served with veal, chicken and steak.

content has to be high, since the various essences that go into vermouth would otherwise not be soluble in the mixture.

The exact formulas used in making vermouths are trade secrets, but the approximate make-up of a typical vermouth, Vermut di Torino, is as follows: to a base of neutral white wine are added Moscato d'Asti (a dessert wine), neutral grain spirits and bitters. Burnt sugar is added to the vermouth to make it red, and in order to make it dry the fermentation process is carried to the point where all the grape sugar is converted to alcohol.

Turin is the headquarters of many vermouth manufacturers—Martini & Rossi, Cora and a number of others. One of the most widely known is Cinzano, a firm founded in the middle of the 18th Century by Francesco Cinzano. It has since expanded greatly; Cinzano's main operations have moved out of the capital of Piedmont to occupy an entire village, appropriately named Cinzano. The company also maintains plants outside of Italy, but they are not in on the secret of the Cinzano blend of ingredients. They receive this essential part of the drink in sealed cans from the plant in Santa Vittoria, just next door to the town of Cinzano, and add it to wines produced in their own areas. The original formula of Francesco Cinzano remains a secret said to be known only by two men, the president of the company and the manager of Cinzano's main plant.

The village of Cinzano, which lies practically in the town of Santa Vittoria, in Cuneo province, is a model modern settlement on the banks of the Tanaro River, where 200 families of Cinzano employees live. It includes what used to be the hunting lodge of King Victor Emmanuel II, which is now used for company receptions. In the Cinzano cellars cut into the hill beneath Santa Vittoria is stored enough wine to float an ocean liner. Cinzano's best foreign customers reside in South America, where vermouth is consumed not only as an apéritif but often drunk throughout the meal, a habit that horrifies French connoisseurs.

Not a mainland Frenchman (he was Corsican by birth) and not known as an epicure, Napoleon fought a battle at Marengo in Piedmont in 1800 and ate a famous meal afterward. Having defeated the Austrians and pursued them until darkness fell, he told his cook to whip up some supper. Far from the supply wagons (so the story goes) the cook had to improvise; all he could find in the war-ravaged countryside were three eggs, four tomatoes, six crayfish, a small hen, some garlic, oil and a saucepan. The materials were so scanty that in desperation the cook used everything he had foraged, though he had to admit that some of the ingredients (chicken and crayfish) swore at each other. Napoleon liked the combination all the same, and having feasted on it, told the cook, "You must feed me like this after every battle." The cook was pleased, but feeling, as a Frenchman, that the crayfish did not belong with the chicken, he served the dish one day without the crayfish. A non-Frenchman, Napoleon noticed the omission and was angry. "It will give me bad luck," he said, and he sent the dish back. The cook restored the crayfish, and it remains the traditional garnish for the dish, but like Napoleon's cook, most French restaurants really feel it should be left out. In Piedmont, however, history is respected. While the dish (sans crayfish) remains basically French, you can get chicken Marengo in fancy restaurants such as the Cambio in Turin, but if you order it, it will invariably be made with crayfish.

The elegant Ristorante del Cambio, in the Piedmontese capital of Turin, is considered the finest restaurant in the region.

CHAPTER IX RECIPES

To serve 10 to 12

A 3-pound fresh beef tongue
A 1-pound *cotechino* sausage or
  other uncooked, garlic-flavored
  pork sausage
A 2-pound boneless rump or chuck
  beef roast, trimmed, rolled and tied
  securely
A 2-pound boneless rump or leg veal
  roast, trimmed, rolled, and tied
  securely
4 onions, peeled and quartered
4 carrots, peeled and cut in half
4 celery tops with leaves
8 parsley sprigs
1 bay leaf
1 tablespoon salt
6 peppercorns
A 2½- to 3-pound whole chicken

Bolliti Misti
MIXED BOILED MEATS

In a large soup pot or kettle, cover the tongue completely with cold water. Bring to a boil over high heat, then reduce the heat and partially cover the pot. Simmer the tongue for about 3 hours, or until the meat shows no resistance when it is pierced with the tip of a sharp knife. Drain the tongue of all the liquid, and skin it with a sharp knife, cutting away the fat, bones and gristle at its base.

Lay the sausage flat in a large pan and cover it with cold water. With the tip of a sharp knife or a small skewer, prick the sausage in 5 or 6 places to release some of the fat from the sausage and to prevent it from bursting as it cooks. Bring the water to a boil, then lower the heat and simmer the sausage, uncovered, for another 45 minutes. Remove it from the pan when it is done and put it aside.

Place the beef, onions, carrots, celery tops, parsley, bay leaf, salt and peppercorns in an 8- to 10-quart soup pot or kettle. Pour in enough cold water to cover the meat completely and bring it to a boil over high heat. Skim off any foam that rises to the surface. Reduce the heat and partially cover and simmer the beef for 1 hour before adding the veal. Let the meats simmer together for another 30 minutes, skimming the surface fat as necessary. Then add the chicken and, after 15 minutes, the tongue and sausage.

Simmer partially covered for 20 to 30 minutes longer, or until all of the meats are tender. With tongs, transfer the beef, veal, chicken, tongue and sausage to a carving board. (If you wish, strain the broth, discarding the vegetables and seasonings, and serve it as a soup course with pasta in it.) With a sharp knife, peel the skin from the sausage. Then carve the sausage, beef, veal and tongue into thin, even slices and arrange these attractively on a large heated platter. Carve the chicken into serving pieces and arrange with the sliced meats. Serve hot, accompanied by *salsa verde (Recipe Booklet).*

To serve 4 to 6

1 pound imported Fontina or Gruyère
  cheese, cut in small chunks (about
  4 cups)
1 teaspoon cornstarch dissolved in
  ½ cup milk
¼ teaspoon salt
⅛ teaspoon white pepper
3 egg yolks
1 canned white truffle, sliced paper thin
  (optional)
4 to 6 slices white French or Italian
  bread toasted, buttered and cut
  diagonally into triangles

Fonduta
HOT MELTED CHEESE WITH TOAST

Put the small chunks of cheese, the cornstarch and milk mixture, and salt and pepper into a heavy 2- to 3-quart saucepan. Cook over low heat, stirring constantly, for about 5 minutes, or until the cheese melts; it will probably be somewhat stringy.

Beat the egg yolks very lightly for a few seconds with a whisk or a rotary or portable electric beater. Spoon about ¼ cup of the hot cheese mixture into the yolks and beat them vigorously. Pour the mixture slowly back into the pan, beating constantly, and continue cooking the cheese mixture over low heat until it becomes runny and smooth and finally begins to thicken to a heavy cream. Ladle immediately into heated shallow ramekins or bowls.

If you use the truffle, arrange slices on top of the *fonduta.* Stand the toast triangles around the inside edges of the ramekins or bowls. Serve at once, while the *fonduta* is hot.

A delectable cocktail dip, *bagna cauda* reposes among vegetables and breadsticks.

Bagna Cauda

HOT ANCHOVY AND GARLIC DIP

Soak the vegetable strips in a bowl of ice cubes and water for an hour to crisp them. Pat dry with paper towels and arrange on a platter with the romaine leaves, tomatoes and mushrooms. Cover with plastic wrap and refrigerate. Arrange the bread sticks on a separate plate and set aside.

In a heavy 1-quart enameled or stainless-steel saucepan, bring the cream to a boil and cook it, stirring frequently, for about 15 to 20 minutes, or until it has thickened and has reduced to about 1 cup.

Choose a 3- or 4-cup enameled or flameproof earthenware casserole that fits over a candle warmer, spirit lamp or electric hot tray. On the stove, melt the butter in the casserole over low heat; do not let it brown. Add the anchovies and garlic, then the reduced cream and the optional truffle, and bring the sauce to a simmer, stirring constantly. Do not let it boil. Serve the *bagna cauda* at once, accompanied by the cold vegetables and the bread sticks. To eat, pick up a vegetable or bread stick with your fingers and dip it into the hot sauce. If the butter and cream separate as the sauce stands, beat with a wire whisk. (You may substitute almost any raw vegetable you like for *bagna cauda:* fennel sticks, cauliflower or broccoli flowerets, white turnip wedges, or red or white radishes.)

To serve 6

1 cucumber, peeled, seeded and cut into 2-by-½-inch strips
2 carrots, peeled and cut into 2-by-½-inch strips
1 sweet red pepper, seeded and cut into 2-by-½-inch strips
1 green pepper, seeded and cut into 2-by-½-inch strips
4 celery stalks, cut into 2-by-½-inch strips
1 bunch scallions, trimmed and cut into 2-inch lengths
A small head of romaine, broken into separate leaves
12 cherry tomatoes
¼ pound fresh mushrooms, whole if small, quartered if large
Italian bread sticks

2 cups heavy cream
4 tablespoons butter
8 flat anchovy fillets, drained, rinsed and finely chopped
1 teaspoon finely chopped garlic
1 canned white truffle, finely chopped (optional)

157

Fit for royalty (or a commoner with a king's taste): baked trout in a bed of mushrooms, topped with bread crumbs and scallions.

To serve 4

4 cleaned, whole trout,
   ½ to ¾ pound each, with heads
   and tails left on, or substitute
   thoroughly defrosted frozen trout
Salt
Freshly ground black pepper
Flour
6 tablespoons butter
2 tablespoons olive oil
½ pound fresh mushrooms, thinly
   sliced
1 teaspoon lemon juice
¾ cup thinly sliced scallions (white
   part plus 2 to 3 inches of green)
¼ cup fresh white bread crumbs (made
   from about 1 slice French or Italian
   bread)

Trotelle alla Savoia
BAKED TROUT WITH MUSHROOMS

Preheat the oven to 425°. Wash the trout, inside and out, under cold running water and pat them dry with paper towels. Season the trout lightly with salt and pepper, then roll them in flour and brush or shake off the excess. In a heavy 10- to 12-inch skillet, melt 2 tablespoons of butter with the oil over high heat. When the foam subsides, add the trout and cook them for 4 to 5 minutes on each side, or until they are golden brown. Carefully transfer the trout to a plate. In a stainless-steel or enameled skillet, melt another 2 tablespoons of butter over moderate heat. Add the sliced mushrooms, sprinkle them with lemon juice, and shaking the skillet almost constantly, cook for about 3 minutes, or until they glisten with butter and are slightly softened. With a slotted spoon, remove the mushrooms from the skillet and spread them over the bottom of a buttered ovenproof baking dish just large enough to hold the 4 trout in one layer. Melt 1 tablespoon of butter in the skillet, add the scallions and cook them for 1 minute. Then

158

with a slotted spoon transfer them to a bowl. In the remaining tablespoon of butter, and in the same skillet, lightly brown the bread crumbs.

Arrange the browned trout (adding any juices that have accumulated on the platter) on top of the mushrooms in the baking dish. Sprinkle them with the crisped bread crumbs and spread the scallions on top. Bake on the middle shelf of the oven for 10 minutes, or until the crumbs and scallions are brown. Serve directly from the baking dish.

Dolce Torinese
CHILLED CHOCOLATE LOAF

Lightly grease the bottom and sides of a 1½-quart loaf pan with vegetable oil and invert the pan over paper towels to drain. In a heavy 1- to 1½-quart saucepan, melt the chocolate over low heat, stirring constantly. When all the chocolate is dissolved, stir in the rum and remove the pan from the heat. Cool to room temperature.

Cream the soft butter by beating it vigorously against the sides of a large heavy mixing bowl until it is light and fluffy. Beat in the sugar and then the egg yolks, one at a time. Stir in the grated almonds and cooled chocolate. In a separate bowl, beat the egg whites and salt with a rotary beater or wire whisk until they are stiff enough to cling to the beater in soft peaks. With a rubber spatula, fold them into the chocolate mixture. When no streaks of white show, gently fold in the cut-up biscuits, discarding the biscuit crumbs. Spoon the mixture into the greased loaf pan and smooth the top with a spatula to spread it evenly. Cover tightly with plastic wrap and refrigerate for at least 4 hours, or until the loaf is very firm.

Unmold the loaf an hour or so before serving time. To do so, run a sharp knife around the sides of the pan and dip the bottom into hot water for a few seconds. Place a chilled serving platter upside down over the pan and, grasping both sides, quickly turn the plate and pan over. Rap the plate on the table; the loaf should slide out easily. If it does not, repeat the whole process. Smooth the top and sides of the unmolded loaf with a metal spatula, then return it to the refrigerator. Just before serving, sieve a little confectioners' sugar over the top. Cut the loaf into thin slices and serve it, if desired, with whipped cream.

To serve 8

½ pound semisweet chocolate, cut in small pieces
¼ cup rum
16 tablespoons (½ pound) soft unsalted butter
2 tablespoons "superfine" sugar
2 eggs, separated
1½ cups grated blanched almonds (about 5 ounces)
Pinch of salt
12 butter biscuits (Petits Beurre or Social Tea), cut into 1-by-½-inch pieces
Confectioners' sugar
½ cup heavy cream, whipped (optional)

Riso al Limone
BOILED RICE WITH LEMON

In a large soup pot or kettle, bring the water and salt to a bubbling boil over high heat. Pour in the rice in a slow stream so that the water never stops boiling. Stir once or twice, then reduce the heat to moderate and boil the rice uncovered and undisturbed for about 15 minutes, or until it is tender. Test it by tasting a few grains. As soon as the rice is done, drain it thoroughly in a large colander.

Over low heat, melt the butter in a 1-quart flameproof casserole and immediately add the hot drained rice. In a bowl, beat the eggs with a fork until they are well combined. Then beat in the cheese and lemon juice. Stir this mixture into the rice and cook over very low heat, stirring gently with a fork, for 3 or 4 minutes. Serve at once while the rice is still creamy.

To serve 4

6 quarts water
3 tablespoons salt
1 cup plain white raw rice, preferably imported Italian rice
2 tablespoons butter
3 eggs
1 cup freshly grated imported Parmesan cheese
4 teaspoons lemon juice

X

Naples and the Deep South

Outside a Naples restaurant where pizza is sold in oval pies of three feet and longer, a young delivery boy proudly displays the city's most famous dish. A family-sized order like this is about 40 inches long.

In the late 1920s, I drove from Naples to Pompeii. The *autostrada* that bypasses the city today did not exist then, and we had to thread our way through a labyrinth of narrow, twisting streets that took us occasionally into the courtyards of apartment houses. There I saw homemade macaroni hung out to dry like the family washing—at the mercy of dust, dirt, insects and the depredations of passing pigeons, children and dogs.

With that kind of image in mind, critical travelers long castigated Naples as the proverbial home of *dolce far niente* (literally, "sweet do-nothing"), with only the "picturesqueness" of dirt and squalor to recommend it. But today Naples is a boom city with a busy port—the second most important in Italy after Genoa's—and soaring clusters of new buildings and factories where most of the city's macaroni is now made by machine. Moreover, even in the past Naples was by no means a city of sweet do-nothings; the fact is that what the world knows as "Italian" cooking originated in the industrious minds and hands of Neapolitans who took along their native cuisine to all the lands to which they emigrated in the sad days when Italy was a country to leave rather than to enjoy.

Perhaps the most famous example of the Neapolitan style of cooking is pizza, so popular in the U.S. that it has even been reintroduced to Naples —largely, it must be said, for consumption by tourists—but the reintroduction has also rekindled flagging local interest in the dish. The style is also deliciously exemplified in the region's macaroni and spaghetti, in its piquant sauces and in its *gelati* and *granite* (ice creams and ices). Inexpensive, hearty and highly varied, the Neapolitan cuisine stands for the cooking of all southern Italy; Naples is the culinary capital of the south as indisputably as Bologna is the capital of the cooking of the north.

There are of course strong contrasts between the two cuisines, that of the north being based on abundance, that of the south on recollections of poverty, leavened by a natural exuberance.

Humble foods, necessarily forced into a prominent place in the southern diet, are given compensatory piquancy and glamor by a southern love for life. By painting a ring-shaped, cakelike loaf of bread with beaten eggs before baking, the Neapolitans give it a polished glaze upon which they impose flamboyant designs—fruit, flowers or religious symbols. Spaghetti and macaroni are enriched with tasty sauces like *pizzaiola*, a piquant mixture of herbs and tomatoes *(page 175)*. Even in the poorest parts of the south the ingenuity of housewives brings remarkable changes to such simple materials as tomatoes, peppers, eggplant or zucchini—combining them, stuffing them, using them in sauces—a further indication of the hand-to-mouth quality of life in the southern part of Italy. To this day, habits of frugality endure. I recently had a visit in Paris from two deep-south residents of Cosenza, in Calabria. I tried to introduce them to the subtleties of French cooking, but they proved reluctant. "We don't eat much meat," one of them explained. "In Calabria, our habits are vegetarian." One was a lawyer and the other an engineer (and both were in upper-income brackets). Nonetheless, they asked for mineral water with their meals because they were "not used to drinking much wine."

The south, it must be said, is not a land of great wines. To me, at least, its well-known wines are unimpressive. For instance, the name Lachrima Christi (tear of Christ), produced from grapes grown on the slopes of Vesuvius, had made me expect something special, but it proved disappointing. The vintage with no reputation at all is what the traveler should experiment with. In the Naples area every hillside is cloaked with vines, but the individual land holdings are so tiny that their wine often is not even named, and few of them produce enough wine to justify commercial exploitation. The wine is often consumed on the spot by the maker. I remember stopping at the Accidie Hotel, near Vico Equense, which absorbed the entire output of the small vineyard it owned on a neighboring hill. From my window one day I watched two workmen press the grapes in a small building behind the hotel. It was a very small-scale operation, doubtless obsolete. The men clung to two long levers protruding from a large metal cylinder, thrust them down, raised them, and then pushed them down again. Later, sitting by the edge of the water, looking across the Bay of Naples at Vesuvius, I tasted the previous year's produce from the same vineyard. The white was agreeable, dry and light, just the thing to drink in the open air on a warm sunny day, with the Tyrrhenian Sea twinkling before you. The red was excellent, warm, with a slight peppery taste.

The Campania region, in which Naples lies, is superior to the rest of the south in wine; its agriculture in general gives it an advantage over the other regions of the south. Because of its fertile volcanic soil, the Romans called the area the Campania Felix (the Fortunate Country). Here wheat, maize and millet grow abundantly and vegetables reach enormous sizes. The fertility of the land is taken advantage of; where fruit or olive trees stand in widely spaced rows, beans, cabbage, broccoli or tomatoes may grow between them.

And vines may be allowed to climb over the trees. Frequently, three crops are harvested each year from the same land.

Apart from the Campania, there are few other pockets of great fertility. In most of the south, a region with a primarily agricultural economy, farming must be carried on under most difficult conditions. The terrain is mountainous and there is not much water. After the fortunate Campania, Apulia is the luckiest of the seven southern regions in climate and amount of arable land. And by the injustice of nature, Apulia is also richest in food from the sea—the fertile element that helps to save the south from hunger.

The resources of the sea include swordfish, eels, sardines, anchovies and mullet—which is very good baked with black olives and capers *(page 178)*. Apulia has the longest coastline (500 miles) of any Italian region and, where it pushes the heel of the Italian boot between the Adriatic and the Ionian Seas, is bounded by water on three sides. But all the southern regions have coastal areas and fishing ports. Without them, the inhabitants could hardly survive. Unfortunately, however, the fresh fruits of the sea do not always travel very far inland. Too often in this rude region, contact with the sea is limited to a narrow strip of land along the coast. Beyond that, the ground mounts so swiftly and transport is so slow that seafood often is not available almost within sight of the water.

It is no wonder, then, that the coast is much more densely populated than the interior, and those who do live on the coast are fortunate indeed. They reside in the part of Italy where men first learned to cultivate oysters on a large scale—in the lovely coastal Lake Lucrino, just south of Naples. A local story has it that oyster cultivation had to be interrupted in Lake Lucrino in 37 B.C., when General Marcus Vipsanius Agrippa, building a military base, linked it by tunnel and canal to sulphurous Lake Averno (the site of Vergil's entrance to Hades). The waters from Averno (whose name derives from the Latin *avernus*, "without birds," presumably because birds had learned to avoid the fumes rising from its surface) destroyed the oysters in Lucrino. Whether that story is true, the industry was in fact almost ruined in 1922, when underground gases broke through the Lucrino's east bank. Happily, however, the beds are thriving today. So are those of the Gulf of Taranto, in Apulia, which were established roughly 300 years ago, and whose oyster farmers use methods much the same as their ancestors'. The Gulf of Taranto is on the Ionian Sea, between the Mare Piccolo (Little Sea) and the Mare Grande (Great Sea). A lagoon fed both by fresh water and by salt water seeping in from the Mediterranean, the Mare Piccolo has an ideal combination of water for producing tasty oysters. The Mare Grande is part of the salt-water Gulf of Taranto, but it is sheltered by a curve of the coast, by

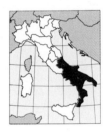

Naples and the surrounding Campania region offer southern Italy's best cooking. There are pizza, sausage and spaghetti, plus macaroni with clam, meat, tomato or garlic sauce. Apulia stuffs eggplant with various cheeses, anchovies, capers, olives and garlic. Calabria slices up eggplant and seasons it with garlic, oil, parsley and pepper. The coastal towns all boast superior mixed-fish stews.

islands and by breakwaters. Baby oysters are started in the Mare Grande and
moved to the Mare Piccolo to fatten as they grow to maturity. The entire
process takes from 18 months to two years. At present, Taranto produces
more than five million oysters a year, along with mussels, clams and other
shellfish.

Inevitably all of the coastal towns have their fish soups. A particularly
tasty *brodetto* of the Abruzzi is a stew consisting of several kinds of fish
seasoned with onion, garlic, parsley, tomatoes, bay leaves, and most important of all, the white vinegar for which the Abruzzi is noted. Naples has its
zuppa di pesce alla marinara, a similarly mixed fish stew seasoned with
garlic, parsley and tomatoes and poured over slices of fried bread placed
in the soup plate. There is also *zuppa di vongole (page 179)*, made the
same way, but with clams or mussels used as a base instead of fish.

Once away from the coast, fish soups tend to disappear, but as in many
poor rural regions, some sort of soup continues to be a mainstay of the
meal. Inland in Calabria, where cooking is based largely on pasta and vegetables, the mainstay of any meal is likely to be a vegetable soup thickened
with pasta. A Calabrian jingle about local soups sums it up: *Sette cose fa la
zuppa: /Cura fame e sete attuta, /Empie il ventre, /Netta il dente, /Fá dormire, /Fá
smaltire /E la guancia colorire. /*(Soup does seven things: /it appeases your
hunger, /slakes your thirst, /fills your stomach, /cleans your teeth, /makes
you sleep, /helps you digest, /and puts color in your cheeks.)

164

Also helping to blunt the hunger so general in the south is the all-pervasive pasta. As a 19th Century writer put it, "God provided pasta as the basis for a whole meal." The citizens of Bari, in Apulia, at one time felt so strongly about their pasta that they revolted to defend it—at least according to legend. The uprising started in July 1647, when the ruling Spaniards, having taxed everything else they could think of, hit upon the instantly unpopular idea of imposing a tax on flour. After a week's fighting, the Spaniards abolished the tax. But there is some doubt whether the men of Bari were defending their pasta or their women; they had put up with the tax until Spanish soldiers were sent into the kitchens to monitor the amounts of flour used. The gallant Spaniards, it appeared, found it less interesting to inspect the flour than to talk to the ladies, and that was perhaps a more plausible explanation for the rebellion.

Because pasta is so important, its variations and complications have been developed ad infinitum. Although the south is closely identified with the manufactured tubular types of pasta whose special quality often derives from the clear mountain water used in making them, there is plenty of homemade pasta too.

The basic refinement for pasta, of course, is sauce. Naples offers spaghetti and macaroni *con le vongole,* that is, with clam sauce *(Recipe Booklet).* The clam is not quite like other clams, for the *vongola* is a small shellfish something like a snail. Other Neapolitan favorites are spaghetti (or maca-

Adriatic oysters and mussels are raised in the beds of the Mare Piccolo, the tidal inlet at Taranto. The young shellfish are first strung on ropes of braided hemp and then suspended from racks near the water's edge so that they hang just below the surface. As they mature, they are transferred to deeper water. In the picture above, the camera lens—half in and half out of water—caught a string of mature mussels being lifted from the water.

Glowing in the deep southern sun, *frutta* (fruit) and *verdura* (vegetables) decorate a grocery entrance at Alfedena, a village in Abruzzi.

roni) *al sugo* (with meat sauce), or *al pomodoro* (with tomato sauce), to give only the most common examples from an endless list. There are numerous varieties of tomato sauce; most favored in Naples is spaghetti in a *pommarola 'ncoppa*, pasta topped with a sauce of fresh tomatoes, with onions, bacon and garlic browned in olive oil. Capri makes a specialty of *spaghetti ai totani (totano* is a member of the squid family, known in English as calamary). In Apulia, the sauces used on spaghetti, macaroni and other varieties of pasta often have one characteristic in common—vegetables added to a meat sauce base. The vegetables may be cabbage and turnip sprouts or artichokes—as in *timballo di maccheroni*, a sort of pasta pie made of *mozzarella*, mushrooms, peas, chicken giblets, sausage and meatballs. Pimentos turn up in spaghetti *alla zappatora* (peasants' spaghetti). The cooks of Apulia usually use garlic with great discretion. Their spaghetti *alla zappatora,* however, reeks of garlic, and also is thick with pepper, which makes it food for strong men. The first mouthful gives you the impression that you are eating fire. But as soon as your palate has become sufficiently anesthetized by the hot ingredients, you begin to appreciate its rich flavor. Not only robust and tasty, it is capable of being thrown together very quickly.

Despite the region's special appetite for pasta, bread is as important a staple in the south as it is elsewhere in Italy. Because it has so often carried people through periods of drought and hardship, bread is identified in the minds of the people with Christ the Life Giver, and given almost reverential treatment. If a piece of bread is dropped on the floor, peasant people will pick it up immediately, kiss it, and return it to the table for eating. Bread, not money, is the traditional gift for beggars. Southern bread, in addition, has another quality; it is made not with commercial brewers' yeast but with yeast produced in groups of households. When the time comes to make bread, the youngest member of a family is sent to the house of a neighbor who has just finished making bread. He brings home some of the leftover dough, which then is set to ferment in his own house and used as yeast for the new bread. In turn, some of the dough used in making this bread is set aside to give to another neighbor in need of yeast for tomorrow's baking. In effect, the yeast used in much of the south's bread baking has been in use for generations; dough made with it is slower to rise than that made with commercial yeast. But for good reason this bread is highly prized; its flavor is beyond compare. In Apulia, as in other parts of the south, the homemade loaf is beginning to lose ground to the commercial product, but the resistance to factory-made bread is still strong.

Bread is combined with cheese in one of the most typical of Neapolitan dishes, *mozzarella in carrozza*—"mozzarella in a carriage" *(page 177)*. It is a *mozzarella* cheese sandwich, dipped in flour and beaten egg, and fried. It should be eaten scalding hot. *Mozzarella* is a very special cheese, made from milk obtained from the large white cattle seen grazing everywhere along the coastal plain south of Naples. Aversa, Salerno and Battipaglia are reputed to produce the best *mozzarella,* but everywhere in the south you see it in grocery windows, swimming in its own milk in large bowls.

It is for their cheese and milk that cattle are most prized in the south. The meat is far too lean and stringy for the pot, and the animals are too valuable both as property and as a source of food on the hoof. True, a well-known specialty of Naples is *bistecca alla pizzaiola (page 178)*, but the dish is less renowned for the quality of the beefsteak than for the interest of the sauce. *Costolette di maiale alla pizzaiola*, a similar specialty of Naples, a pork chop dish *(page 178)*, is more representative of southern meat dishes, at least for more affluent people. Chicken is an even more frequently encountered dish, in part because chickens can be obtained free. One simply asks a neighbor to set three or four fertile eggs under a hen at brooding time and reciprocates the favor with one's own hen at some later time. Feeding chickens, moreover, is no problem; they are left in the streets to scratch for themselves. Chicken recipes are countless, in consequence; one of the best from the south is *pollo alla cacciatora (page 179)*.

Though they must be eaten fresh, innards are also cheap and nourishing. One Apulian dish—called *quagghiarid* in the local dialect—is sheep tripe stuffed with lamb's liver, salami, cheese and parsley mixed with eggs. In Calabria, the specialty of the Catanzaro area is *morseddu*—pig or calf giblets seasoned with tomato and hot red peppers and spread over a bread roll. A more tractable southern dish from the same tradition is *rognoncini trifolati*, lamb or veal kidneys sliced extremely thin and sautéed *(page 176)*.

These southern dishes, clearly, are simple, solid, country food. The vegetables that go with them are also in the rustic tradition of home cooking—the *cucina casalinga*. The most favored are tomatoes, eggplant, artichokes and peppers. The eggplant is ubiquitous in the south, unsurprisingly; the

Near Bitonto, a principal center of olive-oil production, a mountain of green and black olives is reduced to small hills before being hauled away for pressing into oil.

Continued on page 171

Tomatoes, tied in bunches and hung along a wall to dry, will be eaten throughout the winter until the next crop is harvested.

At a farm near Naples, tomatoes are picked, boxed and hauled away in high-wheeled oxcarts. The tomatoes of the Italian south have a rich color and piquant flavor that are ideal for making the well-beloved sauce.

Golden Apples: Italian Staple Born in America

It is not true that southern Italians cannot cook anything without adding tomatoes to it, but no cook south of Rome would care to prepare many meals without tomatoes and no family would be happy without its daily intake of tomato sauce. The tomato was introduced into Europe from the New World in the 16th Century. The French called it *pomme d'amour*, or love apple; Italians described it as *pomodoro*, or golden apple, because the first tomatoes were yellow. The small, sweet red varieties grown in Italy today thrive especially well in the southern sun, leading to the proud Italian claim that the country's tomatoes are the best in the world.

A batch of tomatoes, shown cooking in a caldron, will be skinned and bottled to be made into tomato sauce —a daily necessity in the farm households of southern Italy, where it gives sparkle to the ubiquitous pasta.

169

Potatoes, a basic ingredient of a variety of dishes, including *gnocchi,* stews and croquettes, are harvested near Naples.

vegetable's chief horticultural demands are 120 reasonably warm days between frost and frost, which the southern climate unfailingly provides. One frequently prepared dish is *parmigiana di melanzane (page 177)*; one might think that having achieved that delicious combination of cheese and eggplant, nothing further could be done with eggplant; not so. The southern Italian ways to cook or prepare eggplant are uncountable. In Apulia eggplant is stuffed with anchovies, capers, olives and garlic. In Calabria the combination is not very different—tomato, anchovies, garlic, olive oil, parsley. Here also one finds *melanzane marinate*, eggplant treated as mushrooms sometimes are—chopped small, and seasoned with vinegar, basil, garlic, oregano and pepper *(Recipe Booklet)*. Peppers appear, especially in the Naples area, as *peperoni imbottiti*, stuffed with olives, capers, anchovies and bread crumbs, topped with more bread crumbs, and baked in the oven. Spinach, chopped and cooked in a mold *(page 176)*, often appears as *sformato*, a kind of light pudding or soufflé.

Such entrée and vegetable dishes, hearty as they are, would not completely satisfy a true southern appetite; the south also indulges a well developed sweet tooth on special occasions like weddings and christenings when even the poorest family finds it possible to stretch the budget. Pastry, so sweet as to be cloying to some tastes, is found everywhere. In Calabria, you have *turdiddi*, biscuits of flour, eggs and white wine, fried in oil, dipped in honey, and frosted with sugar or chocolate. The similar *mostaccioli* cookies are made of flour, sugar, almonds and chocolate, and shaped in designs: hearts, fish, colts. Apulia has sweets of ancient origin—*cartellate*, ribbons of sweetened dough soaked in honey; "ladies' mouths"—cream puffs with white frosting, and *passoliate*, a dry cake of almond paste and raisins. Naples offers *sfogliatelle*, flaky pastries filled with cream, chocolate or jam and delicately flavored with lemon, orange and rose; *pastiera napoletana*, puff pastry made either with wheat or barley, *ricottone* cheese, sugar and candied peel; *struffoli* with honey; the rum cake known as *babá*, an Italian variant on the well-known French *baba au rhum*.

No list of the sweet delicacies of the south—and of Naples in particular —would be complete without mention of some of Italy's greatest contributions to gastronomy: variations on ice cream, *dolce far niente* originated by the country's neighbors in the Near East but brought to perfection by southern Italians. While the patricians of Classical Rome were familiar with a kind of ice cream—snow carried down from mountaintops and flavored with juices made from pressed fruits—Italian ice creams as we know them today were not widely known until the 18th Century. Anomalously, they first titillated palates in Paris, where enterprising southern Italians began selling them on that broad, lovely avenue known as the Boulevard des Italiens. One Signor Velloni, a Neapolitan, enjoyed such success with an ice cream shop on the Boulevard des Italiens that he opened several others in Paris, overextended himself and went bankrupt. His enterprises came into the hands of his first assistant and fellow Neapolitan, a gentleman named Tortoni, whose son created *biscuit tortoni*, that sweet, crowning achievement of southern Italian meals. In addition, it was the younger Tortoni whose gastronomic experiments led to the creation of such other masterpieces as *granite* and *gelati (pages 180-181)*, those superb cooling finales to the warming meals of the south of Italy.

On the roof of his shale-rock, conically topped *trullo*, or hut, a form of building dating to prehistoric times, Luigi Tateo inspects drying walnuts destined for dessert dishes.

Pizza

To make 4 ten-inch pizzas

2 packages active dry yeast
Pinch of sugar
1¼ cups lukewarm water
3½ cups all-purpose or granulated
    flour
1 teaspoon salt
¾ cup olive oil
Corn meal
2 cups tomato and garlic sauce (*page
    175*)
1 pound *mozzarella* cheese, coarsely
    grated or cut in ¼-inch dice
½ cup freshly grated imported
    Parmesan cheese

Sprinkle the yeast and a pinch of sugar into ¼ cup of lukewarm water. Be sure that the water is lukewarm (110° to 115°—neither hot nor cool to the touch). Let it stand for 2 or 3 minutes, then stir the yeast and sugar into the water until completely dissolved. Set the cup in a warm, draft-free place (a turned-off oven would be best) for 3 to 5 minutes, or until the yeast bubbles up and the mixture almost doubles in volume. If the yeast does not bubble, start over again with fresh yeast.

Into a large bowl, sift the all-purpose flour and salt, or pour in the granulated flour and salt. Make a well in the center of the flour and pour in the yeast mixture, 1 cup of lukewarm water and ¼ cup of the olive oil. Mix the dough with a fork or your fingers. When you can gather it into a rough ball, place the dough on a floured board and knead it for 15 minutes, or until smooth, shiny and elastic. (If you have an electric mixer with a paddle and dough hook, put the ingredients in a bowl and, at medium speed, mix with the paddle until combined. At high speed knead them with the dough hook for 6 to 8 minutes.) Dust the dough lightly with flour, put in a large clean bowl and cover. Set the bowl in a warm, draft-free spot for 1½ hours, or until the dough has doubled in bulk.

Now preheat the oven to 500°. Punch the dough down with your fists and break off about one fourth of it to make the first of the 4 pizzas. Knead the small piece on a floured board or pastry cloth for a minute or so, working in a little flour if the dough seems sticky. With the palm of your hand, flatten the ball into a circle about 1 inch thick. Hold the circle in your hands and stretch the dough by turning the circle and pulling your hands apart gently at the same time. When the circle is about 7 or 8 inches across, spread it out on the floured board again and pat it smooth, pressing together any tears in the dough. Then roll the dough with a rolling pin, from the center to the far edge, turning it clockwise after each roll, until you have a circle of pastry about 10 inches across and about ⅛ inch thick. With your thumbs, crimp or flute the edge of the circle until it forms a little rim. Dust a large baking sheet lightly with corn meal and place the pizza dough on top of it. Knead, stretch and roll the rest of the dough into 3 more pizzas. Pour ½ cup of the tomato sauce on each pie and swirl it around with a pastry brush or the back of a spoon. To make a cheese pizza, sprinkle the sauce with ½ cup of grated *mozzarella* and 2 tablespoons of grated Parmesan. Dribble 2 tablespoons of the olive oil over the pizza and bake it on the lowest shelf or the floor of the oven for 10 minutes, or until the crust is lightly browned and the filling bubbling hot.

ALTERNATIVE GARNISHES: You may top the pizza with almost any sort of seafood, meat or vegetable you like, using or omitting the *mozzarella* or Parmesan. Swirl the pie with ½ cup of tomato sauce first, as for a cheese pizza. Then top with such garnishes as shrimp, anchovies, sausage or *peperoni* slices, prosciutto slivers, tiny meatballs, garlic slices, strips of green pepper, capers, whole or sliced mushrooms. They may be used alone or in suitable combinations. Dribble 2 tablespoons of olive oil over the pizza after garnishing and before baking it.

All of the ingredients surrounding the pie in the picture at the far right can be used in various combinations to garnish a pizza. Reading clockwise from upper left the ingredients are: chopped beef, *peperoni* (sausage), *prosciutto* (dry cured ham), mushrooms and salami, capers, green peppers, garlic, shrimp and anchovies.

The Art of Baking a Pizza

1 Mix flour, yeast, water, salt and olive oil for pizza dough.

2 Gather the dough into a large ball on a floured board.

3 Knead the dough by pushing with heel of one hand.

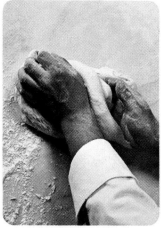

4 Now reverse the process, kneading with the other hand.

5 Place the dough in a bowl in a warm spot, and cover it.

6 When the dough has doubled in bulk take it out.

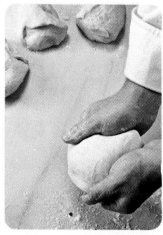

7 Divide the dough into quarters to make pies.

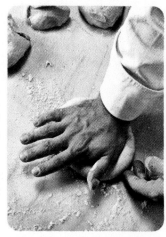

8 Press down with palm on a piece, flattening it.

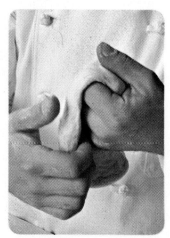

9 Turn dough in your hands and stretch it out.

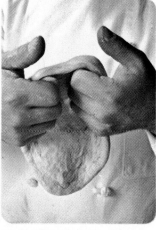

10 Hold the dough and let its weight stretch it.

11 Use a rolling pin to work it into a circle.

12 Pour on tomato sauce, sprinkle with grated cheese. Dribble olive oil over cheese, and bake. The finished pie is pictured at right.

Salsa Pizzaiola

TOMATO AND GARLIC SAUCE

In a 3- to 4-quart enameled or stainless-steel saucepan, heat the 3 tablespoons of olive oil and cook the finely chopped onions in it over moderate heat, stirring frequently, for 7 or 8 minutes. When the onions are
soft and transparent but are not brown, add the tablespoon of finely
chopped garlic and cook for another 1 or 2 minutes, stirring constantly.
Then stir in the coarsely chopped tomatoes and their liquid, the tomato
paste, oregano, basil, bay leaf, sugar, salt and a few grindings of black
pepper. Bring the sauce to a boil, turn the heat very low and simmer
uncover, occasionally, for about 1 hour.

When finished, the sauce should be thick and fairly smooth. Remove
the bay leaf. Taste and season the sauce with salt and freshly ground
black pepper. If you wish a smoother texture, purée the sauce through a
food mill, or rub it through a sieve with the back of a large wooden
spoon.

To make about 3 cups

3 tablespoons olive oil
1 cup finely chopped onions
1 tablespoon finely chopped garlic
4 cups Italian plum or whole-pack
    tomatoes, coarsely chopped but
    not drained
1 six-ounce can tomato paste
1 tablespoon dried oregano, crumbled
1 tablespoon finely cut fresh basil or
    1 teaspoon dried basil, crumbled
1 bay leaf
2 teaspoons sugar
1½ teaspoons salt
Freshly ground black pepper

To serve 4

8 lamb kidneys (or 3 veal kidneys)
2 tablespoons butter
4 tablespoons olive oil
2 teaspoons finely chopped garlic
2 tablespoons finely chopped fresh
   parsley, preferably the flat-leaf
   Italian type
2 tablespoons lemon juice
Salt
Freshly ground black pepper

To serve 4 to 6

5 tablespoons butter
2 tablespoons fine dry bread crumbs,
   made from French or Italian bread
3 tablespoons finely chopped onions
1 ten-ounce package chopped frozen
   spinach, thoroughly defrosted,
   squeezed dry and chopped again—
   or ¾ pound fresh spinach, cooked,
   drained, squeezed and finely
   chopped
3 tablespoons flour
1 cup milk
Freshly ground black pepper
3 egg yolks
¼ cup freshly grated imported
   Parmesan cheese
Salt
3 egg whites

Rognoncini Trifolati
SAUTÉED SLICED KIDNEYS

With a small sharp knife, carefully peel off the thin membrane that covers each veal kidney and cut away the knob of fat under it. (If you are using lamb kidneys, they need not be peeled.) Then cut the kidneys crosswise into paper-thin slices. In a heavy 10- to 12-inch skillet, melt the butter with the olive oil. As soon as the foam subsides, toss in the kidneys and cook them over moderately high heat, stirring and turning the slices constantly, for 2 minutes. Then add the garlic and parsley and cook, stirring constantly, for another 1 or 2 minutes, or until the kidneys and garlic are lightly browned. Pour in the lemon juice and let it boil up once, then turn off the heat. Taste the sauce and season it with salt and pepper. Serve the kidneys immediately from a heated platter.

Sformato di Spinaci
SPINACH MOLD

With 1 tablespoon of butter, grease the top pan of a double boiler (it should be large enough to hold at least 1 quart), or preheat the oven to 325° and butter a 1-quart charlotte mold or other plain metal mold with a cover. Dust the bottom and sides of the pan with bread crumbs and tap the pan lightly to knock out the excess. In a heavy 8- to 10-inch skillet, melt 2 tablespoons of butter over moderate heat and in it cook the onions, stirring frequently, for 7 or 8 minutes, or until they are transparent but not browned. Stir in the spinach and cook, stirring constantly, for 2 or 3 minutes. When all of the moisture has cooked away and the spinach begins to stick lightly to the pan, remove the skillet from the heat.

Melt the remaining 2 tablespoons of the butter in a heavy 3- to 4-quart saucepan. Remove from the heat and stir in the flour. Then pour in the milk, stirring with a whisk until the flour is partially dissolved. Return the pan to low heat and cook, stirring constantly, until the sauce boils and becomes thick and smooth. Remove from the heat and beat in the egg yolks, one at a time, whisking until each one is thoroughly blended before adding the next. Stir in the cheese and the onion-and-spinach mixture, and season with salt and pepper to taste. Allow it to cool slightly. Now beat the egg whites until they are stiff enough to form unwavering peaks when the beater is lifted from the bowl. Stir a heaping spoonful of egg whites into the sauce to lighten it, then gently fold in the remaining egg whites. Ladle the mixture into the buttered pan or mold.

To cook the *sformato* in the double boiler, place the top pan in simmering water deep enough to come almost all the way up its sides. Cover and cook slowly over barely simmering water. To cook in the oven, place the mold in a pot and add enough simmering water to reach about ¾ of the way up the sides of the mold. Cover and bake on the middle shelf of the oven, regulating the heat to keep the water at the barest simmer. Either way, the *sformato* should be just firm to the touch in about 1 hour. To serve, uncover the pan and wipe the outside dry. Run a knife or narrow spatula around the inside of the pan. Place a serving plate upside down over the top of the pan and, grasping both sides firmly, invert the two. Rap the plate sharply on the table and the *sformato* will slide out easily. Serve at once.

Mozzarella in Carrozza
DEEP-FRIED CHEESE SANDWICHES

ANCHOVY SAUCE: (This sauce is optional, but if you are going to use it, you must prepare it first. There will not be time to make it after the sandwiches are finished.) Melt the butter over low heat in a heavy 6- to 8-inch skillet, taking care not to let it brown. Stir in the chopped anchovies, parsley, capers and lemon juice, and keep the sauce warm until the sandwiches are ready to serve.

MOZZARELLA IN CARROZZA: Heat 3 to 4 inches of oil or shortening to 375° in a deep-fat fryer or large heavy saucepan. Using a cookie cutter or a small glass, cut the slices of French or Italian bread into 3-inch rounds. Then slice the *mozzarella* cheese ¼ inch thick; the slices should be a little smaller than the circles of bread. Make sandwiches of the bread and cheese.

In a small mixing bowl beat together the 4 eggs and 3 tablespoons of milk. Pour a cup of milk into another bowl and spread the bread crumbs on a sheet of wax paper. Dip each sandwich in the milk briefly, press the edges of the bread together to seal them, then coat both sides of the sandwiches thoroughly with bread crumbs. To seal the edges even more securely, roll the sandwiches slowly through the bread crumbs like cartwheels. Dip the sandwiches, one at a time, in the egg mixture, then fry them in the hot oil until they are golden brown on each side. Drain on paper towels and serve while still hot.

If you are using the hot anchovy sauce, serve it spooned over the hot sandwiches.

To serve 4 to 6

ANCHOVY SAUCE (optional)
8 tablespoons (1 quarter-pound stick) unsalted butter
4 flat anchovy fillets, finely chopped
1 tablespoon finely chopped fresh parsley
2 teaspoons capers, coarsely chopped
2 teaspoons lemon juice

MOZZARELLA IN CARROZZA
Vegetable oil or shortening for deep frying
A 1-pound loaf sliced French or Italian bread
1 pound *mozzarella* cheese
4 eggs
3 tablespoons milk
1 cup milk
1 cup fine dry bread crumbs

Parmigiana di Melanzane
EGGPLANT PARMESAN

Preheat the oven to 400°. Choose a shallow 1½- to 2-quart baking dish that is attractive enough to serve from and rub it with oil.

Sprinkle both sides of the eggplant slices with salt (to draw out their moisture) and spread them out in one layer on a platter or board. After 20 to 30 minutes, pat the eggplant dry with paper towels. Dip each slice in flour and shake or brush off the excess.

In a heavy 10- to 12-inch skillet, heat ¼ cup of olive oil until a light haze forms over it and brown the eggplant slices a few at a time, working quickly to prevent them from soaking up too much oil. If the oil cooks away, add more. As the eggplant browns, transfer the slices to fresh paper towels to drain.

Now pour ¼ inch of the tomato sauce into the oiled baking-and-serving dish. Spread the drained eggplant slices over the sauce, top them with a layer of *mozzarella* cheese, and sprinkle over it part of the grated Parmesan cheese. Repeat with 1 or 2 more layers (depending on the capacity of the baking dish), but be sure to finish up with layers of the tomato sauce, *mozzarella* and Parmesan. Cover the dish snugly with foil and bake in the middle of the oven for 20 minutes. Remove the foil and bake uncovered for 10 minutes longer.

OPTIONAL: Put the dish under a hot broiler for a few seconds to brown the cheese on top, but do not overcook it or the cheese will become rubbery. Serve directly from the baking dish.

To serve 4

1½ pounds eggplant, peeled and cut in ½-inch slices
Salt
Flour
¼ to ½ cup olive oil
2 cups tomato sauce *(page 47)*
8 ounces *mozzarella* cheese, thinly sliced
½ cup freshly grated imported Parmesan cheese

Costolette di Maiale alla Pizzaiola
BRAISED PORK CHOPS WITH TOMATO AND GARLIC SAUCE

To serve 6

4 tablespoons olive oil
6 center-cut loin pork chops, cut
   1 to 1½ inches thick
1 teaspoon finely chopped garlic
½ teaspoon dried oregano, crumbled
¼ teaspoon dried thyme, crumbled
½ bay leaf
½ teaspoon salt
½ cup dry red wine
1 cup drained canned tomatoes,
   puréed through a sieve or food mill
1 tablespoon tomato paste
½ pound green peppers, seeded and
   cut in 2-by-¼-inch strips (about
   1½ cups)
½ pound fresh mushrooms, whole if
   small, quartered or sliced if large

In a heavy 10- to 12-inch skillet, heat 2 tablespoons of olive oil until a light haze forms over it. Brown the chops in this oil for 2 or 3 minutes on each side and transfer them to a plate. Pour off almost all of the fat. In it cook the garlic, oregano, thyme, bay leaf and salt for 30 seconds, stirring constantly. Add the wine and boil briskly to reduce it to about ¼ cup, scraping in any bits of meat or herbs in the pan. Stir in the tomatoes and tomato paste and return the chops to the skillet. Baste with the sauce, cover, and simmer over low heat, basting once or twice, for 40 minutes.

Meanwhile, heat the remaining oil in another large skillet. Fry the green peppers in the oil for about 5 minutes, stirring frequently. Add the mushrooms and toss them with the peppers for a minute or two, then transfer them to the pan with the pork chops. Cover and simmer for 5 minutes. Simmer uncovered, stirring occasionally, for 10 minutes longer, until the pork and vegetables are tender and the sauce is thick enough to coat a spoon heavily. (If the sauce is too thin, remove the chops and vegetables and boil the sauce down over high heat, stirring constantly.) To serve, arrange the chops on a heated platter and spoon the vegetables and sauce over them.

Triglie alla Calabrese
BAKED RED MULLET WITH BLACK OLIVES AND CAPERS

To serve 4

6 tablespoons butter
3 tablespoons capers, thoroughly
   washed and drained
2 tablespoons slivered black olives
4 red mullets, red snappers or ocean
   perch, ½ to ¾ pound each, cleaned
   with heads and tails on
Salt
¼ cup olive oil
2 teaspoons dried oregano, crumbled
Freshly ground black pepper
2 tablespoons lemon juice
2 tablespoons finely chopped fresh
   parsley, preferably the flat-leaf
   Italian type

Preheat the oven to 425°. In a 6- to 8-inch skillet melt 4 tablespoons of butter over low heat until it becomes a light brown, but do not burn it. Stir in the capers and olives and remove from the heat. Wash the fish quickly, inside and out, under cold running water and dry with paper towels. Salt the inside of each fish lightly. In a shallow flameproof 12-inch baking dish, heat the oil and the 2 remaining tablespoons of butter over moderate heat until it begins to sizzle. Stir in the oregano and a few grindings of black pepper. Roll the fish in the herbed fat. Then place the dish on the middle shelf of the oven and bake, basting the fish with the hot fat every 5 minutes, for 20 to 30 minutes, or until the fish are firm to the touch. With a slotted spatula, carefully transfer them to a heated platter. Warm the butter and caper sauce, stir in the lemon juice and parsley and pour it over the fish.

Bistecca alla Pizzaiola
PAN-BROILED STEAK WITH TOMATOES AND GARLIC

To serve 4

4 tablespoons olive oil
1 teaspoon finely chopped garlic
2 cups peeled, seeded and coarsely
   chopped fresh tomatoes (about
   1½ pounds)
1 teaspoon dried oregano, crumbled
½ teaspoon salt
Freshly ground black pepper
A 3-pound T-bone, porterhouse or
   sirloin, cut 1 inch thick

Heat 2 tablespoons of olive oil in a medium-sized skillet or saucepan until a light haze forms over it. Remove the pan from the heat, add the garlic and, with a spoon, turn it about in the oil for about 30 seconds. Add the tomatoes, oregano, salt and a few grindings of pepper and cook over moderate heat, stirring frequently. In about 5 minutes most of the liquid from the tomatoes will have boiled away. Remove the pan from the heat.

In a heavy 12- to 14-inch skillet, heat the remaining 2 tablespoons of olive oil, again until a light haze forms over it. Over high heat, brown the steak in the oil for 1 or 2 minutes on each side, turning it with kitchen tongs, then lower the heat to moderate and spoon the tomato sauce over and around the meat. Cover and cook for 6 to 10 minutes, or until the steak is done to your taste. (Test by pressing it with a finger—when the steak is slightly resilient, neither soft nor firm, it is medium rare—or you can make a small incision near the bone with the tip of a sharp knife and judge by the redness of the meat.)

To serve, scrape the tomato sauce off the top of the steak into the skillet and transfer the steak to a carving board. Simmer the sauce left in the skillet for 1 or 2 minutes, scraping in any browned bits of meat and sauce clinging to the bottom of the pan. Taste for seasoning. Carve the steak, arrange the slices on a heated platter and moisten each slice with a little sauce.

Pollo alla Cacciatora
BRAISED CHICKEN WITH BLACK OLIVE AND ANCHOVY SAUCE

To serve 4

Wash the chicken quickly under cold running water and pat the pieces dry with paper towels. Season the pieces with salt and a few grindings of pepper.

In a heavy 10- to 12-inch skillet, heat the olive oil until a haze forms over it. Brown the chicken a few pieces at a time, starting them skin side down and turning them with tongs. Transfer the browned pieces to a plate. Now pour off almost all of the fat from the skillet, leaving just a thin film on the bottom. Add the onions and garlic and cook them over moderate heat, stirring constantly, for 8 to 10 minutes, or until they are lightly colored. Add the wine and vinegar and boil briskly until the liquid is reduced to about ¼ cup. Then pour in the chicken stock and boil for 1 or 2 minutes, stirring constantly and scraping in any browned bits that cling to the pan. Return the browned chicken to the skillet, add the oregano and bay leaf, and bring to a boil. Cover the skillet, reduce the heat and simmer, basting occasionally. In about 30 minutes, the chicken should be done; its juice will run clear when a thigh is pierced with the tip of a sharp knife.

To serve, arrange the pieces of chicken on a heated platter. Discard the bay leaf and boil the stock left in the skillet until it thickens slightly and has the intensity of flavor desired. Stir in the black olives and anchovies and cook the sauce for a minute or so longer. Pour the sauce over the chicken.

A 2½- to 3-pound chicken, cut up
Salt
Freshly ground black pepper
2 tablespoons olive oil
¼ cup finely chopped onions
1 teaspoon finely chopped garlic
½ cup dry white wine
2 tablespoons wine vinegar, preferably white
½ cup chicken stock, fresh or canned
½ teaspoon dried oregano, crumbled
1 bay leaf
1 tablespoon slivered black olives, preferably Mediterranean style
3 flat anchovy fillets, rinsed in cold water, dried and chopped

Zuppa di Vongole
FRESH CLAM SOUP

To serve 4

Heat the olive oil in a heavy 2- to 3-quart saucepan. Add the garlic and cook, stirring, over moderate heat for about 30 seconds. Pour in the wine, add the tomatoes, and bring to a boil. Then reduce the heat and simmer the sauce, partially covered, for 10 minutes.

Meanwhile, scrub the clams thoroughly and drop them into about ⅛-inch of boiling water (approximately 1 cup) in a heavy 12- to 14-inch skillet. Cover tightly and steam the clams over high heat for 5 to 10 minutes, or until they open. With tongs or a slotted spoon, transfer the clams, still in their shells, to 4 large heated soup plates. Strain all the clam juice in the skillet through a fine sieve lined with cheesecloth into the simmering tomato sauce. Cook for 1 or 2 minutes, then pour the soup over the clams and sprinkle chopped parsley on top. Serve at once.

NOTE: If the amount of liquid called for in the ingredients sounds insufficient, do not worry. The shellfish produce their own liquid in the cooking.

6 tablespoons olive oil
1 teaspoon finely chopped garlic
½ cup dry white wine
3 pounds firm ripe tomatoes, peeled, seeded, gently squeezed of excess juice, and coarsely chopped (about 3 to 4 cups)
2 dozen small hardshell clams in their shells
1 cup boiling water
4 tablespoons finely chopped fresh parsley, preferably the flat-leaf Italian type

To make about 1½ pints of each flavor

LEMON ICE
2 cups water
1 cup sugar
1 cup lemon juice

ORANGE ICE
2 cups water
¾ cup sugar
1 cup orange juice
Juice of 1 lemon

COFFEE ICE
1 cup water
½ cup sugar
2 cups strong *espresso* coffee

STRAWBERRY ICE
1 cup water
½ cup sugar
2 cups fresh ripe strawberries, puréed
    through sieve or food mill
2 tablespoons lemon juice

To make 1 to 1½ quarts of each flavor

VANILLA ICE CREAM
2 cups light cream
2-inch piece of vanilla bean or
    1 teaspoon vanilla extract
8 egg yolks
½ cup sugar
1 cup heavy cream

PISTACHIO ICE CREAM
2 cups light cream
8 egg yolks
6 tablespoons sugar
2½ tablespoons ground or crushed
    shelled pistachio nuts
1 cup heavy cream
7 drops green food coloring
5½ tablespoons chopped shelled
    pistachio nuts
¼ cup ground blanched almonds

COFFEE ICE CREAM
2 cups light cream
2-inch strip of fresh lemon peel
8 egg yolks
6 tablespoons sugar
2 tablespoons *espresso* coffee
2 cups heavy cream

Granite
FLAVORED ICES

In a 1½- to 2-quart saucepan, bring the water and sugar to a boil over moderate heat, stirring only until the sugar dissolves. Timing from the moment the sugar and water begin to boil, let the mixture cook for exactly 5 minutes. Immediately remove the pan from the heat and let the syrup cool to room temperature.

Depending on which of the flavored ices you want to make, stir in the lemon juice, or the orange and lemon juices, or *espresso* coffee, or the puréed strawberries and lemon juice. Pour the mixture into an ice-cube tray from which the divider has been removed.

Freeze the *granita* for 3 to 4 hours, stirring it every 30 minutes and scraping into it the ice particles that form around the edges of the tray. The finished *granita* should have a fine, snowy texture. For a coarser texture that is actually more to the Italian taste, leave the ice-cube divider in the tray and freeze the *granita* solid. Then remove the cubes and crush them in an ice crusher.

NOTE: If you use frozen strawberries rather than fresh ones, make the syrup with only ¼ cup of sugar.

Gelati
ICE CREAMS

VANILLA: In a 1½- or 2-quart enameled or stainless-steel saucepan, bring the light cream and the vanilla bean almost to a boil over low heat. (If you are using vanilla extract, do not add it now.) Meanwhile combine the egg yolks and sugar in a bowl. Beat them with a whisk, rotary or electric beater for 3 to 5 minutes, or until they are pale yellow and thick enough to fall from the whisk or beater in a lazy ribbon. Then discard the vanilla bean from the saucepan and pour the hot cream slowly into the beaten egg yolks, beating gently and constantly. Pour the mixture back into the saucepan and cook over moderately low heat, stirring constantly with a wooden spoon, until it thickens to a custard that lightly coats the spoon. Do not allow the mixture to boil or it will curdle. Stir in the heavy cream, and if you are using the vanilla extract instead of the vanilla bean, add it now. Strain the custard through a fine sieve into a mixing bowl and allow it to cool to room temperature.

Now pack a 2-quart ice cream freezer with layers of finely crushed or cracked ice and coarse rock salt in the proportions recommended by the freezer manufacturer. Add cold water if the manufacturer advises it. Then pour or ladle the cooled *gelato* into the ice cream can and cover it. If you have a hand ice cream maker, let it stand for 3 or 4 minutes before turning the handle. It may take 15 minutes or more for the ice cream to freeze, but do not stop turning at any time, or the *gelato* may be lumpy. When the handle can barely be moved, the ice cream should be firm. If you have an electric ice cream maker, turn it on and let it churn for about 15 minutes, or until the motor slows or actually stops.

To harden the *gelato*, scrape the ice cream from the sides down into the

These frozen desserts include chocolate, pistachio, coffee and vanilla ice creams and coffee, lemon, strawberry and orange ices.

bottom of the can and cover it very securely. Drain off any water that is in the bucket and repack it with ice and salt. Let it stand for 2 or 3 hours.

PISTACHIO: Heat the light cream and beat the egg yolks and sugar together. Add the ground pistachio nuts and make the custard as above. Then stir in the heavy cream and vegetable coloring, and strain this mixture. Add the chopped pistachio nuts and ground almonds. Cool and freeze.

COFFEE: Heat the light cream with the lemon peel and beat the egg yolks and sugar together. Discard the peel and make the custard as described above. Add the *espresso* coffee (instant or freshly brewed) and heavy cream; strain, cool and freeze.

CHOCOLATE: Heat the milk, beat the egg yolks and sugar together, and make the custard as described above. Then stir in the heavy cream, melted chocolate and vanilla extract. Strain, cool and freeze.

CHOCOLATE ICE CREAM
2 cups milk
4 egg yolks
10 tablespoons sugar
2 cups heavy cream
4 ounces semisweet chocolate, melted
½ teaspoon vanilla extract

181

XI

The Islands: Where It Began

In traditional costume, a Sardinian girl prepares to serve one of the island's favorite delicacies, suckling pig. On the table are a round of sheep's milk cheese and a stack of the flat Sardinian bread known—for its thin, crackling texture—as *carta di musica* (sheets of music).

The world of the Italian kitchen ends where a great deal of it began—on the islands of Sicily and Sardinia. There, more than 2,000 years ago, Sicilians discovered the secrets of Greek cooking from their Greek conquerors, even as Sardinians learned the culinary art of their Phoenician invaders. Both islands elaborated on what they found, turned it, twisted it, added a smidgen of Arabian cookery here, a touch of African there, lots of Roman innovations everywhere (aromatic sauces with the pasta in Sicily, myrtle with the roast pig in Sardinia), until each had made a cuisine quite distinct from the other. Thereafter each would teach the Romans, and thus the world, something about cooking.

All this evolved on two islands—Sicily the largest in the Mediterranean and Sardinia the second largest—that also knew large patches of poverty, poverty complicated in Sicily's case by endless feuds between landless peasants and moneyless landlords and in Sardinia's by centuries of governmental neglect. On both islands many people still subsist solely on pasta and bread. Some of the most intriguing dishes on their menus result from imaginative efforts to make a little go a long way.

The two islands also share a certain insular conservatism, a clinging to their own ancient culinary tradition, and they ignore much of what goes on in the kitchens of other Italian regions. But apart from these similarities each island is separate unto itself and has its own personality.

Sicily is a mountainous island of spectacular scenery, beloved of tourists and dotted with the ruins of Greek temples. Sardinia, rich in medieval churches, is a rolling land of low hills that gives an un-island-like impression of vast and empty space. On Sicily live five million passionately alive Italians whose ever-recurrent political dream is to rise up and throw the mainland Italians out of Sicily. On the other hand, the one and a half million Sardinians, despite many recent infusions of mainland blood, are a reserved and taciturn folk who spend long, lonely days tending flocks of sheep and goats on far-off hillsides. They remind many visitors less of bubbly Italians than of silent, dour Spaniards—although they are as fervent Italian patriots as was Giuseppe Garibaldi, who exploded off the island to win the south for modern Italy.

Both islands have mines and a little industry; but both must farm and fish for their sustenance. Sicily raises lush crops of citrus fruits, garden vegetables and olives and the grapes that produce Mamertino, the wine that drew the praises of Julius Caesar and the Classical poet Martial. There is little meat but there is a considerable amount of wheat in Sicily and since the weather turns warm early in the year, Sicilians have a time advantage over other European farmers so that the first arrival of tender Sicilian peas in the markets of Paris, London and Bonn is everywhere considered a harbinger of spring.

Like Sicily, Sardinia fishes for tuna and swordfish, grows garden truck and the grapes that end up as Cannonau, Angheluruju, Monica and other distinguished wines. But her principal work is pastoral and some 2.5 million sheep —almost a third of all the flocks in Italy—are in Sardinia. Sardinians also tend goats that provide some of the island's most typical dishes—*corda*, for instance, long strips of young kid (or occasionally lamb) tripe cooked on the spit, grilled or stewed with peas and beans. There is plenty of beef, pork and lamb in the island's diet and much cheese. From the area of Gallura comes *casu marzu*, which means "rotten cheese" but which cheese connoisseurs pronounce delicious. *Fiore sardo,* flower of Sardinia, is the *grana*-type cheese Sardinians prefer to eat with their pasta.

The most famous creations of the Sicilian cuisine are sweets and pastries. A taste for sophisticated sweets was introduced into the island in the Ninth Century by the Saracens, who were then its occupiers. In fact, *cannoli,* which are cylinders of pastry filled with creamed cheese, candied fruits and chocolate, were originally called *cappello di turco,* or Turkish hats, reflecting the fact that the invaders from the East were often referred to as Turks. But soon Sicilian cooks turned the Saracen sweets into an elaborate and purely Sicilian art form, and some have since acquired symbolic significance. At weddings candied almonds are thrown at the bride and groom to cries of "May your life be fruitful and sweet." Like *cannoli, cassata,* a layer cake, with filling and cake so subtly combined *(page 192)* that it is sometimes difficult to tell where one leaves off and the other begins, was once served only at such feasts of renewal as Christmas and Easter. Today, they are also served at weddings, to signify the beginning of a new way of life. And in a rite that cultivates a sense of family worth and continuity, little Sicilian children search their homes on All Souls' Day for hidden gifts and cookies called *ossi di morti,* or bones of the dead. The *ossi di morti* and the gifts were hidden, the children are told, by the spirits of dead members of the family, to reward them for having been good boys and girls in the year just past.

Sicilians do not bake only cake. Homemade bread, now becoming rare in so many parts of the world, is still commonplace in Sicily. The typical loaf is cartwheel-shaped and is baked in a small, igloo-shaped oven erected near the fireplace in most Sicilian kitchens. In the base of the oven is a compart-

ment for storing the long-handled baking tools: a mop, an iron bar, a metal rake and wooden shovels with round scoops big enough to hold a generous pizza. The Sicilian wife sets firewood ablaze in the oven and moves it about from spot to spot with the iron bar until most of the wood is consumed and the oven is uniformly hot. Then she moves the fire outside the oven with the rake, cleans the oven with a dry mop lest cinders be baked into her bread, and puts the bread or pizza dough into the oven on the shovels. She sets a removable metal door in place and rakes the remainder of the fire against the door to keep the oven hot during the baking. In addition to the usual cartwheel-shaped loaf, she has endless other forms and sizes: lozenge shapes, sandwich rolls, flat buns, unleavened bread that is soaked in oil and eaten with salt fish. She also bakes two types of a bun known as *vasteddi*. The *vasteddi maritati*, or married *vasteddi*, is a round bun sprinkled with cumin seeds and filled with a layer of *ricotta* cheese, two layers of pork strips, pork spleen fried in lard and a layer of bacon. The other type, *vasteddi schietti* (unmarried), has a slightly leaner filling.

The Sicilians learned to make bread from the Greeks centuries ago. But their fondness for bread has never lessened the appeal of pasta. The island's most famous pasta is *pasta con sarde,* or pasta with sardines, cooked Palermo style. Other Sicilian specialties are *farsu magru (Recipe Booklet)* and *caponata (page 195)*. The first is a beef or veal roll stuffed with hard-boiled eggs and spices. The second is diced eggplant cooked in a strongly seasoned tomato sauce. It can in the hands of a careful cook become a masterpiece. The secret is that all the ingredients—eggplant, peppers, tomatoes, onions and celery— each with the amount and kind of seasoning peculiarly suited to it must be cooked separately according to a schedule that will bring their various cooking requirements to completion at the same moment. Then vinegar, capers, olives, a little tomato sauce and a bit of anchovy sauce are added, and the result is one of the subtlest dishes I ever tasted in Italy; its decisive element was care in the kitchen.

Fish, either alone or combined with such dishes as *caponata,* is important in the Sicilian diet. Syracuse, the ancient Greek-founded city once ruled by the tyrant Dionysius, might be considered the capital of Sicilian seafood. When I sat down in the Bandiera restaurant there and asked the proprietor to serve me small portions of the great specialties of his city, he gave me seven or eight dishes, all of them seafood. I remember especially the *insalata di mare* (salad of the sea) composed of mussels, prawns and squid. I also recall another noble dish, black mussels baked in their shells with olive oil, cheese and bread crumbs, subtly fragrant with herbs whose names the cook refused to reveal. Syracuse likes not only salt-water fish but fresh-water fish as well. The city is the site of the Spring of Arethusa, famous since Classical times. It is named for the nymph Arethusa, beloved of the river god Alpheus who pursued her to the present site of Syracuse, taking pains, during the chase, to keep his river waters from mingling with those of the sea. So the large natural spring echoes the ancient legend, for it is located so close to the sea that only a massive wall keeps the salt water from mingling with the fresh. It teems with fish, especially the gray mullet that appears in so many wonderful Sicilian meals.

Sicilians eat little meat and most of that in the form of cured sausage, which the farmers take with them, along with bread, cheese and wine, into

Sicily and Sardinia, Italy's largest islands, dine differently. Sicily, an open country, grows its food on wheat farms and in truck gardens, vineyards and citrus orchards. The pride of the cooks of Sicilian Catania is *caponata*, diced eggplant with peppers, tomatoes, onions and celery to which, in Palermo, pine nuts are added. Sardinia, a pastoral land, raises almost a third of all the sheep in Italy. Sardinians roast them whole on spits over outdoor fires.

Rococo cakes of marvelously intricate design worked around the names of the bride and groom are traditional at Sardinian weddings. The cookies above the cake, called *cuoricini*, or little hearts, are also served at weddings.

the fields for lunch. One fresh pork sausage, *salsiccia cotta sotta la cenere*, is cooked in heavy brown paper in the ashes on the hearth. The paper keeps the ashes from sticking to the sausage.

In Sardinia the meals are heartier. This is the land of cooking *a fùrria fùrria*, meaning to turn and turn again. Whole animals—wild boar, suckling pigs, baby lambs and young goats—are skinned, cleaned and spitted lengthwise on a rough rod, perhaps a tree branch sharpened at both ends. Then they are set beside a fire made of juniper, olive and mastic wood. The flame must not touch the roast. No herbs are used. As the animal is turned and roasted it is impregnated with distinctive, delicate aromas and tastes from the wood fire. The Sardinians also use wood fires to cook *a carrargiu*, "in a hole." A hole as large as the whole pig, lamb or kid is dug in the ground, and a fire set in it to dry out the surrounding earth. When the fire burns down, the ashes are cleaned out of the hole and it is lined with myrtle branches. The animal is laid on the myrtle and covered with more branches, after which the hole is closed with earth and a fire is started on top.

There is also in Sardinia much hunting for the table. The ranks of *muflone*, wild sheep found here and in nearby Corsica, have been depleted by hunting Sardinians and are now protected by law. But the wild boar—blacker, smaller and more ferocious than his mainland counterpart, but much sweeter tasting —remains plentiful, as does the bear. Hares and birds like partridges and thrushes can be legally taken through the autumn. They are often boiled with all their innards, then placed piping hot in small bags lined with myrtle leaves and allowed to absorb the fragrance.

In Sardinia, which once shared with Sicily the title of Rome's granary, bread remains a major staple. The special bread is *pane carasau*, also known as *carta di musica*, or music paper, because it is thin and breaks, showing cracks like the ruled staffs on music paper. Stacks of it, made from unleavened dough, have been carried into the fields by Sardinian herdsmen for centuries.

Sardinia has all the pasta the rest of Italy has, from *gnocchi* through ravioli and spaghetti, as well as spicy sauces old and new. Sardinia also has some specialties of its own: *culingiones*, ravioli stuffed with *ricotta* cheese, spinach, eggs and saffron and served with a meat or tomato sauce and grated cheese; *culuriones de patata*, ravioli made of potato dough flavored with onions and peppermint; *pillas*, layers of pasta and hashed meat, prosciutto, bland cheese and egg moistened with wine, covered with tomato sauce and baked in the oven; and *succu tundu*, also called *fregula*, tiny saffron-flavored pasta balls cooked in consommé.

This island, which gave its name to the sardine, offers in addition lobster and eels from the sea and trout from its mountain streams. One other pleasant product of Sardinian waters is a curious little appetite stimulator —*buttariga*, dried mullet eggs and tuna.

Sardinia is a tranquil peaceful place, deep rooted in the past. Its herdsmen still wear the *mastruca*, a coat made of two or three goatskins sewn together that was first described by Plautus in his *Poenulus* and later by Cicero in *Pro Scauro*. Its fishermen still fish with wooden hooks and tridents.

These centuries-old techniques, much more clearly visible in Sardinia than in Sicily, stand witness to the heritage that lies at the base of all Italian cooking. Behind the cooking of ancient Rome lay the cooking of the still more ancient Etruscans. Through southern Italy and Sicily came the pre-Roman influences of Greece and, later, those of Arabia. And via Sardinia came contributions from the East.

Thus the traditional cuisine of the Italian islands, and of Sardinia in particular, is archaic, not in the sense of being primitive, but of being historic and unspoiled—a reflection today of the imagination and skills of the peasants of long, long ago, the people who walked these fields and fished these waters in Classical and Preclassical times. In Sardinia little that is basic ever changes; the wars and invasions of the long centuries wash away, leaving few traces. Man stands meditative and tranquil before that which supplies him sustenance; the fields and the animals and the sea. Everything—the skies, stony pastures, the march of the seasons and the generations—is worthy of a lifetime's grave attention and appreciation. There is no hurry. Here, with perception, one can see how it was when the world was simultaneously innocent and uncontrolled, when men ate primarily for the strength to survive and contest, and almost never for pleasure. It is not the beginning of food and cooking, but it is about as near as we can get to the beginning.

Biscuits of hand-mixed flour, eggs, baking powder, vanilla, milk, oil and lemon rind are brought to village ovens for baking.

Family Feast in Sicily

Cakes in fanciful shapes filled with chocolate and crowned with candied fruits; cylinders of golden crust wrapped around chocolate paste blended with vanilla; a pink and green almond loaf embedded with cherries, orange peel and pistachio nuts; wine jellies in the forms of saints, shields and flowers. These are the glories of the kitchens of Sicily. Small wonder then that Sicilians at table keep their eyes firmly fixed on the important course, the dessert. In Sicily the finest wines, like Marsala and the various *moscati,* are sweet dessert wines. Family feasts (and hardly a day passes in Sicily without a good reason for a family feast) bring out the best in the island's cooks. Here, in pictures taken on a small farm near the city of Messina, the aunts of little Rosaria Calcabotta help to celebrate her first Holy Communion.

The guest of honor, young Rosaria carries dessert biscuits to table *(right).* Above, she smiles shyly at her family as the wine is opened.

Nothing goes better with vanilla or peach ice cream cones than Sicilian puppets performing any one of the 500 plays from the epic of *Orlando Furioso*. Elaborately carved kings and knights clank about in these plays—as the crowned Charlemagne and his friends and foes are doing at the Acireale Theater (*right*). Giants, dragons, ogres and eagles abound and someone is always leaping astride the hippogriff and cantering off to the moon. But the best parts are the fights: swords flash on high, and heads roll all over the stage until a youngster can hardly tell whether he is slurping his own vanilla or his neighbor's peach—and it hardly matters.

Cassata alla Siciliana

SICILIAN CAKE WITH CHOCOLATE FROSTING

To serve 8

A fresh pound cake about 9 inches
long and 3 inches wide

1 pound *ricotta* cheese

2 tablespoons heavy cream

¼ cup sugar

3 tablespoons Strega or an
orange-flavored liqueur

3 tablespoons coarsely chopped mixed
candied fruit

2 ounces semisweet chocolate, coarsely
chopped

CHOCOLATE FROSTING

12 ounces semisweet chocolate, cut
in small pieces

¾ cup strong black coffee

½ pound unsalted butter, cut into
½-inch pieces and thoroughly
chilled

With a sharp, serrated knife, slice the end crusts off the pound cake and level the top if it is rounded. Cut the cake horizontally into ½- to ¾-inch-thick slabs. Rub the *ricotta* into a bowl through a food mill, or use a coarse sieve and a wooden spoon; beat with a rotary or electric beater until smooth. Beating constantly, add the cream, sugar and Strega. With a rubber spatula, fold in the candied fruit and chocolate. Center the bottom slab of the cake on a flat plate and spread generously with the *ricotta* mixture. Place another slab on top, keeping sides and ends even, and spread with more *ricotta*. Repeat until all cake slabs are reassembled and the filling has been used up. End with a plain slice of cake on top. Gently press the loaf to make it compact. Do not worry if it feels wobbly; chilling firms it. Refrigerate for 2 hours, or until the *ricotta* is firm.

Melt 12 ounces of chocolate with the coffee in a small heavy saucepan over low heat, stirring constantly until the chocolate has completely dissolved. Remove from heat and beat in the butter, 1 piece at a time. Beat until the mixture is smooth, and chill until thickened to spreading consistency. With a metal spatula, spread the frosting evenly on the top, sides and ends of the *cassata*, swirling it decoratively. Cover loosely with plastic or foil and refrigerate the *cassata* for at least a day before serving.

1 For a *cassata*, cut a pound cake into thick, horizontal slices.

2 Next step is to chop 2 ounces of baking chocolate into coarse pieces.

3 Smooth the lumpy *ricotta*, and add flavorings, chocolate and fruit.

4 Use this mixture as a filling between the thick slices of pound cake.

5 Cover the tops and sides with large helpings of the chocolate frosting.

6 Use a pastry tube to decorate the cake with buds and floral vines.

Bradamante, the lady warrior of the *Orlando Furioso* puppet cycle, draws her battle sword for a worthy cause: to cut into a true Sicilian *cassata*.

To serve 4

4 firm ripe tomatoes, 3 to 4 inches in
diameter (about 2 pounds)
Salt
2 tablespoons olive oil
¼ cup finely chopped onions
½ teaspoon finely chopped garlic
1 cup fresh white bread crumbs (made
from 2 slices of French or Italian
bread)
4 anchovy fillets, drained, soaked in
cold water for 10 minutes, dried
and finely chopped
1 seven-ounce can tuna (preferably
Italian style, packed in olive oil),
broken into small pieces
3 tablespoons finely chopped fresh
parsley, preferably the flat-leaf
Italian type
2 tablespoons capers, thoroughly
washed and drained
6 finely chopped black olives
(preferably Mediterranean style)
1 tablespoon freshly grated imported
Parmesan cheese
Finely chopped fresh parsley

To serve 4

2 live 1½- to 2-pound lobsters,
split in half lengthwise
¼ cup olive oil
¼ cup finely chopped onions
1 teaspoon finely chopped garlic
1 cup dry white wine
1½ pounds firm ripe tomatoes,
peeled, seeded, gently squeezed of
excess juice, and coarsely chopped
(about 2 cups)
1 tablespoon finely chopped fresh
parsley
1 teaspoon dried oregano, crumbled
¼ teaspoon crushed dried red pepper
½ teaspoon salt

Pomodori alla Siciliana
BAKED TOMATOES STUFFED WITH ANCHOVIES, TUNA AND BLACK OLIVES

Preheat the oven to 375°. Slice about ¼ inch off the top of each tomato. Using your index finger or a teaspoon, scoop out all of the pulp and seeds inside the tomatoes, leaving hollow shells about ¼ inch thick. Salt the insides of the tomatoes and turn them upside down over paper towels so that they will drain.

Meanwhile, heat the 2 tablespoons of olive oil in a heavy 8- to 10-inch skillet and in it cook the finely chopped onions and garlic over moderate heat, stirring frequently, for 7 or 8 minutes, or until the onions are transparent but not brown. Stir in the fresh white bread crumbs, anchovy fillets and pieces of tuna fish and cook, stirring constantly, for another 1 or 2 minutes. Remove the skillet from the heat and add the finely chopped fresh parsley, capers and olives. If the mixture looks too dry and crumbly, add 1 or 2 more teaspoons of olive oil. Spoon the stuffing mixture into the hollowed tomatoes, sprinkle them with the tablespoon of grated Parmesan cheese and a few drops of olive oil.

Arrange the stuffed tomatoes in one layer in a lightly oiled 8- to 9-inch shallow baking dish and bake them on the middle shelf of the oven for 20 to 30 minutes, or until they are tender but not limp and the crumbs on top are brown and crisp. Serve the tomatoes hot or cold, sprinkled with a little chopped parsley. They may be served as part of the *antipasto* or as a separate vegetable course.

Aragosta fra Diavolo
LOBSTER BRAISED WITH WINE AND TOMATOES

Remove and discard the gelatinous sac (or stomach) near the head of each lobster and the long intestine attached to it. Then remove and set aside the greenish brown tomalley (or liver) and the black caviarlike eggs (or coral) if there are any. With a heavy sharp knife or kitchen scissors, cut off the claws and gash the flat underside of each large claw with the flat of a knife. Remove and discard the small claws and the antennae.

In a heavy 12- to 14-inch skillet, heat the olive oil until a light haze forms over it. Add the lobster bodies and large claws and cook them over high heat for 3 or 4 minutes, turning them once or twice with tongs. Transfer the lobsters to a plate.

Pour off almost all of the fat from the skillet, leaving a thin film on the bottom. Add the onions and garlic and cook them over moderate heat, stirring frequently, for 7 or 8 minutes, or until the onions are transparent but not brown. Add the wine and boil it briskly over high heat, stirring constantly, until it is reduced in volume to about ½ cup. Add the tomatoes, parsley, oregano, red pepper and salt and bring the mixture to a boil, stirring constantly. Return the lobsters to the skillet, cover and cook over moderate heat for 8 to 10 minutes, basting every few minutes. Just before serving, press the tomalley and coral through a fine sieve and stir them into the hot sauce. Let the sauce simmer for a minute or 2 without boiling. Taste the sauce and season it with salt and pepper if necessary.

To serve, arrange the pieces of lobster on a deep heated platter and spoon the sauce over them.

Vitella alla Sarda
BRAISED VEAL WITH TOMATO SAUCE AND BLACK OLIVES

Preheat the oven to 350°. Soak the anchovies in cold water for 10 minutes, then pat them dry with paper towels and cut them into 1-inch pieces. Stir the garlic and 1 tablespoon of parsley together and roll the anchovy pieces in this mixture. With a small sharp knife, cut deep incisions in the veal and insert the pieces of anchovy.

Heat the oil in a heavy flameproof casserole or Dutch oven that is large enough to hold the veal comfortably. In it, over high heat, brown the meat on all sides. Then transfer it to a plate. Add the onion, carrots and celery to the fat remaining in the casserole and, stirring frequently, cook the vegetables over moderate heat for 7 or 8 minutes, or until they color lightly. Pour in the wine and cook over high heat for 2 or 3 minutes, stirring constantly and scraping in any browned bits that cling to the bottom and sides of the pan. Return the veal to the casserole and add the chicken stock. Bring to a boil over moderate heat, cover, and cook in the middle of the oven for 1½ hours, or until the veal is tender when pierced with the tip of a sharp knife.

Transfer the veal to a carving board, cut off the strings and sprinkle the outside of the roast with ½ cup of chopped parsley. Carve the veal into slices ¼ inch thick and arrange these, slightly overlapping, in 1 or 2 rows on a heated serving platter. Working quickly, strain the braising stock through a fine sieve into a small saucepan, pressing down hard on the vegetables before discarding them. Skim as much fat as possible from the surface and then boil the sauce briskly over high heat, stirring frequently, until it has been reduced to about 1 cup. Taste and season it with lemon juice and salt and pepper if needed. Spoon the stock over the sliced veal. Bring the tomato sauce to a simmer in a small saucepan, stir in the slivered black olives and serve it separately in a warm sauceboat along with the veal.

To serve 6

4 flat anchovy fillets
1 teaspoon finely chopped garlic
1 tablespoon finely chopped fresh parsley
A 3-pound boneless veal roast, securely tied
¼ cup olive oil
½ cup finely chopped onions
¼ cup finely chopped carrots
¼ cup finely chopped celery
½ cup dry white wine
1 cup chicken stock, fresh or canned
½ cup finely chopped fresh parsley, preferably the flat-leaf Italian type
½ to 1 teaspoon lemon juice
Salt
White pepper
1½ cups tomato sauce *(page 47)*
1 tablespoon slivered pitted black olives, preferably Mediterranean style

Caponata
COLD EGGPLANT APPETIZER

Sprinkle the cubes of eggplant generously with salt and set them in a colander or large sieve over paper towels to drain. After about 30 minutes, pat the cubes dry with fresh paper towels and set them aside.

In a heavy 12- to 14-inch skillet, heat ¼ cup of the olive oil. Add the celery and cook over moderate heat, stirring frequently, for 10 minutes. Then stir in the onions and cook for another 8 to 10 minutes, or until the celery and onions are soft and lightly colored. With a slotted spoon, transfer them to a bowl. Pour the remaining ¼ cup of olive oil into the skillet and over high heat sauté the eggplant cubes in it, stirring and turning them constantly for about 8 minutes, or until they are lightly browned. Return the celery and onions to the skillet and stir in the vinegar and sugar, drained tomatoes, tomato paste, green olives, capers, anchovies, 2 teaspoons salt and a few grindings of pepper. Bring to a boil, reduce the heat, and simmer uncovered, stirring frequently, for about 15 minutes. Stir in the pine nuts. Now taste the mixture and season it with salt and pepper and a little extra vinegar if necessary. Transfer the *caponata* to a serving bowl and refrigerate it until ready to serve.

To make about 8 cups

2 pounds eggplant, peeled and cut into ½-inch cubes (about 8 cups)
Salt
½ cup olive oil
2 cups finely chopped celery
¾ cup finely chopped onions
⅓ cup wine vinegar mixed with 4 teaspoons sugar
3 cups drained canned Italian plum or whole-pack tomatoes
2 tablespoons tomato paste
6 large green olives, pitted, slivered and well-rinsed
2 tablespoons capers
4 flat anchovy fillets, well rinsed and pounded into a paste with a mortar and pestle
Freshly ground black pepper
2 tablespoons pine nuts

To serve 4

5 egg yolks plus 1 whole egg
2 tablespoons sugar
½ cup Marsala

To serve 6 to 8

MARINADE
3 cups dry white wine
¼ cup olive oil
¼ cup finely chopped parsley,
  preferably the flat-leaf Italian type
1 bay leaf, crumbled
⅛ teaspoon ground allspice
⅛ teaspoon ground nutmeg
1 tablespoon salt

A 4-pound boneless beef chuck or
  bottom round roast at least 4 inches
  in diameter, trimmed, rolled and
  tied securely in 3 or 4 places
2 tablespoons butter
2 tablespoons olive oil
1 cup dry white wine
2 cups beef stock, fresh or canned
2 tablespoons finely chopped fresh
  parsley
1 flat anchovy fillet, drained, rinsed
  and finely chopped
¼ teaspoon lemon juice
Salt
Freshly ground black pepper

Zabaione
CUSTARD WITH MARSALA

Combine the 5 egg yolks, 1 whole egg and 2 tablespoons of sugar in the top of a double boiler above simmering water or in a medium-sized heat-proof glass bowl set in a shallow pan of barely simmering water. Beat the mixture with a wire whisk or a rotary beater until it is pale yellow and fluffy. Then gradually add the Marsala and continue beating until the *zabaione* becomes thick enough to hold its shape in a spoon. This process may take as long as 10 minutes.

Spoon the *zabaione* into individual dessert bowls, compote dishes or large stemmed glasses, and serve it while it is still hot.

Manzo alla Sarda
BEEF MARINATED AND BRAISED IN WHITE WINE

In a large glass, porcelain or stainless-steel bowl, combine the 3 cups of white wine, ¼ cup of olive oil, ¼ cup of finely chopped parsley, bay leaf, ground allspice and nutmeg, and salt. Place the rolled and securely tied beef in the mixing bowl and turn it over in the marinade until it has become thoroughly moistened on all sides. Marinate the beef for at least 6 hours at room temperature or for about 12 hours in the refrigerator, turning the beef occasionally.

Preheat the oven to 350°. Remove the beef from the marinade and pat it completely dry with paper towels, but do not discard the marinade; set it aside to be used again later. Over moderately high heat, melt the butter with the oil in a flameproof casserole that is just large enough to hold the beef comfortably. When the foam subsides, add the beef and brown it on all sides, turning it with 2 wooden spoons. Transfer the browned meat to a plate and discard all but a thin film of the browned fat from the casserole. Pour in the marinade and boil it briskly over high heat until it has reduced to about 1 cup, meanwhile using a wooden spoon or rubber spatula to scrape in any browned bits clinging to the bottom and sides of the pan. Return the beef to the casserole and add 1 cup of white wine and the 2 cups of beef stock. The combined liquid should come about ⅓ of the way up the side of the meat; add more beef stock if necessary. Bring the casserole to a boil over high heat, cover, and place in the middle of the oven. Braise the beef for 2 to 2½ hours, turning it over in the casserole 2 or 3 times. When it is tender enough to be easily pierced with the tip of a sharp knife, transfer the roast to a cutting board.

Pour the braising liquid through a fine sieve into a 1½- to 2-quart saucepan. Let it settle for a minute or so, then with a large spoon skim off as much surface fat as possible. Boil the braising liquid briskly over high heat, stirring occasionally, until it has reduced to about 2 cups. Stir in 2 tablespoons of finely chopped parsley, the chopped anchovy and lemon juice. Taste the sauce and season it with salt and pepper if needed. Cut the strings off the beef and carve the roast into thin, even slices.

Arrange the slices of beef, slightly overlapping, in a row on a heated platter. Moisten them with a few tablespoons of the hot sauce and pass the rest separately, in a sauceboat.

Rich, steaming *zabaione*, a wine-egg custard, fills a dessert cup.

Glossary

ABBACCHIO (ahb-BAHK-yoh): suckling lamb that has been fed on milk and never tasted grass

ACCIUGHE (ahk-CHOO-gay), **ALICI** (ah-LEE-chee): anchovies

ACETO (ah-CHEH-toh): vinegar

AFFOGATO (ahf-foh-GAH-toh): steamed or poached

AFFUMICATO (ahf-foo-mee-KAH-toh): smoked or cured

AGLIO (AH-l'yoh): garlic

AGNELLO (ah-N'YEHL-lo): lamb that has been weaned

AGNOLOTTI (ah-n'yo-LOHT-tee): literally, "little fat lambs"; pasta similar to ravioli with meat filling

AGRODOLCE (ah-gro-DOLL-cheh): sour and sweet; bittersweet, sourish

AL DENTE (ahl DEN-teh): literally, "to the tooth," term used to describe the point at which pasta is properly cooked; it has the quality of being slightly resistant; underdone

ANGUILLA (ahn-GWEE-lah): eel

ANIMELLE (ah-nee-MEHL-leh): sweetbreads

ANITRA (AH-nee-trah): duck, drake

ANTIPASTO (ahn-tee-PAHS-toh): literally, "before the meal"—hors d'oeuvre, or a first course

ARAGOSTA (ah-rah-GO-stah): spiny lobster

ARANCIO (ah-RAHN-choh): orange

ARISTA (ah-REE-stah): roasted loin of pork. The word *arista* may be derived from the Greek word *aristos*, meaning "best." According to legend, 15th Century Greek Orthodox prelates exclaimed "Aristos!" when served a loin of pork at an eating place in Florence, a name that stuck as *arista*.

ARROSTO (ah-ROH-sto): a roast of meat

BACCALÀ (bahk-kah-LAH): dried, salted cod

BARBABIETOLE (bar-bah-b'yeh-TO-leh): beets

BASILICO (bah-ZEE-lee-ko): basil

BATTUTO (baht-TOO-toh): base for soups, stews, etc., made of finely chopped vegetables, herbs and salt pork or oil

BICCHIERE (beek-K'YEH-reh): a glass; used as a measurement in Italian cookbooks, equaling approximately one cup

BISCOTTI (bee-SKOT-tee): literally, "twice baked"; cookies or biscuits

BISTECCA (bee-STEHK-kah): beef or veal steak

BOLLITO (bohl-LEE-toh): boiled; boiled meat

BRACIOLA (brah-CHOH-lah): cutlet or steak

BRASATO (brah-ZAH-toh): braised

BRODETTO (broh-DET-toh): soup generally containing pieces of fish

BRODO (BROH-doh): broth

BRODO RISTRETTO (BROH-doh ree-STRET-toh): consommé

BUDINO (boo-DEE-no): pudding

BUE (BOO-eh): beef

BURRO (BOOR-ro): butter

CACCIAGIONE (kahk-chah-JO-neh), **SELVAGGINA** (sehl-va-JEE-nah): game

(ALLA) CACCIATORA ([AHL-lah] kah-chah-TOH-rah): "hunter's style"; meat or fish cooked in a sauce that includes tomatoes, scallions, mushrooms, bay leaves and red or white wine

CAFFÈ ESPRESSO (kahf-FEH ess-PRESS-so): strong, black coffee made by forcing steam through ground coffee

CAFFELATTE (kahf-feh-LAT-teh): a drink of hot milk and coffee in equal parts

CALAMARI (kah-lah-MA-ree), **CALAMARETTI** (kah-lah-ma-RET-tee): squid, tiny squid

CALDO, MOLTO CALDO (MOHL-toh KAHL-doh): warm, hot

CANNELLA (kah-NEH-lah): cinnamon

CANNOLI (kah-NO-lee): tubes of crisp pastry filled with *ricotta* cheese, chocolate and candied fruit

CAPITONE (kah-pee-TOH-neh): large eel

CAPPERI (kahp-PEH-ree): capers

CAPPONE (kahp-PO-neh): capon

CAPPUCCINO (kahp-poo-CHEE-no): coffee and hot, beaten milk

CAPRETTO (kah-PRET-toh): kid

CARCIOFO (kar-CHOH-fo): artichoke

CARDO (KAR-doh): cardoon, vegetable of the thistle family

CARNE (KAR-neh): meat

(ALLA) CASALINGA ([AHL-lah] kah-sa-LEEN-ga), **CASERECCIO** (kah-seh-REH-choh): homemade

CASSATA (ka-SA-tah): an ice-cream dish made of a hard shell of cream or chocolate enclosing lighter ice cream

CASSATA ALLA SICILIANA (ka-SA-ta AHL-la see-chee-L'YA-nah): a rich Sicilian poundcake with layers of *ricotta* cheese and decorated with thick chocolate frosting

CASTAGNA (ka-STA-n'yah): chestnut

CAVOLFIORE (ka-vohl-FYOH-reh): cauliflower

CAVOLO (ka-VO-lo): cabbage

CECI (CHEH-chee): garbanzo beans, chick-peas

CEDRO (CHEH-d'roh): citron

CERVELLA (cher-VEHL-lah): brains

CETRIOLO (cheht-R'YOH-loh): cucumber

CHIODI DI GAROFANO (K'YOH-dee dee gah-RO-fa-no): cloves

CICORIA (chee-KO-r'yah): chickory

CINGHIALE (cheen-G'YAH-leh): wild boar

CIOCCOLATO (chee'yoh-ko-LA-toh): chocolate

CIOTTO (kohs-CHOH-toh): leg of lamb

CIPOLLA (chee-POHL-lah): onion

CIPOLLINA (chee-pohl-lee-nah): pearl onion

CODA DI BUE ALLA VACCINARA (KO-da dee BOO-eh AHL-la vah-cheen-AH-ra): oxtail, butcher's style

CONDITO (kohn-DEE-toh): seasoned, tasty

CONIGLIO (koh-NEEL-yoh): rabbit

CONTORNI (kohn-TOR-nee): vegetables accompanying the main course, or garnishes

CORATELLA (ko-ra-TEHL-lah): innards; heart, lungs, liver and kidney

COSCETTO (kohs-CHET-toh), **COSCIA** (KOHS-chah): leg

COSTATA (kohs-TAH-tah): rib chop

COSTOLETTA (kohs-toh-LET-tah), **COTECHINO** (koh-teh-KEE-no): highly spiced pork sausage

COTOLETTA (ko-toh-LET-tah): chop or cutlet

COTTO (KOT-toh): cooked, done

COZZE (KOH-t'seh): mussels

CREMA (KREH-mah): custard

CROSTA (KROHS-tah), **CROSTATA** (krohs-TAH-tah), **CROSTATINA** (krohs-tah-TEE-nah): crust, pie crust, tart

CROSTINO (krohs-TEE-noh): crouton, or a small piece of toast

CRUDO (KROO-doh): raw

CUCCHIAIO (kook-YI-yo), **CUCCHIAINO** (kook-yah-EE-no): large spoon, small spoon (terms used in Italian cookbooks); roughly equivalent to a tablespoon and a teaspoon

DATTERI DI MARE (DAHT-teh-ree dee MAH-reh): "sea dates," a type of shellfish

DOLCE (DOHL-cheh): sweet

DOLCI (DOHL-chee): sweets, cakes

DORATO (doh-RAH-toh): golden brown (a cooking instruction)

DRAGONCELLO (drah-gohn-CHEL-lo): tarragon

ERBA (EHR-bah): herb

FAGIOLI (fah-JO-lee): dried kidney beans

FAGIOLINI (fah-jo-LEE-nee): string beans, French beans

FARCITO (far-CHEE-toh): stuffed

FARINA (far-REE-nah): flour

FAVE (FAH-veh): broad beans

FEGATINI DI POLLO (feh-gah-TEE-nee dee POHL-loh): chicken livers

FEGATO (feh-GAH-toh): liver

(AI) FERRI ALLA GRIGLIA ([eye] FER-ree ahl-lah GREEL-yah): grilled

FETTA, FETTINA (FET-tah, fet-TEE-nah): slice

FILETTO (fee-LET-toh): fillet

FINOCCHIO (fee-NO-k'yoh): fennel

FONDI DI CARCIOFO (FOHN-dee dee kar-CHOH-fo): artichoke hearts

FORMAGGIO (for-MAH-jo): cheese

FORNO, AL FORNO (FOHR-no, ahl FOHR-no): baked

FREDDO (FRED-doh): cold

FRESCO (FRESS-ko): fresh, uncooked

FRIGGERE (FRIJ-jeh-reh): to fry

FRITTATA (free-TAH-tah): omelet

FRITTO (FREET-toh): fried

FRITTURA (freet-TOO-rah): fried food

FRUTTA (FROO-tah): fruit

FRUTTI DI MARE (FROO-tee dee MAH-reh): "fruit of the sea"; an assortment of shellfish

FUNGHI (FOON-ghee): mushrooms

GAMBERETTI (gahm-beh-RET-tee): small shrimp

GAMBERI (GAHM-beh-ree): shrimp

GELATO (jeh-LAH-toh): ice cream

GHIACCIATO, (g'yah-CHAH-toh): ice; iced

GHIACCIO (G'YAH-ch'you), **GNOCCHI** (N'YOHK-kee): dumplings

GNOCCHI ALLA ROMANA (N'YOHK-kee ahl-lah ro-MAH-nah): dumplings made from semolina and baked in the oven

GNOCCHI DI PATATE (N'YOHK-kee dee pah-TAH-teh): dumplings made of potato and flour

GNOCCHI DI RICOTTA (N'YOHK-kee dee ree-KOHT-tah): dumplings made of *ricotta* and flour

GNOCCHI VERDI (N'YOHK-kee VEHR-dee): dumplings made from a mixture of spinach flour and *ricotta* cheese; specialty of northern Italy

GRANCHIO (GRAHN-k'yo): crab

GRANITE (grah-NEE-teh): Italian flavored ices

GRAPPA (GRAHP-pah): brandy made by fermenting the pressings of grapes after the juice, or must, has been drawn off

GRISSINI (grees-SEE-nee): bread sticks

IMBOTTITO (im-boht-TEE-toh): stuffed

IMPANATO (im-pah-NAH-toh): breaded

INDIVIA (een-DEE-vee-ah): endive

INSALATA (een-sah-LAH-tah): salad

INSALATA DI POMODORO (een-sah-LAH-tah dee po-mo-DOH-ro): salad with tomato

INSALATA MISTA (een-sah-LAH-tah MEE-stah): mixed salad

INSALATA VERDE (een-sah-LAH-tah VEHR-deh): green salad

LARDO (LAR-doh): salt pork

LARDO AFFUMICATO (LAR-doh ahf-foo-mee-KAH-toh): bacon

LATTE (LAHT-teh): milk

LATTUGA (laht-TOO-gah): lettuce

LAURO (la'OO-ro): bay leaf

LEGUMI (leh-GOO-mee): vegetables

LENTICCHIE (len-TEEK-k'yeh): lentils

LEPRE (LEH-preh): hare

LESSO (LESS-soh): boiled meat

LIMONE (lee-MOH-neh): lemon

LUMACHE (loo-MAH-keh): snails

MAGGIORANA (mah-joh-RAH-nah): marjoram

MAGRO (MAH-gro): lean

MAIALE (mah-YAH-leh): pork

MAIONESE (mah-yo-NEH-zeh): mayonnaise

MANDORLE (MAHN-dor-leh): almonds

MANZO (MAHN-dzo): beef

(ALLA) MARINARA ([AHL-lah] mah-ree-NAH-rah): "sailor style," sauce used in southern Italian cooking, including tomato, garlic, oil, oregano

MARINATO (mah-ree-NAH-toh): marinated

MAZZACUOGNI (mah-tsah-KWO-n'yee): very large prawns (mazzancelle in Roman dialect)

MELANZANA (meh-lahn-DZAH-nah): eggplant

MELONE (mel-LO-neh), POPONE (po-PO-neh): melon

MENTA (MEHN-tah): mint

MERLUZZO (mehr-LOO-t'zo): cod

MIELE (M'YEH'leh): honey

MILLE FOGLIE (MEEL-leh FOHL-yeh): literally, "a thousand leaves"—flaky pastry

MINESTRA (mee-NEH-strah), MINESTRE (mee-NEH-streh): soup or pasta course

MINESTRONE (mee-neh-STRO-neh): vegetable soup with pasta or rice

MISTO (MEE-sto): mixed

MORTADELLA (mor-tah-DEL-lah): large spiced pork sausage

MUSCOLI (MOO-sko-lee): mussels

NOCE MOSCATA (NOH-che moh-SKAH-tah): nutmeg

OCA (OH-kah): goose

OLIO (OH-l'yo): oil

ORIGANO (oh-REE-gah-no): wild marjoram, oregano

OSTRICHE (OHS-tree-keh): oysters

PALOMBACCI (pah-lohm-BAH-chee): game pigeons

PANE (PAH-neh): bread

PANINO (pah-NEE-noh): bread roll

PANNA (PAHN-nah): cream

PANNA MONTATA (PAHN-nah mohn-TAH-tah): whipped cream

(ALLA) PARMIGIANA ([AHL-lah] par-mee-JAH-nah): with Parmesan cheese

PARMIGIANO (par-mee-JAH-no): Parmesan cheese; also called formaggio di grana (for-MAH-jo dee GRAH-nah)

PASTA (PAH-stah): basically a dough of flour and water used to make noodles; generic name for pasta products, from spaghetti to cannelloni

PASTA ALL'UOVO (PAH-stah ahl-lwo-vo): dough of flour and water and eggs—egg pasta

PASTA ASCIUTTA (PAH-stah ahs-CHOOT-tah): "dry pasta"—pasta served plain or with a little sauce

PASTA IN BRODO (PAH-stah een BROH-do): pasta served as part of a soup

PASTELLA (pah-STEL-lah), PASTETTA (pah-STEHT-tah): batter for deep-fat frying

PASTICCERIA (pah-stik-CHEH-ree-yah): pastry

PASTICCIO (pah-STIK-ch'yo): baked dish with a crust on top

PASTINA (pah-STEE-nah): small pasta for soup

PATATA (pah-TAH-tah): potato

PEPE NERO (PEH-peh NEH-ro), PEPE ROSSO (PEH-peh ROHS-so): black pepper, red pepper

PEPERONCINI (peh-peh-rohn-CHEE-nee): dried or fresh hot red peppers

PEPERONI (peh-peh-RO-nee): green peppers or red sweet peppers (pimiento); also, in the U.S. only, a spicy sausage

PESCE (PEHS-cheh): fish

PESTO (PEHS-toh): paste of fresh basil, Parmesan cheese, garlic, and thinned with olive oil, served in soup or over pasta. A specialty of Genoa

(A) PIACERE ([AH] p'yah-CHEH-reh): cooked to your pleasure, to your taste

PIGNOLI (peen-YO-lee): pine nuts

PISELLI (pee-ZELL-lee): peas

(ALLA) PIZZAIOLA ([AHL-lah] peedz-eye-YO-lah): with tomato sauce, garlic, oregano, black pepper

POLLO (POHL-lo): chicken

POLPETTE (pohl-PEHT-teh): meatballs

POLPETTONE (pohl-peht-TOH-neh): meat loaf

POMODORO (po-mo-DOH-ro): tomato

PORCHETTA (pohr-KEHT-tah): roasted whole suckling pig

PREZZEMOLO (pred-DZEH-mo-lo): parsley

PROSCIUTTO (pro-SHOO-toh): ham

RAGÙ (rah-GOO): meat sauce, stew

RIPIENO (reep-YEH-no): stuffing; filled or stuffed

RISO (REE-zoh), RISOTTO (ree-ZOHT-toh): rice, rice dish

ROSMARINO (rohz-mah-REE-no): rosemary

SALAME (sah-LAH-meh): salami

SALE (SAH-leh): salt

SALMÌ (sahl-MEE), IN SALMÌ (een sahl-MEE): sauce for game bird dishes

SALSA (SAHL-sah): sauce

SALTARE (sahl-TAH-reh): sauté

SALVIA (SAHL-v'yah): sage

SCALOPPINE (skah-lo-PEE-neh): thin slices of veal

SCAMPI (SKAHM-pee): a type of shrimp native to the Adriatic Sea

SECCO (SEHK-ko): dry

SEDANO (SEH-dah-no): celery

SEMIFREDDO (SEH-mee-FREH-do): mousse, chilled pudding

SEMOLINO (seh-mo-LEE-no): a coarse meal made from wheat

SEPPIA (SEHP-yah): cuttlefish

SOFFRITTO (sohf-FREET-toh): soup or stew base made of vegetables and herbs; the cooked battuto

SOGLIOLA (sohl-YO-lah): sole

SPEZIE (SPEDZ-yeh): spices

SPEZZATINO (spedz-zah-TEE-no): stew; literally. "cut into little pieces"

SPIEDINO (sp'yeh-DEE-no), SPIEDO (SP'YEH-doh), ALLO SPIEDO (AHL-lo SP'YEH-doh): skewer, spit, roasted on a spit

SPUMANTE (spoo-MAHN-teh): generic term for sparkling wines (e.g., Asti Spumante, Lambrusco)

SPUMONE (spoo-MO-neh): light, foamy ice cream made with egg whites or whipped cream

STRACOTTO (strah-KOHT-toh): pot roast

STUFATO (stoo-FAH-toh): stew; literally, "cooked on the stove"

SUGO (ZOO-go): gravy or sauce

TACCHINO (tahk-KEE-no): turkey

TARTUFI (tar-TOO-fee): truffles

TESTA (TEH-stah): head

TIMO (TEE-mo): thyme

TONNO (TOHN-no): tuna fish

TORRONE (tohr-RO-neh): nougat

TORTA (TOHR-tah): cake

TRIGLIA (TREEL-yah): red mullet

TRIPPA (TREEP-pah): tripe

TROTA (TRO-tah): trout

UCCELLETTI (oo-chel-LET-tee), UCCELLINI (oo-chel-LEE-nee): small birds, usually roasted and served whole

(IN) UMIDO ([een] OO-mee-doh): stewed in gravy

UOVO (WO-vo): egg; TUORLO D'UOVO (TWOR-lo DWO-vo): egg yolk; BIANCO D'UOVO (B'YAHN-ko DWO-vo): egg white

UVA (OO-vah): grapes; UVA PASSA (OO-vah PAHS-sah): raisins

VITELLO (vee-TEL-lo): milk-fed, very young veal

VITELLONE (vee-tel-LO-neh): young beef

VONGOLE (VOHN-go-leh): clams

ZAFFERANO (dzahf-feh-RAH-no): saffron

ZAMPONE (dzahm-PO-neh): highly spiced pork sausage encased in the skin of a pig's foot

ZEPPOLE (DZEHP-po-leh): sweets similar to those eaten on St. Joseph's Day in Rome; also a Neapolitan fritter

ZUCCHERO (DZOO-kek-ro): sugar

199

Recipe Index: English

NOTE: An R preceding a page refers to the Recipe Booklet. Size, weight and material are specified for pans in the recipes because they affect cooking results. A pan should be just large enough to hold its contents comfortably. Heavy pans heat slowly and cook food at a constant rate. Aluminum and cast iron conduct heat well but may discolor foods containing egg yolks, wine, vinegar or lemon. Enamelware is a fairly poor conductor of heat. Many recipes therefore recommend stainless steel or enameled cast iron, which do not have these faults.

In recipes that call for cheese, imported ones are recommended. Most domestic versions lack the authentic taste, aroma and texture.

Recipe Index: Italian

General Index
Numerals in italics indicate a photograph of the subject mentioned.

Abruzzi, 7, *map* 163, 164, *166*
Academy of Cooking, 36, 119, 121
Academy of Wines and Grapes, 71
Accidie Hotel, 162
Accumoli, 58
Acini di Pepe, 41, *42*
Acireale Theater, *190-191*
Adige River, *map* 105, 107
Agnolotti, 34, 41, *43*, 152
Al dente, 46
Alba, 150, *153*
Alexander III, Pope, 139
Alfedena, *166*
Alla fiorentina, 69-70
Alla milanese, 137, 144
Alla romana, 53, 56
Alto Adige, 109
Amatrice, 59
America, foods from, 13, 25, 169
Anchovies, 37, 122, 124, *127*, 163;
    for pizza, *172-173*
Ancona, *map* 55, 61
Anellini, 41, *42*
Antipasto, *32*
Antrodoco, 59
Aosta, *map* 151
Apicio restaurant, 104
Apicius, 19, 22
Appetizer, 187. *See also Antipasto*
Appian Way, 54, *map* 55, *56-57*
Apulia, *map* 163, 165, 166, 167,
    171; *quagghiarid*, 167
Arabs, 20-21, 24, 187
Arcimboldi, Giuseppe, 136, 138
Arezzo, 70, *map* 71, 78
Artichoke heart omelet, 70
Artichokes, 10, 55, 123, 167; Greek
    style, 109
Ascoli Piceno, 61
Asiago cheese, *93*
Asparagus, 23, 37, 86, 87, 120,
    136
Austria, influence of, 104, 109, 137

Bagna cauda, *148*, 152, *157*
Bandiera restaurant, 185
Barbarossa, Frederick, 120, 139
Barbaresco, *77*, 153
Barbera, 152
Bardolino, *77*, 104
Bari, *map* 163, 165
Barolo, *77*, 153
Basil, sweet, 37, 120
Bass, *114-115*
Battuto, 30, 99, 129, 142
Bay of Gaeta, *map* 55, 58
Bean(s), 18, 23, 25, *68*, 70-71, 162;
    alla romana, 56-57
Beef, *bolliti misti*, 152; braised in
    stock and red wine, 135; *cannel-*
    loni, 63; Italian, 38, 70, 71;
    stewed, in Lombardy, 137
Bel Paese, 38, *93*, 137, 139
Belvedere Fort, *68*
Bergamo, 92, 136
Besciamella, 62, *63*, 99
Bignè, 54, 57
Birds, 38; small, *110*, 138, 187
Biscuit tortoni, 38, 171
Blond, Georges, 23
Boar, wild, 10, 38, 79, *84*, 152, 186,
    187
Boats, fishing, 124, *126*, 127
Bolliti misti, 152
Bologna, 38, 84, *map* 87; cuisine of,
    22, 36, 85, 86, 87
"Boloney," 38, 87
Bozzi, Ottorina Perna, 135, 136
Bradamente, *193*
Brandy, Italian, 152, 153
Bread, 13, 21, 23, 89, 138-139, 162,
    182, 184-185, 187
Bread sticks, 150, 157
Brenner Pass, *map* 105, 110
Bressanone, 110, *111*
Broccoli, 10, 56, 162
Brolio, *77*

Brolio Castle, 71, *72, 73*
Buffalo, water, 90; and *mozzarella*,
    94-95, 96-97
Burano, 105
Butcher shops, *14, 17,* 18-19, 84
Butter, areas cooking with, *map* 35,
    36, 136, 137

Cabbage, 18, 162
Caciocavallo, 92
Caesar, Julius, 11, 89, 136, 153, 184
Caffè alla Borgia, 107
Caffè Dante, 107
Caffè espresso, 108, *109*
Caffè Motta, 134
Cakes, 23, 49, 61, 78, 107, 171, 184,
    186, 188, *192, 193*
Calabria, 162, *map* 163, 164, 167, 171
Calf's liver with onions, sautéed,
    104
Cambio, Ristorante del, *155*
Campania region, 162, *map* 163
Campari, 140
Cannelloni, 34, 41, *43*
Capellini, 34, 41, *42*
Capon, 23, 54; "fast-day," 122
Caponata, 32, 185
Cappelletti, 34, 41, *43,* 86-87
Capri, *map* 163, 166
Cassata, Sicilian, 184, *193*
Cattle, 38, 70, *74-75,* 86, 167
Caviar, Po River, 105
Celery, 37, 60, 136, 157
Cellini, Benvenuto, saltcellar, *8*
Cerasuolo del Piave, 104
Cheese, 13, 20, 23, 38, 55, 58, *90-91,*
    137, 139, 151, 171, 184; Asiago,
    93; Bel Paese, *93,* 139; for cook-
    ing, 92, 93, 94; *fontina, 93,* 151;
    for grating, *93;* Gorgonzola, *93,*
    109, 139; *mascarpone,* 109;
    mozzarella, 56, *93, 94-95, 96-97,*
    167; Parmesan, 86, 87, 88, *90,*

    139-140; Parmigiano Reggiano,
    93; pecorino, 54, 56, 58, *93;*
    provatura, 55-56; *provolone, 91,*
    93; ricotta, 93; Robiole, 151;
    romano, 129; *sardo,* 129; sheep's
    milk, *182;* sour, 123; table, *93;*
    Taleggio, *93; Toma veja,* 151;
    types of, 90-91, *93*
Cheese balls, deep-fried rice-and-,
    64
Cherries, 18, 26, 86, *87*
Chestnuts, 78, 108, 152
Chiana Valley, 70, *map* 71, 78
Chianina cattle, *70*
Chianti, 7, 71, 77
Chianti Brolio, 71, *73*
Chicken, 19, 23, 38, 78, 167;
    Marengo, 154
Chicken giblets, 152, 166
Chirico, Giorgio de, 105
Chocolate(s), 55, 60; frosting, Sicil-
    ian cake with, *192, 193;* ice cream,
    181; pampepato di cioccolatto,
    89
Christmas delicacies, eels, 53, 54, 79,
    123; cassata, 184, *192, 193; noci-*
    ata, 59; *panettone,* 134, 139; rolls,
    89; *torrone,* 139; *tortellini,* 86
Cinqueterre, 121, 124
Cinzano, 154
Clams, 37, *123,* 164
Clement VII, Pope, 25
Cod, 55, 61, 79, 106, 122-123; Leg-
    horn seafood stew, 79
Coffee, 107; iced, 136; introduction
    of, 24-25, *102;* to make, *108, 109*
Colomba restaurant, 104, 105
Columbus, Christopher, 25, 119
Comacchio, *map* 87, 89
Como, *map* 137
Conchiglie, 34, 41, *43*
Conchigliette, 41, *42*
Cookbooks, 19, 22, 109, 135

Credits and Acknowledgments

The sources for the illustrations in this book are shown below. Credits for the pictures from left to right are separated by commas, from top to bottom by dashes.

All photographs by Fred Lyon from Rapho Guillumette except:
Cover—Fred Eng. 4—Bottom left Charles Phillips, right Velio Cioni. 8—Walter Sanders courtesy the Kunst-historisches Museum, Vienna. 12, 13—Drawing by Domenico Gnoli. 14, 15—Drawings by Domenico Gnoli, Matt Greene. 16, 17—Alinari, Florence (2)—Fototeca Unione, Rome. 21—Frank Lerner courtesy the Metropolitan Museum of Art. 27—Emmett Bright. 28, 29—Charles Phillips. 35—Constructed by Nicholas Fasciano, cartography by Lothar Roth, photographed by Charles Phillips. 42, 43—Fred Eng. 45, 46—Charles Phillips. 58—Velio Cioni. 66—Bottom Charles Phillips. 70—Velio Cioni. 77—Fred Eng. 93—Fred Eng. 98—Charles Phillips. 101—Charles Phillips. 109—Drawings by Matt Greene. 114, 115—Charles Phillips. 122—Charles Phillips. 128—Charles Phillips. 130—Charles Phillips. 131, 132—Richard Jeffery. 138—Derek Bayes. 158—Richard Jeffery. 174—Center row left Charles Phillips (2). 55, 71, 87, 105, 121, 137, 151, 163, 185—Maps by Lothar Roth; base map courtesy Ginn and Company, Boston, Mass.

For their help in the production of this book the editors wish to thank the following, all in New York City: Sam Aaron, President, Sherry-Lehmann, Inc., Wine and Spirits Merchants; Bazaar de la Cuisine, Inc.; Tina Bellusci, Mamma Leone's Restaurant, Restaurant Associates; Charles Berlitz; Bloomingdale's; Nicholas de Santis, Associate Editor of *Trade with Italy;* Francesco Ghedini, who served as a text consultant; Ginori Fifth Avenue; Dr. Renato Guerrieri, Travel Commissioner, Italian Government Travel Office; Hammacher-Schlemmer; Jean's Silversmiths, Inc.; Lord and Taylor; Manganaro Foods; Michael Manteo; and Pampered Kitchens, Inc. Thanks are also due to Corning Glass Works, Corning, N.Y.

Sources consulted in the production of this book include: *The Talisman Italian Cookbook,* by Ada Boni; *Italian Bouquet* by Samuel Chamberlain; *Italian Food* by Elizabeth David; *The Best of Italian Cooking* by Nika S. Hazelton; and *The Italian Cookbook* by Maria Luisa Tagliente.

Printed in U.S.A.